ALSO BY SETH DAVIS

Equinunk, Tell Your Story:
My Return to Summer Camp

WHEN MARCH WENT MAD

WHEN MARCH WENT MAD

THE GAME THAT TRANSFORMED BASKETBALL

★

SETH DAVIS

TIMES BOOKS   HENRY HOLT AND COMPANY   NEW YORK

Times Books
Henry Holt and Company, LLC
Publishers since 1866
175 Fifth Avenue
New York, New York 10010
www.henryholt.com

Henry Holt® is a registered trademark of
Henry Holt and Company, LLC.

Library of Congress Cataloging-in-Publication Data

Davis, Seth.
  When March went mad : the game that transformed basketball / Seth Davis.—1st ed.
    p. cm.
  ISBN-13: 978-0-8050-8810-6
  ISBN-10: 0-8050-8810-5
  1. NCAA Basketball Tournament—History. 2. Basketball—United States—
History—20th century. 3. Michigan State University—Basketball—History.
4. Michigan State Spartans (Basketball team)—History. 5. Indiana State University—
Basketball—History. I. Title.
  GV885.49.N37D38 2009
  796.323'630973—dc22   2008047628

Henry Holt books are available for special promotions and
premiums. For details contact: Director, Special Markets.

First Edition 2009

Designed by Kelly Too

Printed in the United States of America
1   3   5   7   9   10   8   6   4   2

For Sweet Melissa

NO.	NAME	POS.	HT.	YR.	HOMETOWN
11	Terry Donnelly	G	6-2	Junior	St. Louis, Mo.
12	Mike Brkovich	G	6-4	Soph	Windsor, Ont.
33	Earvin Johnson	G	6-8	Soph	Lansing, Mich.
32	Gregory Kelser	F	6-7	Senior	Detroit, Mich.
31	Jay Vincent	C	6-8	Soph	Lansing, Mich.

Reserves

NO.	NAME	POS.	HT.	YR.	HOMETOWN
10	Gregory Lloyd	G	6-1	Junior	Lansing, Mich.
15	Ron Charles	F	6-7	Junior	St. Croix, U.S. Virgin Islands
21	Donald Brkovich	F	6-6	Frosh	Windsor, Ont.
23	Michael Longaker	G	6-1	Junior	Warren, Mich.
24	Jamie Huffman	G	6-3	Soph	Lansing, Mich.
35	Robert Gonzalez	F	6-7	Frosh	Detroit, Mich.
42	Rick Kaye	F	6-7	Soph	Livonia, Mich.
43	Gerald Gilkie	F	6-5	Soph	Detroit, Mich.

Head coach: George M. (Jud) Heathcote

Assistant coaches: Bill Berry

Dave Harshman

Fred Paulsen

Trainer: Clint Thompson

Head student manager: Darwin Payton

★ INDIANA STATE SYCAMORES (33–0) ★

NO.	NAME	POS.	HT.	YR.	HOMETOWN
22	Carl Nicks	G	6-2	Junior	Chicago, Ill.
23	Steve Reed	G	6-3	Soph	Warsaw, Ind.
33	Larry Bird	C	6-9	Senior	French Lick, Ind.
40	Brad Miley	F	6-8	Junior	Rushville, Ind.
42	Alex Gilbert	F	6-8	Junior	East St. Louis, Ill.

Reserves

NO.	NAME	POS.	HT.	YR.	HOMETOWN
5	Bob Ritter	G	6-3	Junior	Indianapolis, Ind.
10	Scott Turner	F	6-6	Frosh	Bedford, Ind.
15	Rod McNelly	G	6-2	Frosh	Speedway, Ind.
20	Rich Nemcek	G	6-6	Junior	Hammond, Ind.
24	Tom Crowder	F	6-5	Senior	Cayuga, Ind.
30	Bob Heaton	G	6-5	Junior	Clay City, Ind.
32	Eric Curry	C	6-9	Junior	Chicago, Ill.
44	Leroy Staley	G	6-5	Senior	Tampa, Fla.

Head coach: Bill Hodges

Assistant coaches: Mel Daniels

                    Terry Thimlar

Trainer: Bob Behnke

Assistant trainer: Rick Shaw

WHEN MARCH WENT MAD

PROLOGUE

On Sunday evening, March 25, 1979, the NBC Sports production team gathered in a conference room at the Hotel Utah in Salt Lake City to go over the game plan for the following night's NCAA men's basketball championship game. George Finkel, the game producer, spoke first. He laid out the manner in which he and his broadcasting team of Dick Enberg, Al McGuire, and Billy Packer would be presenting the contest between Michigan State and Indiana State.

The next person to speak was Don McGuire (no relation to Al), who produced the pregame, halftime, and postgame segments that were hosted by Bryant Gumbel. Before beginning a career in television, McGuire had worked as the sports information director at the University of New Mexico, where the associate athletic director was a man named Bob King. King had since moved on to become head basketball coach at Indiana State University, but before the start of the 1978–79 season, he developed an aneurysm in his brain and had to undergo emergency surgery. That forced King to hand over the reins to his young assistant, Bill Hodges, who despite having no previous head coaching experience had guided the Sycamores to a stunning 33–0 record and a berth in the national championship game. Now, McGuire told the group that he wanted to air a story on King, the incapacitated head coach, during NBC's pregame segment on Monday night.

McGuire was abruptly interrupted by Don Ohlmeyer, the executive producer of NBC Sports. A large, domineering, and sometimes bombastic man, Ohlmeyer had spent a decade at ABC Sports learning at the knee of the legendary producer Roone Arledge. While working for the popular, eclectic program *Wide World of Sports*, Ohlmeyer learned the importance of developing a story line to pump up interest in a sporting event.

"Nobody cares about Bob King," Ohlmeyer said to Don McGuire. "What about Magic and Bird?"

Ohlmeyer was referring to Earvin "Magic" Johnson and Larry Bird, the All-American stars at Michigan State University and Indiana State, respectively. An uncomfortable silence fell on the room. "Well," McGuire said, "Dick, Al, and Billy are going to be talking a lot about those two during the game. And we've got a highlights piece set to music ready to go for halftime."

"Well, you're going to do them in the pregame, too," Ohlmeyer snapped. "Those guys are the stars here. That's who people want to see."

Ohlmeyer's edict left McGuire in a bit of a pickle. In the first place, he now had less than twenty-four hours to put together a quality piece. More problematic was Bird's notorious antipathy toward the media. He had gone through most of the season without speaking to the press, and McGuire had no idea whether Bird would consent to be interviewed so close to tip-off.

The following morning, Don McGuire sent Packer and a camera crew to the University of Utah's Special Events Center, where the Indiana State Sycamores were just completing their game-day shootaround. Fortunately for NBC, Bird agreed to answer a couple of questions. Packer began by asking him how he felt about playing for the national championship.

"Well, this is probably the biggest game I'll ever play in my life," Bird replied in his high-pitched Hoosier twang, which made "life" sound like "lahff." As he spoke, Larry looked not at Packer but straight ahead and slightly downward. He had a disconcerting habit of resisting eye contact with people he didn't know well.

Bird continued, "I just feel like I'm representing not only myself and my team, but we're representing our school and our town, Terre Haute. It means so much to me just to even be here that we're gonna give it all we got, and we're gonna try our hardest to win."

"You know," Packer said, "a lot of people were surprised yesterday, Larry, when you mentioned you played ball with Magic Johnson in the World Invitational Tournament." Packer was referring to the tournament the two of them played for Team USA the previous summer that culminated with a game against a squad from Russia in Lexington, Kentucky.

Larry cracked a wry smile. "Well, you know me and Magic played in that game, and you know it's funny 'cause Magic's such a great passer, but he wouldn't give me the ball. And you know I need the ball."

The interview had been surprisingly pleasant and light. Larry left the court with his team, and the Michigan State Spartans strode into the arena. Packer knew there was no concern over whether Magic Johnson would consent to an interview. The broadcaster had never dealt with an athlete who so enjoyed the give-and-take with the media.

"It's a dream come true, really, for me," Johnson said in answer to Packer's first question. "I won a state title [in high school] back in my home state, and then my next accomplishment was going to the NCAA and playing a game like tonight in the finals. It's a dream come true, and like I said, it's an awful important game. I just hope we play up to par and win the game."

Packer then told Magic what Bird had said about him. Johnson flashed the bright ivory smile that would soon earn him millions of dollars. "Well, I hope he don't think I'm gonna pass it to him tonight, either. But I thought I passed him the ball. Maybe he forgot."

Don McGuire was pleased to hear that Packer's excursion had been successful. He now had enough material to make NBC's pregame show an all-Magic-and-Bird affair. In retrospect, it seems inconceivable that anyone involved in producing the game could have failed to recognize the significance of the impending confrontation between these two compelling characters. Ohlmeyer, however, possessed an innate sense of theater that allowed him to see beyond the attraction the game would have for a hard-core basketball audience. He knew that if NBC could draw in the casual sports fan, and even the nonsports fan, the network would have something bigger than just a game. It would have an event.

By one measure, the impact of the 1979 NCAA championship game would be apparent a few days later. Nielsen Media Research reported that the contest had generated a 24.1 rating, which meant that nearly a quarter of all television sets in America were tuned in that night. Thirty years later, that remains the highest Nielsen rating for any basketball game, college or pro, in the history of the sport. Thanks to the proliferation of channels that has taken place since then, it's unlikely the number will ever be surpassed by another basketball game. Consider that the 2008 NCAA final between the University of Memphis and the University of Kansas yielded a 12.1 Nielsen rating, a healthy number by modern standards. When Magic's and Bird's former pro teams, the Los Angeles Lakers and the Boston Celtics, met in the 2008 NBA Finals, it was hailed as a dream scenario for the league. Yet the highest rating any of the six games delivered was a 10.7.

While the success that Magic and Bird later enjoyed in the pros added retrospective luster to their first meeting, it does not account for the intense interest the two of them generated that night. Those millions of viewers had no idea they were watching the birth of the most storied rivalry in modern American sports. They were simply drawn in by the dramatic story line ripped straight out of the Old Testament: little Indiana State, which had competed in the NCAA's Division I for only ten years, was taking on Michigan State, the mighty Big Ten team, for the title. That concept might not have been so titillating if they were playing a best-of-seven series, but the one-and-done format of the NCAA tournament made it irresistible. Anything could happen, the thinking went, so you'd better watch. "This was a classic David versus Goliath story," Ohlmeyer says. "It made people feel like this was a once-in-a-lifetime event."

"It was testimony to America's fervor for the underdog," Dick Enberg says. "Here comes Indiana State and this big blond guy and four chemistry majors. The argument was, they played in a minor league. Are they really that good? And they're matched up against the Big Ten power. Dramatically speaking, it was truth strangling fiction."

Bird's story strangled fiction by itself. Many people knew the skeletal details—small-town farm boy drops out of Indiana University, spends a year working on a garbage truck, resurfaces at Indiana State, and leads the Sycamores through a storybook undefeated season—but before the championship game, Indiana State had played on national television just three times. The 1979 NCAA final gave many Americans their first glimpse of Bird. "You didn't get to see everybody [on television] all the time. So in those days, it was a big treat when the tournament finally rolled around," says Bob Ryan, the longtime sportswriter for the *Boston Globe*. Bird's tight-lipped approach to the media only added to his allure. "There was just enough known about Bird and just enough unknown," says Lynn Henning, who was a columnist at Michigan State's hometown paper, the *State Journal*. "A little mystery goes a long way."

Bird was so underexposed that his roommate and teammate at Indiana State, Bob Heaton, would later say that up until the championship game he had friends in Denver (where Heaton had played before transferring to Indiana State) who thought Larry was black. This touches on another aspect of Bird's matchup with Magic that drew in the big audience. The two central protagonists were both highly skilled big men who wore the number 33, but the similarities ended there. Magic was black; Bird was white. Magic loved being the center of attention; Bird was painfully shy. Magic grew up in urban Lansing; Bird was the hick from French Lick. Magic played for the big state school in the high-profile Big Ten; Bird toiled in obscurity for the small college that competed in something called the Missouri Valley Conference.

Most of all, America tuned in to the 1979 NCAA championship game in record numbers because people understood that these two young men played a unique, exquisite style of basketball. It wasn't their physical gifts that drew folks in. Magic and Bird weren't especially quick or agile, and neither man would be a candidate for the high jump. Yet they were intense competitors and great thinkers on the court. Those qualities manifested themselves in the prettiest play of all: the pass. More than anything, Magic and Bird were great passers. They were truly something to see.

"Magic was a six-eight point guard and that was certainly unique, but it wasn't as if he was David Thompson. It wasn't as if he was Michael Jordan," says Dave Kindred, who covered the game for the *Washington Post*. "He succeeded because he knew how the game was played, and so did Bird. I'm not going to deny they were great athletes or had great hand-eye coordination, but they weren't preternaturally gifted athletes. Watching them was watching basketball the way it should be played."

On that Monday evening, more than two thousand miles from where Indiana State and Michigan State were taking the court in Salt Lake City, the general counsel of the National Basketball Association was settling in front of a television in the living room of his home in Scarsdale, New York. The NBA was in the midst of a terrible season beset by sagging attendance, plummeting TV ratings, and the growing perception that white America would never buy in to a sport dominated by black players. David Stern wouldn't become the NBA's commissioner for another five years but, as he watched Magic and Bird go at it that night, he couldn't help but hope the pro game was about to get a badly needed boost. "We were very excited at the NBA that these two extraordinarily gifted athletes that were generating this much attention were coming our way," he says.

Some eighty miles northeast of Stern's home, a dozen or so ambitious, young wannabe television executives were wrapping up another long day of work in their cramped offices in Bristol, Connecticut. They had spent the day continuing their preparations for the launch of a new cable television venture, the Entertainment and Sports Programming Network, which would soon be known as ESPN. The official launch date was September 7, and the channel's founder, Bill Rasmussen, had signed a deal a few weeks before with NCAA executive director Walter Byers to broadcast all the NCAA championship contests that were not being aired by one of the big three networks. The deal gave ESPN the rights to use NBC's feed of the early rounds of the NCAA tournament, beginning in 1980. "We kept telling ourselves, this time next year we're going to do the games leading up to this one," Rasmussen says. "Having a contract with the NCAA was huge to us at that point. Our network was really built on college basketball."

From his courtside seat at the scorer's table in Salt Lake City, Dave Gavitt sensed he was glimpsing into a bountiful future for the sport. Gavitt, the soft-spoken, whip-smart athletic director at Providence College, was serving his first season as a member of the NCAA men's basketball committee, and having participated in the NCAA's negotiations with ESPN, he understood better than most the potential that the emergence of cable television offered. Over the previous few months, Gavitt had secretly met with coaches and administrators from Georgetown University, St. John's University, and Syracuse University in hopes of convincing them to join Providence in a new basketball conference that would comprise schools located in the major television markets of the northeast. Gavitt did not realize how quickly his brainstorm would come to fruition—the Big East would begin competing during the 1979–80 season—but as the Magic-Bird faceoff got under way, he sensed his idea was coming along at an opportune time. "Television had the ability to take something big and make it bigger," Gavitt says. "We felt like we were on the cusp of that with college basketball and the NCAA tournament."

As Stern, Rasmussen, and Gavitt watched the 1979 NCAA championship game, each was optimistic that it would have a positive impact on his own corner of the basketball world. But because they could not perceive all the external forces aligning that night, they could not fully comprehend what was really happening.

The game of basketball was about to change forever.

The 1979 NCAA championship game helped to catapult college basketball, and especially the NCAA tournament, into the national consciousness. In fact, the game kicked off a six-year stretch that could fairly be characterized as the golden era of the NCAA tournament. Between 1979 and 1985, the tournament introduced to the country six players who would dominate the NBA over the next two decades: Magic Johnson, Larry Bird, Isiah Thomas, Michael Jordan, Patrick Ewing, and Hakeem Olajuwon. That period also included two of the greatest championship-game upsets in sports history: North Carolina State over Houston in 1983 and Villanova over Georgetown in 1985.

In 1979, the NCAA tournament was expanded to include forty teams (up from thirty-two the year before). The tournament was expanded twice more over the next five years—to forty-eight teams in 1980 and to sixty-four in 1985. With the exception of the addition of the sixty-fifth team to accommodate an opening-round game in 2001, the tournament has not been expanded since.

The television rights fees have undergone a similar explosion. The 1979 NCAA tournament grossed $5.2 million in TV revenue. That figure doubled when NBC renewed its contract for two years in 1980. When CBS wrested the rights from NBC prior to the 1982 tournament, it paid $48 million for three years. CBS's price doubled again when it forked over $96 million for another three years in 1985. The fees grew so fast that in 1999 CBS and the NCAA agreed to an eleven-year, $6 billion deal that commenced with the 2003 tournament.

During the late 1960s and early 1970s, the NCAA tournament had built its popularity on the dominance of John Wooden's UCLA Bruins, who won ten championships in twelve years. Many observers worried that the tournament would falter when that run ended in 1975, but the Magic-Bird championship game firmly stamped the NCAA tournament as the place where stars are born and the impossible becomes possible. It also came at a most propitious moment: the dawn of the cable TV era that would be dominated by ESPN, when administrators like Dave Gavitt were maneuvering to acquire more exposure for their universities, during a period when the NBA had so much room to grow under its soon-to-be new commissioner David Stern. As the NBA prospered in the 1980s thanks to the Magic-Bird rivalry, the league continued to offer a forum where fans could enjoy the great athletes they first discovered during the month of March.

Thus, as Indiana State and Michigan State convened at center court in Salt Lake on March 26, 1979, all the pieces were falling into place to transform basketball. The only thing those pieces lacked was a catalytic event to transform the interest into true madness. "The college game was already on the launching pad," Al McGuire said. "Then Bird and Magic came along and pushed the button."

1

They had a hand signal. Whenever Earvin Johnson was somewhere he didn't want to be, when he was surrounded by autograph seekers he couldn't turn down or glad-handers he didn't have the heart to shoo away, he would turn to Charles Tucker, his friend and mentor since childhood, and touch his hand to the brim of his cap. That meant it was time to go. And that was what Tucker was waiting for on April 22, 1978, as he and Earvin sat in a conference room in Kansas City and discussed a potential contract agreement between Johnson and the NBA's Kansas City Kings.

Earvin was fresh off a brilliant freshman season at Michigan State University. He had led the Spartans to their first outright Big Ten title in nineteen years. He had helped them reach the NCAA tournament's Mideast Regional final, where they lost 52–49 to the University of Kentucky, the eventual champion. Johnson, however, had been uncharacteristically sloppy in that game, scoring just 6 points on 2-for-10 shooting and making several costly mistakes down the stretch. Yet that did not dissuade him from considering the possibility of turning professional. At the Spartans' annual spring banquet a few weeks before, Johnson gave his strongest indication yet that he was leaning toward leaving college. "If the money's right and a few other things are right, I'd probably have to go," he said. One unnamed associate was quoted in the local newspaper, the *State Journal,* as saying that Johnson was "almost 70 percent sure he wants to turn pro, but he's thinking big money right now. He's not going for peanuts."

Johnson was undeniably a huge talent. Yet his uneven performance in the NCAA tournament solidified some nagging doubts about just how well his unique blend of skills would translate to the NBA. "The kid's got a long way to go," said Bob Kauffman, the general manager of the Detroit Pistons. "I hope he doesn't take a chance and ruin himself." Larry Donald, the revered columnist for *Basketball Weekly*, wrote that "knowledgeable scouts will tell you they worry about his shooting ability. They see Earvin as the kind of player who might someday make a winner into a champion, but he's never going to make a loser into a winner. No guard can."

Perhaps it was those misgivings or just the financial realities of operating a franchise in a league that was struggling to remain afloat that kept Kansas City's general manager, Joe Axelson, whose team owned the second overall pick in the draft, from offering the big money that young Earvin was hoping for. The meeting was already delicate since Axelson was violating the NBA's rule forbidding its teams from trying to lure college players into the draft. (Though Axelson told NBA commissioner Larry O'Brien that no financial terms were discussed, Johnson later revealed to the *State Journal* that Axelson had offered him a five-year contract worth $225,000 per year.) Finally, after much haggling, Johnson ran out of patience. He looked over at Tucker and touched the brim of his cap. The two of them immediately stood up to leave. "He's a funny dude," Tucker says. "He takes a long time to think about things, but once he makes up his mind, he's ready to go."

Axelson said he would call Tucker the next day to let him know whether he could meet their price. When Axelson called well past the designated hour, Tucker informed him that Johnson had decided to remain in school. Naturally, Michigan State coach Jud Heathcote was elated to hear the news, but the episode reinforced Heathcote's understanding that the temptation of the pros would be even harder for Johnson to turn down a year later. That was the reality he faced heading into the 1978–79 season: the Magic Act was not going to be playing in East Lansing much longer.

Larry Bird was not as inclined as Johnson to test the NBA waters during the summer of 1978, but that didn't matter. His name was among the list of draftable players, thanks to the NBA's "junior eligible" rule, which stated that a player could be selected at the end of his junior season as long as his original high school graduating class had been through four years of college. If the player stayed in school, the team that picked him would have until the day before the next year's draft to sign him to a contract. If no deal could be reached, the player's name would simply go back into the pool. Bird fell under the auspices of the junior eligible rule because he had taken a full year off following his senior year at Springs Valley High School in French Lick, Indiana, before enrolling at Indiana State University.

Like Johnson, Bird was also coming off of a brilliant 1977–78 season. He was ranked second nationally in scoring (30.0 average) and was a consensus first team All-American. For the second straight year, though, he had failed to lead the Sycamores to the NCAA tournament—they lost in the second round of the National Invitation Tournament (NIT)—but that wasn't the reason he wanted to come back to school. He wanted to be the first person in his family to earn a college degree. And when Larry Bird wanted to do something, it was awfully hard to talk him out of it.

Even so, the folks in Terre Haute were plenty nervous. After all, Bird had grown up in one of the poorest families in the poorest county in the state. What's more, the hometown Indiana Pacers owned the third pick in the 1978 draft. Bird had met personally in Indianapolis with the team's coach, Bobby "Slick" Leonard, who was hopeful that Bird would enter the draft so the Pacers could pick him. (Word trickled back to Terre Haute that a case of beer had been consumed during said meeting.) Indiana State president Richard Landini dispatched a member of his staff to Bird's house to encourage him to stay in school. "I'm not going anywhere," Bird told him. "I promised my mom." Sycamores coach Bob King also encouraged Bird to keep a low profile. "They tried to hide Larry a little bit from agents who were coming around and trying to sweet-talk him into going into the draft," recalls Sharel King, the coach's wife. "I don't know where they took him, but he played a lot of golf that summer."

Indeed, Bird was playing golf in, of all places, Santa Claus, Indiana, on June 8, when he received word of his early Christmas present: the Boston Celtics had selected him with the sixth pick in the draft. Celtics general manager Red Auerbach, who called Bird the best-passing big man he had seen since Bill Bradley, assured King that he was not expecting to have Bird's services until the following year. The fact that the Celtics had two first-round draft picks in 1978 gave them the luxury of waiting. Larry, meanwhile, knew nothing of the Celtics' storied tradition. He had heard of Bill Russell, but only because when he was a kid, he and a cousin used to play one-on-one pretending they were Russell and Wilt Chamberlain.

Larry had tried to avoid the media spotlight during his first two seasons at Indiana State, and, even though he knew he'd probably be drafted, he had no desire to talk to reporters about it. Indiana State's sports information office prepared a statement on Bird's behalf for that day. The only thing that needed to be filled in was the name of the team. "I'm very happy that the Boston Celtics have shown enough interest in me to draft me, even though I'm not going to sign until next season," the statement read. "I'll be interested in sitting down to talk things over after Indiana State's '78–79 season has been completed."

Bird was intent on playing out his career at Indiana State, but he also understood the unique leverage his situation presented. He could now leave for the NBA at any moment. So he told King he would come back for his senior year, but on one condition: he did not want to be required to talk to the press. King mulled it over for a good half second before saying yes.

As it turned out, King would not be in a position to deliver on that promise. A few weeks after the NBA draft, King suffered a heart attack in Algona, Iowa, while en route to a coaching clinic. He was hospitalized for three weeks, but he appeared to be on the mend until September, when he started suffering from lingering headaches. His wife asked Bob Behnke, the team's trainer, to come to their house to massage King's neck, but Behnke told her he believed something more serious might be going on.

After several weeks of tests, the fifty-five-year-old King was diagnosed with a bulging aneurysm in his brain. He was told he would need to have surgery as soon as possible, which would leave him incapacitated for the foreseeable future. Since King was also Indiana State's athletic director, he was responsible for deciding who should replace him as acting head coach until he was well enough to return.

King had two assistant coaches, Stan Evans and Bill Hodges, both in their midthirties and both eager to step in. On the surface, Evans was the obvious choice. Unlike Hodges, he had been a college head coach, most recently at Miami Dade (South) Community College, where he coached for two years before King brought him to Indiana State in the spring of 1975. Evans was far more involved in practices and putting together game plans than Hodges was. In fact, as the program's primary recruiter and advance scout, Hodges wasn't even on the bench for many of the Sycamores' games.

Moreover, Evans had a promise from King that he would ascend to head coach whenever King retired, which was presumably going to be at the end of the 1978–79 season. Evans says that King (who died in 2004) gave him that assurance when he hired him from Miami Dade on the condition that Evans bring his star center, DeCarsta Webster, to Indiana State with him. Evans was also the one who recommended to King that he hire Hodges, an Indiana native whose ties around the state would be valuable for recruiting.

Stan Evans might have had all those things going for him, but Bill Hodges had one thing Evans didn't. He had Larry Bird in his corner.

Hodges was the one who made all those recruiting trips to French Lick in the spring of 1975, eventually cajoling Bird, who had dropped out of Indiana University the previous fall, to give college one more try. Hodges was the one who found Bird a job in Terre Haute, who let Bird live in his house until he could move into a dorm room and set him up with a local dentist who performed more than half a dozen root canals on him. Like Bird, Hodges was an Indiana farm boy who chewed tobacco and wasn't above getting into the occasional bar scrape. Where Evans could be aloof and blunt, Hodges was easygoing and conversational. "Larry and Stan really had a strange relationship," says Jimmy Smith, Indiana State's starting point guard during Bird's sophomore and junior seasons. "I don't know that Larry cared for Stan a lot. Stan was a very intelligent business person, but he and Larry didn't get along very well."

Bird wasn't just a returning All-American. He had a one-way ticket to Boston in his pocket, ready to be cashed in at any moment. Nor was he shy about making his preferences known. "Larry wouldn't play if Stan was going to be head coach," Sharel King says. Bird confirmed as much in his 1989 autobiography *Drive*, in which he wrote, "Believe me, I definitely would have left if Bill Hodges hadn't gotten the job."

In the end, Bird's strong preference made the decision easy for King and for Richard Landini, Indiana State's president and its number-one basketball fan. Landini announced Hodges's promotion to interim head coach on October 11, just four days before the start of practice. Two days later, King underwent successful brain surgery, but it was not at all clear when—or if—he would return to work.

Evans, meanwhile, tried to put on his best public face. He was officially "reassigned" to a job as personnel director at the university, claiming all the while that it was his choice. "After thirteen years in basketball, I had acquired sort of tunnel vision. I wanted to pursue some new avenues," he said. Hodges told reporters that he and Evans "had a nice chat last week and he feels like it's better for him. There is no bitterness and no problems internally."

The private reality was much different. On the afternoon of the decision, Evans went to clean out his desk. Since he and Hodges shared adjacent offices, Evans had to walk through Hodges's office to get to his own. "He walked through my office, walked in front of my desk, walked into his office, and he shut the door. I never saw him after that, and I've never seen him since," Hodges says. "We were really close, but he never said one word."

"He stabbed me in the back. I got him the job," Evans says of Hodges. "I wasn't going to work for Hodges. I knew more than him. It was an arrogant move on my part, but I was hurt, disappointed, and shocked."

Thus was Bill Hodges, who was all of thirty-five years old and whose only previous head coaching experience was two years as the freshman coach at Tennessee Tech, handed the keys to a program that included arguably the best player in America. "I don't have any head coaching experience, but I'm not the type of guy to lose sleep at night," he said. "I'm still Coach King's assistant. When he gets well, he'll be the head coach again." Hodges said that his team's goal was "winning the conference, which means an NCAA bid," adding that he was "very close" with Bird. "We have a big brother relationship, but I'll treat him like the rest of the players," he said.

Though Hodges was aware of King's promise to Bird that he would not have to deal with reporters, he asked Bird to accompany him to the Missouri Valley Conference's preseason media day in Des Moines, Iowa. Bird grudgingly agreed, and despite his misgivings he was funny and engaging with the writers. Naturally, many of the questions centered on the coaching change that had taken place three weeks before. "It's not really a problem," Bird said. "They're basically the same type of coach. Coach Hodges's role changed overnight. Used to be he was the guy you'd see if you had problems, like if you wanted to get out of a test or something, but now he is the man."

Bird was joking, but one of the local writers, who was a young part-timer, published it straight-up in the next day's *Terre Haute Tribune*. One of Bird's teachers humiliated him by warning him in front of the whole class that he wouldn't be able to use his status as a basketball player to get out of taking any tests. Bird was irate. When Hodges came into the locker room before practice that afternoon, Bird exploded. This was why he didn't want to deal with the press in the first place, he said. King had promised him he didn't have to do any interviews, and he didn't want to do any more.

Hodges acquiesced. "Coach King gave you his word and I'll stick with it," he said. "But remember, if you're not going to talk to the press, that means any press—including our press. Our friends." That was fine with Larry. Hodges called the local beat writers and informed them that while he would do the occasional interview with radio and television (where he couldn't be misquoted), Bird would not be talking to any more print reporters the rest of the season.

The Sycamores had yet to play their first game, but the season's dynamic was firmly in place. Bill Hodges may have been the head coach, but this was going to be Larry Bird's show.

It was highly unusual for Jenison Fieldhouse at Michigan State to be nearly empty when Earvin Johnson was performing on the court, but that was the case in early October when Lane Stewart, a photographer for *Sports Illustrated*, flew into town to conduct a photo shoot. Johnson was clad in formal wear for the session—a jacket with tails, top hat, white tie and vest, shiny patent leather shoes—as he held a basketball and struck pose after pose. The session was for the cover of the magazine's college basketball preview issue, which was going to be published in late November. A few of Johnson's teammates milled about the gym. "One thing I was struck by as I watched him is that he didn't seem to be shy about it at all," says Mike Longaker, a walk-on junior guard that season. "He could eat it up all day long and still have a big ol' smile on his face. It wasn't an act, either. It's just who he was."

And who he had always been—the center of attention, the life of the party, and the toast of the town of Lansing, Michigan. Johnson first gained notice as a grade-schooler, when he excelled on the playground court down the street from the yellow frame house where he grew up along with his eight brothers and sisters. As an eighth grader at Dwight Rich Middle School, Johnson set a city scoring record with 48 points in a game, even though he sat for most of the fourth quarter. Though Earvin was always big for his age, he developed guard skills during games of full-court one-on-one against his older brother Larry. As a little boy, he relished the idea of attending J.W. Sexton High School, the city basketball power whose building he could see from his bedroom window, and leading its team to a state championship.

That dream was derailed by a school integration program that required Earvin to be bused across town to Everett High School. The busing program was mostly targeted toward the city's eight elementary schools, but since Everett was 92 percent white (and thus in violation of federal guidelines), it was folded into the program. Lansing's busing initiative was not popular in many quarters—five of its supporters on the Board of Education were recalled in a special election—and Earvin was desolate at the idea of playing for Everett, not least because the school had barely made a ripple in basketball. Moreover, his two older brothers, Quincy and Larry, had had bad experiences there. Quincy witnessed protests and a few brick-throwing incidents, and when Larry was cut from the varsity basketball team, he was convinced the decision was racially motivated. (Larry told the coach, George Fox, that his little brother would never play for him.) Johnson's parents, Earvin Sr. and Christine, were concerned enough that they wrote a letter to the school board asking them to grant Earvin a waiver so he could go to Sexton. The request was denied. They considered having Earvin bunk up with friends who lived within Sexton's jurisdiction before deciding that he was better off living at home and going to Everett.

"I was upset," Earvin said in 1977. "I wanted to go to Sexton. All the dudes I played with went to Sexton. I went to every Sexton game. I was a Sexton man, and then they came up with this busing thing."

Fox recalls, "It was very controversial. Racial tension ran high. The white kids didn't want them there, and the black kids didn't want to be there."

Such was the breach that Earvin stepped into when he began his sophomore year at Everett in the fall of 1974. (Like all of the city's high schools, Everett included grades ten through twelve.) During an early basketball practice, Johnson grew livid when an older white teammate appeared to be refusing to pass him the ball. Fox had to restrain Earvin from going after the player. Johnson also recalled an instance when some black female students were, in his view, unfairly cut from the cheerleading squad. He and the other black basketball players threatened to boycott practice until the girls were admitted.

Earvin also struggled academically at first. His feelings of inadequacy were agitated by a school security guard whom the students referred to as John the Narc. According to Earvin, John made a habit of disparaging him, telling him he would never amount to anything. As Johnson wrote in his autobiography, *My Life*, "John the Narc would be shocked to hear it, but I turned him from my enemy into my biggest motivator. Starting in eleventh grade, I worked harder at school than at basketball."

A tipping point in his relationship with Coach Fox came early during Johnson's sophomore season. The junior varsity coach had discovered after a practice that his keys were missing. When he told the players he thought one of them had stolen the keys, it led to a contentious meeting between parents and the school's administration. The meeting ended with plenty of bad feelings but no resolution. Afterward, Fox discreetly approached Johnson and asked him to intervene. "Earvin, you know who's got those keys," he said. "Just get 'em back for us." The next day, Earvin brought Fox the keys. The coach never spoke another word about it.

"We were worried because those kids were going to boycott practice, Earvin included," Fox says. "That helped my relations with Earvin. We accused the right kid, but we never told who it was. We just dropped it, and Earvin respected us for not talking about it."

When Fox first saw Johnson play in junior high school, he wondered why such a big player spent all his time roaming the perimeter. The answer dawned on him the summer before Earvin came to Everett, when Fox organized exhibitions against high school teams from around the state. He thought his young players would take a few lumps, but with Johnson in the fold, Everett dominated by huge margins. Fox realized that his oversized new arrival was by far his team's best ball handler and passer. As unconventional as it seemed, he decided to let Johnson continue to roam the perimeter as well as lead the fast break. "Coach Fox is the one who told him to dribble that basketball," says Jay Vincent, Johnson's rival at Lansing's Eastern High School and later his teammate at Michigan State. "I don't know if there were too many coaches who would let a six-foot-eight guy do that at the time. If he had said get inside and stop dribbling, it would have been a totally different Magic Johnson."

The basketball court also provided a forum to sort out conflicts. For example, Fox had a routine of ending practice with a conditioning drill called a rundown. The players had to trot at a respectable pace, with each player lasting as long as he could until there was only one player left. Johnson was usually the last man standing, but one day a white senior named Randy Shumway told Fox he intended to win. "There's no way," Fox said. "You can't stay with him."

Sure enough, after the other players dropped out, Johnson and Shumway were the only two still running. As they exhausted themselves, the two eventually agreed to call it a tie and walked over to Fox with their arms around each other's shoulders. "I almost cried," Fox says.

Once the high school season began, Johnson made his mark. During a game against conference favorite Parkside High in early January, he poured in 36 points and had 18 rebounds and 16 assists in a 19-point win. That was the second time that Fred Stabley Jr., a young reporter from the *State Journal*, had seen Johnson play. When Stabley interviewed Earvin afterward, he suggested that the youngster needed a flashy nickname to match his dynamic skills. "The Big E is taken by Elvin Hayes, and Julius Erving is Dr. J," Stabley said. "How about if I call you 'Magic'?"

Surrounded by his friends, Johnson was a little embarrassed at the question. "That's fine with me, Mr. Stabley," he said. When Stabley's story appeared in the next day's paper under the headline "Everett Crushes Parkside. Johnson Powers 80–61 Romp," the lead sentence read: "Earvin 'Magic' Johnson sauntered over to the bench, a smile covering his youthful face, and slapped the hands of each one of his teammates."

Stabley continued to use the nickname during his game accounts, and after a few months it took hold. If it added to Earvin's burgeoning celebrity, that was also fine with him. He actually enjoyed standing around after games and signing autographs. He would even sign while sitting in the bleachers before his games started. "I remember one night we were at Grand Ridge, which is pretty much an all-white school. It was the end of the third quarter of the jayvee game, and he's still up there signing autographs," Fox says. "Parents, too. They all took a liking to him. I just went up and I said, 'Folks, I'm sorry, we gotta get him down to the locker room.' And he apologized to them. That's the way he was."

Though Johnson mostly socialized with his black friends who went to Sexton, he also attended quite a few parties thrown by his classmates at Everett—sometimes on the same night. Wherever he was, he often took control of the music using the same authority with which he orchestrated a fast break. "He'd go, 'All right, this is E. J. the Deejay, bringing it to you live from Lansing,'" says Jamie Huffman, Johnson's teammate at Everett. "He liked the spotlight and he liked the ladies. To me, he just always seemed older than he was."

"Going to Everett over Sexton helped Earvin down the road. I'm convinced of that," Fox says. "He learned how to deal with racial problems. He mingled with white kids; he dated white girls if the truth be known, and nobody seemed to mind. He'd have been a different person at Sexton."

Not surprisingly, Earvin was also a big a hit with the local basketball establishment. He was in seventh grade when he was first befriended by Charles Tucker, a psychiatrist and counselor in the Lansing school system. Tucker was a gym rat who played a year and a half in the American Basketball Association and knew all the good ballplayers in town, including the guys at Michigan State. As Earvin got older, Tucker introduced him to some of his professional friends, such as Darryl Dawkins and George Gervin. Tucker soon became a close confidant of Johnson's parents and was the family's conduit to the outside world during Magic's recruitment.

Earvin also had an open invitation to play pickup games with the Michigan State players. Even though he was much younger than the college guys, he shined in those workouts. He sent tongues wagging one day during the summer between his sophomore and junior years when he dunked over Lindsay Hairston, who at the time was one of the best shot-blockers in the Big Ten. On another occasion, during his senior year, Earvin showed up with his right hand wrapped because of an injury. He still dominated play using mostly his left. He became especially close with Michigan State's best player, Terry Furlow, who attended many of Earvin's high school games and took him to a few parties.

Johnson kept his hand in a variety of extracurricular activities at Everett, including the student newspaper. When a reporter from the *Detroit News Sunday Magazine* asked Johnson what he would write about himself, he replied, "I'd write that he likes to get to know people. He's a fun person to talk to. He loves to spend money. He's an outgoing person. He loves to sit down and talk, talk, talk. I guess it would be a long story. You'd probably have to put it in a book."

If anything, Johnson was too enamored of all the attention. His eagerness to please often led him to be overextended. His standard solution was to blow off his obligations without explanation or apology. "The problem with Earvin is he can't say no to anyone," Fox says.

"It was easier for him not to go somewhere than to say no. He stood up a lot of people that way. Then they'd call me up and say, 'Where's Earvin? He was supposed to be here tonight.'"

Johnson was not about to assume a lower profile after arriving at Michigan State in the fall of 1977. He could often be spotted driving around campus in his long brown Buick "deuce-and-a-quarter" convertible, blasting his music for all the world to hear. Just like he did at parties, he seized control of the music that was played in the Spartans' locker room. ("Magic Man" by Heart was a favorite selection.) Two nights a week, he brought his "E. J. the Deejay" act to an off-campus student disco called Bonnie & Clyde's. "People are stopping me to sign autographs for their little brothers or themselves," he marveled that November. "The first day girls just kept coming to my room to say hi and they're glad I came here. When I walk into a classroom I can hear 'em saying, 'That must be Earvin.' They're whispering about me. It's nice because they're behind us one hundred percent."

Michigan State's head basketball coach, Jud Heathcote, encountered similar problems to those George Fox had faced whenever Johnson would skip out on a promise he had made to appear somewhere. "I finally had to tell Earvin [that] you can't tell people you're gonna be there and then not be there," Heathcote says. "To say that he was sorry he didn't show up wouldn't be true. He was concerned he had to be there, but he didn't feel an obligation he had to. He got better at that, but never completely where you knew he'd be someplace he said he would be."

Under most circumstances, all this attention being directed at a freshman would cause jealousy in the locker room. By all accounts, however, that was rarely the case with the Spartans. There were several reasons for this. In the first place, before Johnson arrived, Michigan State had not won anything significant in a long, long time. The upperclassmen had gone 26–28 the previous two seasons, and they ached to play for a winner. "That superseded everything else," says Greg Kelser, a small forward who had been the team's leading scorer and rebounder the year before Johnson arrived. "I had proven that I could play at that level, but for us to get recognition we had to win. We knew with Earvin, the wins would come. He and I clicked right from the very beginning."

It also helped that the Spartans' locker room was filled with players who did not mind playing supporting roles. The player with the most reason to be jealous was Kelser, a lithe six-foot-seven athlete whom Indiana University coach Bob Knight had called the best forward in the Big Ten. Kelser, however, was a reserved, cerebral kid who, as the son of a military man, was not inclined to let his ego hurt the esprit de corps. Jay Vincent, Johnson's roommate and fellow freshman, had gotten used to playing in Magic's prodigious shadow throughout high school, and he was plenty happy to let Johnson take on the role of vocal leader. Terry Donnelly was a lightly recruited six-foot-two guard from St. Louis who says he felt like he had "won the basketball" lottery when Johnson showed up. The sixth man, six-foot-seven sophomore Ron Charles, was a native of the Virgin Islands who brought a laid-back Caribbean sensibility to the whole circus.

But the biggest reason why Johnson's teammates didn't resent his fame was that they genuinely liked him. He treated them with respect, regardless of who they were or how many minutes they played. He hung out with them socially and invited them home to feast on his mother's cooking. "He did not make you feel that he was the superstar and you were the sub," says Mike Brkovich, a six-foot-four guard from Windsor, Ontario. "He joked around with you; he had time for you; he was an ordinary guy in a lot of ways. All the guys on the floor of his dorm room became friends with him. For the two years I played with him, I never once thought Earvin was a prima donna."

Showing how sensitive he could be to his teammates' egos, midway through his freshman year Johnson approached Mick McCabe, a writer for the *Detroit Free Press*, and suggested he write a story about the team's senior captain, Bob Chapman. "I've been around a lot of arrogant players, and Magic was not one of them," Jay Vincent says. "His parents would have never let him get like that."

Nowhere was Magic more magnanimous than on the court. His

entire approach to the game centered on the goal of getting other people to score; he looked for his own shot only when the team really needed him to. He was just as masterful at dishing out confidence. "He had this aura about him that he could get guys to do things they didn't think they were capable of doing," says Edgar Wilson, a former Spartan forward who was a graduate assistant during Magic's freshman year. "He'd set someone else up to score and then pat 'em on the back and say, 'That's what I'm talkin' about!' Those were his favorite words." Adds Brkovich, "There were times in practice where he could take four scrubs and beat the starting five. He just got you going and got you believing in yourself."

On one particularly hot day, Heathcote was putting the players through a full-court, four-on-four drill that was meant to improve their conditioning. Midway through the exercise, Mike Longaker, who was then a sophomore, staggered over to the sidelines and vomited. "As soon as I was done, he grabbed me by the shorts and said, 'Come on, come on, let's go,'" Longaker says. "I remember thinking, this guy is incredibly driven."

Heathcote noticed that, too. "I've always said, not only is Earvin the best player I've ever coached, he's the best player to *coach* I've ever coached," Heathcote says. "All he cared about was winning."

That extended to all manner of competition. When Johnson was sitting in the training room one day where he and Longaker were getting their ankles wrapped, Longaker balled up a wad of tape and tossed it left-handed into a garbage can across the room. "I can do that," Magic said, whereupon he fished the tape out of the garbage, returned to his own table, and attempted the shot until he made it.

Nor was he shy about wielding the sharper edges of leadership. Midway through Johnson's freshman year, Kelser attempted a careless hook shot toward the end of an 82–70 win at Illinois. "Greg, don't take that shot," Johnson barked. Afterward, Kelser confronted Magic in the locker room and asked, "What's your problem?"

"I was just trying to win the game," Johnson replied.

(Years later, during an NBA game between Kelser's Seattle Super-

Sonics and Johnson's Los Angeles Lakers, Kelser was whistled for a foul and slammed the ball down in anger. Johnson dashed over to a referee and yelled, "Tech! Tech!" When Kelser returned to the bench, one of his teammates leaned over and said, "I thought he was your boy.")

In September 1978, the Spartans took a twelve-day trip to Brazil, where they played in an international tournament, winning the gold medal over a Brazilian team that featured a dazzling sharpshooting guard named Oscar Schmidt. When the Spartans returned to campus, word quickly spread among the players that while they were gone, a hotshot freshman named Rob Gonzalez, a highly recruited six-foot-seven forward from Detroit, was bragging during pickup games that he was going to be a big-time star right away. Heathcote had instructed his players to take a few days off after the tournament because he was worried they were worn out, but when Johnson heard of Gonzalez's exploits, he grabbed his sneakers and his teammates and headed over to Jenison Fieldhouse. In game after game, Johnson humiliated the freshman, repeatedly beating him one-on-one and talking trash all the while. Gonzalez was barely a factor in the Spartans' rotation that season, and Kelser, for one, believed it was because Johnson had so badly squashed his confidence.

Magic, however, was all smiles for Lane Stewart, the *Sports Illustrated* photographer who came to town a few days before the start of practice. Stewart prepared for the photo shoot by spending several hours that morning with his assistant hanging rolls of white paper behind a basket to serve as a backdrop. Then he went into the locker room, where Johnson was getting dressed in the formal clothes. He sat next to Johnson and explained what they wanted to accomplish during the session. "The expression on your face should be, 'Gee, Mom, isn't this the silliest thing I have ever done?'" Stewart told him. Johnson smiled and assured Stewart he understood.

When Johnson came onto the court, Stewart wanted to begin by taking a few pictures of him using Polaroid film. That would give Stewart a chance to see how the background and lighting worked against Johnson's face before switching to regular film. He asked Johnson to stand underneath the backboard, then jump up and place the ball in the basket. When Stewart looked at the Polaroid film, he was amazed. "It was perfect," Stewart says. "If we wanted to use that for the cover, we could have. He had great control over his body, but also over his expression. The whole concept could have been ruined with the wrong expression, but Magic's charisma really came through to the camera."

Johnson then spent well over an hour repeatedly jumping and dunking while Stewart snapped almost two hundred pictures. Not once did Stewart think Johnson was getting tired or growing impatient with the shoot. When it was over, Stewart said to his assistant, "If we could sign that kid to a personal contract, we'd be millionaires." The issue hit the newsstands in November, with the cover showing a leaping Johnson laying the ball into the hoop with his arms stretched, his legs splayed, and his megawatt smile beaming for all the world to see. The heading read, "The Super Sophs: Michigan State's Classy Earvin Johnson." He was so excited he went to a few stores in East Lansing just to see what the magazine looked like on the shelves.

Yet when it came to predicting the national champions, *Sports Illustrated*, like most everyone else, chose Duke, the previous year's runner-up. The magazine placed the Spartans fourth in its preseason rankings. The Associated Press had them seventh. Lofty praise, to be sure, but for the Spartans' photogenic superstar, it was not lofty enough. "One of the reasons I [came] to Michigan State was that I love to be the underdog and rise to the occasion," he said. With the occasion of a new season upon him, Earvin Johnson was ready to continue his ascent.

2

Larry Bird and Magic Johnson were actually teammates for a brief time during the summer of 1978, when they competed for a team of American college all-stars that played in the World Invitational Tournament. The final game in Lexington, Kentucky, was broadcast by NBC, giving Bird his first opportunity to play on national television. Unfortunately, because the team was coached by Kentucky's Joe B. Hall, the Kentucky players dominated the starting lineup, relegating both Bird and Magic to nondescript roles coming off the bench.

One of the broadcasters working for NBC that day was Billy Packer, a thirty-eight-year-old former point guard at Wake Forest University who was working his fourth year for NBC. Packer, who watched several of the U.S. team's games and practices, had broadcast two of Michigan State's NCAA tournament games the previous March, so he was already familiar with what Johnson could do. He came away from his first exposure to Bird somewhat underwhelmed. "It never jumped out at me that this Larry Bird was a great player," Packer says. "He was just another guy."

Packer may have had limited exposure to Bird, but even those most familiar with his abilities were skeptical that he could lead Indiana State deep into the postseason. The Sycamores had lost three starters plus their head coach from a team that hadn't even made the NCAA tournament the previous season. At the Missouri Valley Conference's preseason media gathering, the league's writers picked the Sycamores to finish third in the conference. The coaches picked them second, behind Southern Illinois University. The chief barometers for national recognition were the top twenty-five rankings issued by the Associated Press, which was voted on by a panel of writers and broadcasters, and United Press International, which polled forty-two coaches around the country. Indiana State began the season unranked in both polls.

Nor did the major national publications hold the Sycamores in high esteem. The *Sporting News*'s season preview issue that fall included a ranking of the nation's best twenty-five teams, plus a list of more than a dozen that warranted "honorable mention," along with another dozen or so "sleeper" teams to watch out for. Indiana State was nowhere to be found. Though *Playboy* magazine selected Bird for its preseason All-America team for the second straight year, its college basketball expert, Anson Mount, dismissed Bird's supporting cast, writing that the "Sycamores will be inexperienced and Bird will again carry the team with little help. Watch for Bird to be double- and triple-teamed all year."

Bird and Hodges, however, had reason to believe that the team had the talent to challenge for the conference title and the coveted NCAA berth that came with it. The best player among Bird's teammates was Carl Nicks, a six-foot-two junior guard from Chicago. Nicks had attended Indiana State two years before as a freshman, but after a season in which he struggled both on the court and in the classroom, Bob King suggested that he transfer to a junior college. During that freshman season, Nicks had grown to respect Bird as a player, but he didn't always appreciate being on the receiving end of Bird's competitive drive in practice. "Everything was a challenge with him, every day," Nicks says. "Eventually I figured out he was making me a better player, but for a while, it really got under my skin. He'd take me down low and punish me, or he'd drain jumpers in my face and say, 'You can't guard me.' That bothered me big-time." Nicks might have been less bothered if he and Bird had socialized off the court, but Nicks was not a part of Bird's inner circle. "We were from two different worlds," Nicks says. "You could say he was shy, but I just thought he was extremely closed in and private, almost to the point where he had some trust issues. He only trusted guys he grew up with and the teammates he felt comfortable with."

Nicks concedes that he had some trust issues of his own to overcome, stemming mainly from the culture shock he felt after moving from a big city to a midsized, mostly white city surrounded by small rural communities. "I grew up on the South Side of Chicago, and it's like ninety-five percent black there," Nicks says. "I get down there with these southern Indiana types, and I'm thinking, Where the hell am I? I'm a city kid, talking fast, moving fast, and people [in Terre Haute] had the laid-back, beer-drinking southern mentality. It was hard for me to let down my barriers, because I was in shock for a long time."

Nicks says he assumed Larry "wasn't accustomed to being around blacks that much," but he also never thought Bird was a racist. Bird helped bridge the divide by inviting Nicks one weekend morning to go squirrel hunting with his buddies. "I didn't know nothing about shooting no guns," Nicks says. "When I saw a squirrel, I just started firing. I was thinking to myself the whole time, what am I doing out here? And I was scared to death because I thought there might be raccoons or wolves running out there. The other guys were cracking up."

When Nicks got to Gulf Coast Community College in Florida after his freshman season at Indiana State, he blossomed as a player, averaging 22.4 points and 5 assists as a sophomore. Still chastened by King's insistence that he play for a junior college, Nicks considered transferring to a different Division I school. He changed his mind over the summer when he got a call from Bird imploring him to return to Indiana State. "Larry was saying, 'Hey man, if you come back, I think you're the piece we need. We can really do some big-time stuff.' And for some reason, I didn't even hesitate to question him," Nicks says. "That was the first time I can remember Larry being somewhat intimate. I didn't want to pass up an opportunity to play with him again, because I had seen him do some serious stuff my freshman year."

Two other transfers also showed promise. Bob Heaton, a six-foot-five swingman from Clay City, Indiana, had left the University of Denver after the school decided to de-emphasize basketball. He was a gifted scorer with an affable, go-along-to-get-along demeanor, and his country sensibilities meshed so well with Bird that Larry invited Heaton to live with him during his senior year. He also never complained about coming off the bench instead of starting. The other transfer, Alex Gilbert, was a six-foot-eight jumping jack who came from Coffeyville Community College in Kansas. Gilbert was a prolific rebounder who could score around the rim, but his shooting range was nonexistent. Bird claimed that Gilbert was such a lousy ball handler that he literally could not dribble the ball past half-court.

The starting point guard would be Steve Reed, a six-foot-three sophomore who had been a backup the year before. Reed sometimes beat Bird in games of H-O-R-S-E during practice, but he had to be exhorted just to attempt a shot during a game. The other frontcourt starter was Brad Miley, a six-foot-eight junior from Rushville, Indiana, who was a horrendous shooter but whose quick, light feet enabled him to guard all five positions. He quickly became the team's designated stopper as well as the constant butt of Bird's biting sense of humor. (Bird liked to joke that Miley was the "best player to go this far in college without being able to shoot.") Rounding out the seven-man rotation was Leroy Staley, a six-foot-five jitterbug who added another layer of speed and toughness as well as the ability to score in spurts.

Thus did Indiana State consist of one future NBA superstar playing center, a borderline pro prospect in Nicks (he was drafted by the Denver Nuggets in the first round of the 1980 NBA draft and went on to play three years in the league), and a collection of guys with limited, specialized abilities. Those specialties, however, complemented each other beautifully. More important, Bird's teammates not only accepted but embraced their status as subordinate role players. "We all had our own little deal," Heaton says. "I think we all realized that this guy is an All-American college player of the year. We figured, we're lucky to be here; we'll hang on Larry. Just take us there." Nicks adds, "Everybody really knew their role and mastered it. Some guys just never shot the ball, but they didn't gripe about not getting points."

"We didn't have a lot of NBA talent on our team, but we were a team," Bird said. "When you have a team of guys who know their roles and stick to their roles, you can't get any better than that. Yeah, I was the focal point, and I was the one scoring the points and getting the rebounds, but if it wasn't for these other four guys with me, it would have never worked."

While the Sycamores' prospects were obviously going to hinge on Bird's ability to carry them, they dispelled the impression early on that they were a one-man team. On November 19, Indiana State played an exhibition against a team from the Soviet Union that was in the midst of a tour against American colleges, which included wins over Notre Dame, Kentucky, Arkansas, Kansas, Indiana, Purdue, and New Mexico. In a game played on Indiana State's home floor in the Hulman Center before just 6,622 fans (well short of the 10,189 capacity), Bird had 22 points and 13 rebounds but fouled out with 9:25 remaining. Indiana State led by 7 points at the time, and though the Russians scraped back to within 1 point with a little over three minutes to play, the Birdless Sycamores held on and won, 83–79. "If we can beat these guys, we should be able to beat anybody," Nicks said afterward.

In their official season opener six days later, Indiana State blew by Wisconsin's Lawrence University by 43 points. The only dramatic moment came just before tip-off, when each Indiana State player shook hands with Bob King, whose doctor had allowed him to attend his first game. That win set up a major clash on November 27 with the Sycamores' in-state rival, Purdue University, whom they had beaten by 28 points the year before in Hulman Center. It was rare for Indiana State to outclass its Big Ten counterpart, but the Sycamores won this time in West Lafayette, 63–53, behind Bird's 22 points, 15 rebounds, and 5 assists. Though Bird tended to roam the perimeter on offense to take advantage of his shooting and passing abilities, he was technically Indiana State's starting center, and he spent much of the game battling under the boards with Purdue's seven-foot-one center, Joe Barry Carroll. The Sycamores were inefficient on offense (35.5 percent shooting), they were sloppy with the ball (17 turnovers), and they lost the rebounding battle by 3, yet they made up the difference by attacking the goal aggressively on offense, which enabled them to outscore the Boilermakers from the foul line by 12 points. The game wasn't pretty, but the win was a huge boost for the team's confidence. "I'm an old Purdue guy and I knew what the crowd would be like," Hodges said. "I felt like if we could come in here and play within ourselves . . . on our own motivation without our crowd behind us, and play with poise, then we can go and play anywhere on the road with confidence."

From there, Indiana State edged out two regional rivals, winning against the University of Evansville on December 2, 74–70, and then squeaking by Illinois State University 78–76 before a sellout crowd at Hulman Center two days later. The season was young, but a pattern was emerging: great performances by Bird (40 points against Evansville; 31 points and 19 rebounds against Illinois State), a little help from his teammates, a bend-but-not-break devotion to defense, and just enough luck to prevail. Against Illinois State, the Sycamores had trailed 70–62 with just under five minutes remaining but found a way to win thanks largely to Nicks, whose 23 points included the game-winning basket with thirty-eight seconds remaining. Even more important than the points was the hard-nosed mentality that Nicks had brought with him from Chicago's South Side. "This ball club has great character," Hodges said. "I just have to go tell them to play ball. I don't have to say much. I've never been around a bunch of guys with this mental toughness."

Next up for the Sycamores was a quick trip to Florida on December 8 for a two-day tournament at Stetson University. The anticipated arrival of the boys from Terre Haute had not elicited much notice in the Sunshine State. A local newspaper's season preview had provided a list of notable games that would take place in Florida that season, as well as fifteen opposing players worth watching. There was no mention anywhere of Indiana State or Larry Bird. Some thirteen NBA scouts came to watch Bird in action (just in case he didn't come to terms with the Celtics), but barely three thousand fans showed up to see him score 32 and 37 points, respectively, in easy wins over East Carolina and Cleveland State.

The local writers were duly impressed by what they had seen from the unheralded blond kid from Indiana, and they were curious to hear what he had to say—only to be told by Indiana State's sports information director, Ed McKee, that Bird would not meet with them. This begat the somewhat awkward ritual of having the media turn to the other players for stories they wanted to write about Bird. "They brought in me and Carl Nicks to talk to the media, and basically all the questions pertained to Larry," Bob Heaton says. "So we were Larry's mouthpiece. They'd ask, 'What is Larry thinking?' Well how do I know? Afterward I thought, I'm not going to do that again."

Even so, Hodges recognized the potential benefits of Bird's silent treatment. "I caught a lot of flak, but when it comes down to it, it might have been the best thing that happened to our team," he says. "Everybody got a little bit of love. It wasn't all about Larry Bird."

Moreover, Hodges was also starting to believe his team might be much better than anyone realized. On the day the Sycamores beat Cleveland State, Hodges watched Notre Dame, which was ranked No. 3 in the AP poll, defeat No. 2 UCLA by three points. *Shit*, he thought, *we're just as good as they are.* After the Sycamores returned to Terre Haute with a 6–0 record, Hodges walked into the players' lounge, where Bird was watching Kentucky, the defending NCAA champions, play on television. "You know what?" Hodges said. "I think we're as good as them, too." Bird didn't disagree.

That notion would have seemed laughable to many of the fans and experts who followed college basketball across the country. To them, the Missouri Valley Conference was a second-tier league, perennially overshadowed by the huge Midwestern universities that comprised the Big Ten. Moreover, Indiana State was a second-tier program inside its second-tier conference. While the program's history had a little bit of luster—John Wooden had coached there for two years before leaving for UCLA in 1948—it had moved up to the NCAA's highest competitive level, Division I, only in 1969. Indiana State didn't become a full-fledged member of the Valley until 1977, and the only reason the school had been invited to join the league was because Cincinnati, Louisville, and Memphis State had defected to more prominent destinations.

Nor did it help that Bob Knight's Indiana Hoosiers, the 1976 NCAA champions and the signature program in the Big Ten, played just sixty miles to the east, while Purdue, Wooden's alma mater, was located a hundred miles to the north. Even the other second-tier schools in the region like Illinois State, Evansville, and Southern Illinois had more of a winning tradition than Indiana State had. Given that they were still trying to prove they could hang with the big boys in their own neighborhood, and given that the writers and coaches who voted in the national polls had no way of seeing them play unless they lived in the area, the Sycamores would have to have an extraordinary season to be considered among the nation's elite. Teams like Kentucky, UCLA, and Notre Dame were part of a very exclusive club, and the Indiana State Sycamores were clearly not cool enough to be invited inside the velvet ropes. If they wanted to come to the party, they would have to crash it.

While Michigan State was a Big Ten team that had been to the Elite Eight of the 1978 NCAA tournament, that program also suffered from having to play under a shadow cast by an in-state rival. In this case, the shadow came from Ann Arbor, where the University of Michigan, which had lost to Indiana in that 1976 NCAA title game, had established itself as one of the premier programs in the nation. Throughout the 1960s and 1970s, no matter how hard Michigan State tried, it constantly came up short in its quest to overtake its nemesis. Their duel was writ especially large during the 1976–77 basketball season, when Michigan and Michigan State vied intensely to win the services of one Earvin Johnson.

On the surface, it wasn't a fair fight. During Magic's senior year at Everett High, Michigan went 26–4 under coach Johnny Orr and won its fifth Big Ten championship in thirteen years. The Wolverines also possessed a typically strong crop of veterans led by All-American Phil Hubbard, a six-foot-eight forward who had become good friends with Magic. If Johnson joined that group, they would have a real chance to win a national championship his freshman season.

Michigan State, meanwhile, had gone 12–15 that season, making it ten years since its last Big Ten title. The Spartans had not played in the NCAA tournament since 1959. Jenison Fieldhouse, the Spartans' home arena, was so decrepit that coaches were afraid to take recruits there on campus visits. Attendance at home games hovered around five thousand—on a good day. Moreover, the athletic department was in shambles in the wake of a scandal that had landed the football program on NCAA probation. A brief walkout of ten black basketball players in 1975 had led to the firing of the head coach, Gus Ganakas, a year later. When Ganakas was reassigned to another position inside the athletic department, he wrote a letter to Earvin to assure him that he should still come to Michigan State. Johnson, however, was unmoved. He liked Ganakas, and now that the school had dumped him, Johnson figured he was probably headed for Ann Arbor.

A few days after Michigan State announced that it had lured Jud Heathcote from the University of Montana to replace Ganakas, Heathcote got a phone call from Fred Stabley Jr., the *State Journal* writer who had given Johnson his nickname. Stabley asked Heathcote if he knew about the local prodigy. "Sure," Heathcote replied. Then he hung up the phone and asked his assistants to find out who this Johnson fellow was.

It wouldn't take long for Heathcote to learn what all the fuss was about. During his first few months on the job, numerous boosters called to ask if he knew about Magic. He caught his first glimpse that spring while watching Johnson play with the Michigan State team in Jenison Fieldhouse. "He was telling our guys what to do and where to go—and they were listening," Heathcote says. "That amazed me."

Heathcote knew it wouldn't be easy to convince Johnson to play for him. Johnny Orr's top assistant coach, Bill Frieder, who was such a dogged recruiter that even the Michigan State coaches asked him from time to time about whether they should go after certain players, had been pursuing Johnson ever since Frieder first spotted him before he entered high school. "If there was any way to take a tenth grader into the NBA, you could do it with him. He was that good," Frieder says. "He had the same expressions he has always had, the smile on his face, the good attitude on the court. The whole deal."

Frieder scored an early coup when he convinced Johnson to attend Orr's summer basketball camp in Ann Arbor when he was in ninth grade. Frieder also helped persuade him not to play in any major summer showcases like Howard Garfinkel's Five-Star Camp, lest he draw the attention of out-of-town recruiters. But one thing Frieder sensed he would have trouble overcoming was Johnson's close relationship with Charles Tucker, who was a psychiatrist and counselor in the Lansing school system when he first befriended Johnson in the seventh grade. When it came to advice on basketball, Johnson trusted Tucker more than anyone else except his father. By the time Earvin's recruitment heated up, Tucker was teaching at Michigan State. He also played pickup basketball with the Spartan players and was friends with the MSU coaches, especially Heathcote's assistant Vern Payne. "Charles did a great job recruiting Earvin for Michigan State," Frieder says. "You had to go through him to get to the parents. He would not let you get close to the father, and he resented Michigan being around. He was the one who probably put the daggers in us." At one point, Tucker requested a meeting with Orr, but Orr refused. That didn't help.

As Johnson's senior season began at Everett High School, his coach, George Fox, asked him to narrow down his list to about seven schools. Coaches like Louisville's Denny Crum, Indiana's Bob Knight, and Notre Dame's Digger Phelps came through town, but it was often left to Fox to gently break the news that there was very little chance the kid would leave the state of Michigan. After Johnson met with Leonard Hamilton, who was then an assistant at Kentucky, Hamilton came over to Fox's house, sat in front of his fireplace, and gushed over the enthusiasm Magic had expressed for Kentucky. "That don't mean a damn thing," Fox said. "He's that way with everyone. I'm telling you, don't get your hopes up."

Johnson took official visits to the University of Maryland, Notre Dame, and North Carolina State. He was scheduled to go to the University of Southern California, too, but on the day of his visit, a USC assistant called Fox to tell him Earvin wasn't at the Los Angeles airport. When Fox asked Magic what happened, he said he was tired of making visits, so he just decided not to go—without bothering to let the USC coaches know.

Once the basketball season got under way, it was apparent that Johnson was going to attend either Michigan or Michigan State. It helped Heathcote's cause that Lansing Eastern High School's Jay Vincent, who had been good friends with Johnson ever since they started dueling as grade-schoolers, appeared headed for State. Johnson and Vincent were such popular attractions that when their schools played each other for the second time that winter, the game was held not in a high school gym but rather in Jenison Fieldhouse. The contest, unlike those involving the Spartans, drew a raucous sellout crowd and was broadcast live on local television. The local Nielsen rating for that game was only slightly less than the one the station generated for that year's Super Bowl.

Throughout the season, bumper stickers that read "Leading the Way with Earvin and Jay" were popping up around Lansing. The two were regular fixtures at Michigan State games, thanks to the box Heathcote provided for them and their friends. Problem was, that access also gave them a chance to see Heathcote up close, and it was not a pretty sight. The coach chewed out his players, berated the officials, and no matter what was happening on the court he never, ever seemed happy. "I couldn't get a read on Jud and his style," Johnson later said. "I tried, but I couldn't do it."

"I was looking at Jud scream at his players and I was like, Wow, this is going to be a tough coach to play for," Vincent says. "Magic said a few times he didn't know if he could deal with how Coach Heathcote yells."

Fortunately for Heathcote, Charles Tucker was in his corner. "I know ball and I could see he was a competitor," Tucker says. "He was clever. A lot of coaches will pull you out if you make a mistake and forget you're there. Jud would jump up and holler and sit a guy down. But then he'd tell them what they did wrong and send them back in the game."

Needless to say, when it came to recruiting, Heathcote did not ooze charm the way someone like Bill Frieder did. Heathcote was not the type to blandish anyone, and he wasn't going to start with some high school kid. "Jud was not a good recruiter," Fox says. "His attitude was, if they don't want to come here, I don't want 'em here. Of course, he never said that about Earvin. He wanted Earvin bad."

Like Ganakas before him, Heathcote made a point to attend every Everett High School game that he could. One night, he bought a dollar raffle ticket and won a free basketball. Part of the raffle's promotion was that every member of the Everett team would sign the ball, so Heathcote brought it to the locker room after the game. When Johnson signed the ball, he cracked, "That's the only signature he'll ever get from me." Of those days, Heathcote says, "I never felt comfortable with Earvin."

He wasn't much more comfortable back at Michigan State. He got a message one day that Dr. Clifton Wharton, the school's president and the first African American president at a Big Ten university, wanted to meet with him and athletic director Joe Kearney in his office. When the two men arrived, Wharton's assistant told them the president was very upset, though he didn't want to reveal why.

Once the meeting began, Wharton fumed at Heathcote and Kearney. "I do not like the position you've put me in," he said.

Heathcote and Kearney looked at each other. "Mr. President," Heathcote said, "I have no idea what you are talking about."

"Yes you do," Wharton replied. "You are trying to get me involved in the recruitment of Earvin Johnson. You are putting pressure on me to meet with his parents at their house because they do not want to come here to my office. I am not going to their house, and I do not want to be involved."

Heathcote tried to assure Wharton that he had no hand in trying to get him to meet with Johnson's parents—and in fact that such a meeting was pointless because his parents already wanted him to go to Michigan State. Wharton didn't buy that explanation. "Jud was not as innocent in that as he says," Wharton says. "I had heard from other sources that he was carrying on about how I did not want to go to speak to the family, but that was not the central issue. I was very concerned that this be a squeaky-clean recruitment, because given the sanctions that had been imposed on our football program, we had to be like Caesar's wife. I said, 'Heathcote, this is going to be a clean recruitment or else.' He looked at me like, Do you really mean that? I made it clear that if there was a single improper action on his part, he would be gone."

The confrontation was indicative of the pressure that everybody was feeling. When Heathcote and Kearney stepped on the elevator after the meeting, Heathcote turned to his boss and deadpanned, "Hey, Joe, I think the president is a little pissed off at us." That was Heathcote's way of lightening the mood, but Kearney didn't so much as crack a smile.

But whatever deficiencies Heathcote had as a recruiter, the town of Lansing more than made up for them. Wherever Earvin went, he was besieged by friends and family begging him to go to Michigan State. "Earvin had a posse before anyone knew what a posse was," Fox says. "A lot of them weren't basketball players, and many of them weren't in the position to drive to Michigan to watch him. But they could get out to State." It wasn't just kids, either. In February, a group of two dozen local businessmen formed a committee to try to convince

Johnson and Vincent to be Spartans, but President Wharton, ever fearful of attracting more scrutiny from the NCAA, put the kibosh on that effort.

The strain inexorably took its toll on young Earvin. Recruiters were literally showing up on his doorstep, so he wound up spending more time at other people's houses. His phone rang so often, the family had to change the number. "Every time I think I've got a moment to myself, ding-a-ling, there goes the phone," he said. The intensity ticked up after he led Everett to the Class A state championship on March 26. In a thrilling game that sold out Michigan's Crisler Arena and was broadcast on statewide television, Everett defeated Birmingham's Brother Rice High School 62–56, but victory came only after Rice guard Kevin Smith had sent the game into overtime with a banked-in desperation heave from half-court. After the game, the ubiquitous Bill Frieder walked along press row and passed out stat sheets to the media. Johnson was brilliant as usual: 34 points, 14 rebounds, 4 assists, 3 steals.

As the NCAA's spring signing deadline loomed, Johnson remained torn. He showed up one night at Fisher Body, where his father was working his late shift, and asked his dad point-blank what he wanted him to do. "I know you want me to go to Michigan State," Earvin said.

"Yeah, I'd like you to go there because it's close and we'll get to see you," his father said. "But wherever you go, we're going, too. It's all on you, Junior."

In early April, Earvin and his parents traveled to Washington, D.C., to participate in the annual McDonald's All-American Classic. After the game, Fox drank some beers with Heathcote at the hotel and told him he believed Magic was going to Michigan State. "You can't be so close to so many people and just leave town," Fox says.

The community pressure crested on April 17, the day Johnson returned from a two-week stint in Germany, where he competed in an international basketball tournament with a team of American high school players. That morning, a story ran in the *State Journal* announcing that a welcome-home rally for Earvin would be held at

Capital City Airport. Johnson's plane landed at 10:54 p.m., two and a half hours later than originally scheduled. By the time his flight finally touched down, there were more than four hundred people, including Jud Heathcote, waiting to greet him. A surprised Johnson strode onto the speaker's stand and expressed his gratitude. After he spoke, he was presented with a petition of signatures from over five thousand Lansing elementary school students urging him and Vincent to choose Michigan State. The display overwhelmed him. "I thought there might be a couple of reporters and my family at the airport, but nothing like this," he said, brushing a tear from his cheek. "It means a great deal to me to see that a lot of people really care about me."

From his distant but not disinterested perspective, Gus Ganakas saw the coverage of Johnson's homecoming and sensed it was having an impact. "He could say no to Michigan State," Ganakas says, "but he couldn't say no to Lansing."

As D-day approached, Heathcote readied to make his closing argument. Vincent had just announced he was coming to Michigan State, but there was no guarantee that Johnson would follow. Heathcote had arranged with Tucker to meet with him, Magic, and Magic's dad at a restaurant in town. But when Heathcote showed up, nobody else came. "I got hot," Heathcote says. "I said, 'Hey, if he's going to Michigan so be it, but he's gotta tell me.'"

As it turned out, it was just a miscommunication. They got together the next night, Tuesday, April 19. Heathcote knew that Johnson's primary concern was whether he would be able to play guard, so the coach spent most of the night trying to mollify him. "I may be a hayseed from Montana, but I've seen you play enough," Heathcote said. "You will have the ball on the fast break. You will set the offense. You'll probably play forward on defense to take advantage of your rebounding, but you will be the point guard."

That was what Magic wanted to hear, but he still had cold feet. It was up to Vern Payne, the assistant coach who was closest to Magic, to close the deal. Payne, who was African American, was the only member of Ganakas's staff whom Heathcote had retained. At the end of Heathcote's first season, Payne accepted the job as the head coach at Wayne State University in Detroit. He had driven back to Lansing early on the morning of Wednesday, April 20, 1977, so he could see his family and start selling his home. When he stopped to grab breakfast at the Bob's Big Boy restaurant on Troll Bridge Road, he saw Bill Frieder and another Michigan assistant having breakfast. Knowing full well why the two men were in town, Payne decided on the spur of the moment to pay a surprise visit to Everett High School. When Payne got there, he asked a secretary in the front office if she could have Earvin Johnson meet him in the library. A few minutes later, Johnson stepped into the conference room where Payne was waiting, shut the door, and sat in a chair.

Payne began by reminding Johnson that he was now employed by Wayne State, not Michigan State, so he had nothing to gain by being there. "I'm here because I care about you and your decision," he said. "Nobody asked me to come talk to you. In fact, no one even knows I'm in town." Then he moved to dispel Earvin's doubts about Heathcote. "He's a good coach," Payne said. "Don't pay attention to all the swear words and the redness in his face and all the yelling. What's important is what comes out of his mouth, and I'm telling you, he's a very, very good coach. He will help you become a better player."

Aside from that vote of confidence, the crux of Payne's argument centered on the way Earvin would continue to be idolized by the city of Lansing if he stayed. Payne talked about Johnson's family, his friends, his high school coach, even Fred Stabley Jr., the local sportswriter who had covered him in high school. Many of Johnson's close friends still called him Earvin, but Payne called him Magic because, says Payne, "That's who he was." Payne told Johnson he would be a great player wherever he went, but he could be "Magic" only at Michigan State.

"You will have a chance to do some great things that have never been done at Michigan State," he said. "You'll be a trail blazer just like you were at Dwight Rich [Middle School] and at Everett. You won't have that same impact in Ann Arbor or anywhere else."

The meeting lasted nearly an hour. Johnson had a few comments and questions, but mostly he listened. Finally, he surprised both himself and Payne by saying, "Okay, let's do it. Get the papers and I'll sign."

Payne didn't need to hear it twice. He immediately left the school, drove over to Heathcote's office, and informed his now former boss that Johnson had committed to Michigan State. Johnson went to Fox's office to tell him the news. "Yeah, big surprise," Fox said sarcastically. They agreed that Earvin would reveal his choice at a press conference that Friday, two days later. In keeping with Johnson's flair for the dramatic, they decided to hold their secret tight until then.

After school was over that day, Johnson played ball with his friends in Everett's gymnasium. As usual, Bill Frieder sat in the stands and watched. When Johnson was through playing, Frieder followed him into the locker room to make yet another pitch for Michigan. As Johnson spoke about how difficult the decision was, he started to cry. Frieder did not take this as a good sign. He called his boss, Johnny Orr, and said, "I don't think we're going to get him."

The news of the forthcoming press conference sent the fans and local media into a frenzy of speculation. That night, Orr spoke at the annual all-sports dinner held by the University of Michigan Club of Lansing. "I wish I could tell you Earvin's coming to Michigan, but I can't," Orr said. "We don't know because he doesn't know right now."

The next day, Heathcote and one of his assistants, Don Monson, played in a golf tournament at Walnut Hills Country Club, where Heathcote was a member. They spent most of the afternoon dodging queries about Magic's intentions. When a local camera crew buttonholed Heathcote and asked what Johnson had decided, Heathcote lied and said he had no idea. Later that night, a crew from WJIM television glimpsed Heathcote eating dinner in the clubhouse. According to one account, he "was scowling and looking exceedingly irritated as he ate his chicken." (Apparently, this observer did not realize that was simply Heathcote's natural state.)

While Fox wanted to keep his promise to Earvin to hold the decision under wraps, he also wanted to repay the *State Journal* for its loyal coverage during the three years Johnson had played for Everett. So they arranged a secret photo opportunity at Johnson's house late Thursday evening, when he officially signed his letter of intent to Michigan State. The photograph was taken for the *Journal's* afternoon edition, which wouldn't be published until after the press conference was over.

By the time Johnson walked into the principal's office at Everett on Friday morning, he was tired of the whole charade. "Let's get this over with," he said. The classroom where he was to make his announcement was filled with some eighty people, including half a dozen TV cameras. As they waited for Magic to arrive, Joe Falls, a columnist for the *Detroit Free Press*, exchanged guesses with Tim Staudt, a Lansing sportscaster who had worked feverishly, and unsuccessfully, during the previous forty-eight hours to divine Johnson's intentions. "This is the best-kept secret of all time," Staudt told Falls. "I saw Jud Heathcote last night and he looked terrible. I saw Johnny Orr the night before and he looked great. I know it's going to be Michigan. I just know it."

Johnson's press conference was not carried on live television, but the audio was piped through the school's public address system so the entire student body could hear what Johnson was saying. The song "It's a Small World" played over the loudspeakers just prior to his arrival. As he walked into the classroom trailed by Fox, his parents, and Tucker, a man spoke into a television microphone and provided play-by-play. "The door is opening now and here comes Earvin Johnson into the room. . . . He's now walking toward the table where the microphones are. . . . He's sitting down now. . . ."

Johnson shifted his chair. He glanced down at the dozen or so microphones arrayed on the table and smiled. "Am I supposed to talk in all these mikes?" he said. Then he looked across the room and quipped, "Is [sic] there any questions before I get started?" A ripple of nervous laughter ensued. Finally, he said, "No, um, next year I will be, uh, attending Michigan State University." The room burst into a round of applause. A chorus of loud cheers could be heard from classrooms all through the school.

For the next half hour, Johnson patiently answered all the questions about why he was going to Michigan State and how he made his decision. The video of the press conference shows a young man who was clearly at ease in the spotlight, yet one whose elocution was a far cry from the smooth, precise delivery that would define him years later. "I always wanted to go to Michigan State since, I don't know, sixth, seventh grade," he said. "I always went to all the games, you know, and, um, once you get that Spartan in you, I guess it can't come out."

What will be his goals at Michigan State?

"Well, winning the Big Ten and trying to win the NCAA championship, you know. And hopefully going on and getting prepared for the pros."

How close did he come to going to Michigan?

"That was really close to happenin'. I really like the Michigan staff and the players, you know, and, um, it was almost gonna happen. If I had signed earlier, I probably would have went to Michigan because all through the year I was favoring Michigan."

What was the difference?

"I like Michigan State because they were the underdogs. And I'm the kind of player that likes to go into a down type of program and try to lift it up."

How did he feel now that the decision was behind him?

"I feel real good. Maybe the telephone will stop ringing."

George Fox may have felt all along Johnson was going to Michigan State, but many of Johnson's closest friends believed he was headed for Ann Arbor. "Everybody was sort of surprised that day," said Dale Beard, his teammate at Everett. "He didn't tell any of us, and the two of us used to talk about everything. So I was really shocked."

In the end, the visit from Payne proved to be decisive. "Vern was the key," Johnson said years later. "At that point, I was having questions about Jud and was going to Michigan. . . . My heart was always at Michigan State, no question about it. But basketball-wise, Michigan was always on top."

Payne says, "He simply needed someone to pull all the pieces together for him. I think I was able to deal with the questions in his mind and crystallize his thinking."

The announcement finally enabled Heathcote to discuss his prized recruit with reporters. "After I came out of shock, I was tremendously elated," he said. "I've never seen a young man with as much charisma, enthusiasm and charm for basketball." And yet that elation was tinged with a dash of realism. "There's a very good possibility that Earvin will not be here the full four years," Heathcote conceded. "You don't throw away financial security if you can reach your ultimate goal sooner."

Now that the recruitment was officially over, President Wharton felt comfortable calling Johnson's family. He told Johnson's mother, Christine, that he was pleased her son would be playing for Michigan State. Christine answered with a string of polite but distant "Mm-hmms." Wharton added, "And I want to assure you that while he's here, he is going to get a first-rate education."

"Now you're talking," she said.

The reaction from Michigan State fans was predictably electric. The phones at the *Detroit News*'s sports desk rang throughout the day with people seeking to get the latest information. By 11 a.m., more than one hundred people had called Michigan State requesting season tickets, bringing the total requests to over five hundred since the season ended the month before. A lot of pressure accompanied that hype, but that was not foremost in Heathcote's mind. He told some friends he wanted to have a "We Signed Earvin" party at his house. Word spread so fast that eventually more than three hundred people were jammed elbow to elbow into Heathcote's modest home. The soiree ended around four in the morning with Jud and two of his buddies sitting around an ice tub, downing the last of the beers as they toasted their good fortune.

Earvin Johnson had been thrust into the public eye before he had even entered high school. Many teenagers would have wilted under that kind of glare, but Johnson chose the one college where he would face more scrutiny and expectations than anywhere else. Larry Bird, on the other hand, made a completely different choice. Bird's path to Indiana State was unlike the one Johnson traveled to Michigan State precisely because Bird never wanted to be a celebrity. He only wanted to play basketball. Alas, Bird would eventually realize he could not excel at one without becoming the other.

3

The Indiana State Sycamores returned home from their back-to-back wins in Florida with a 6–0 record, and on December 12 they cracked the national rankings for the first time: they were twentieth in the Associated Press poll and sixteenth in the UPI poll. That caused a few members of the national media to trickle into Terre Haute, which, needless to say, was not a welcome development for the team's resident superstar.

Bird had several reasons for erecting his wall of silence. He was acutely sensitive to the possibility that his teammates might get jealous, but he was also fearful that some of the embarrassing details of his past would come to light. "He came from a culture in French Lick where everybody knew everybody, but everybody didn't know everybody's business," says Bob Ryan, the longtime columnist for the *Boston Globe* who coauthored Bird's autobiography in 1989. "As I got to know him, he opened up about certain things. It was amazing what was locked up inside him."

Larry had been intensely shy ever since he was a youngster. According to Jim Jones, his former high school coach, Larry once flunked an English class because he didn't want to give a speech. When his older brother, Mark, was leading Springs Valley High School to a state sectional championship, Larry didn't go to the games because he didn't like crowds. Even his mother, Georgia, used to say that Larry was the only one of her six children whom she often couldn't tell what he was thinking. "Larry only tells you exactly what he wants you to know," she once said.

Larry's upbringing was not exactly the best training ground for facing the klieg lights of the national media. "It would have been difficult to find anyone less prepared to be interviewed than I was when I got to Indiana State," he wrote in *Drive*. The Birds were among the poorest families in French Lick, which was located in the poorest county in the state, Orange County. Throughout Larry's childhood, his father, Joe, was in and out of jobs as he battled alcoholism. He finally landed steady work at the Kimball Piano Factory in town, where he worked as a wood finisher for eight years. Georgia Bird often worked two jobs at a time, usually as a waitress. The Birds rented seventeen houses in eighteen years until they finally bought a house on Washington Street.

"My kids were made fun of for the way they dressed," said Georgia. "Neighbor boys had basketballs or bikes. My kids had to share a basketball. A friend of Larry's would say, 'If you can outrun me down to the post office, you can ride my bike for ten minutes.' Larry used to run his tail-end off."

Though by all accounts Joe was a loving father, he and Georgia fought often, especially when his excessive drinking brought on more financial hardship. They divorced when Larry was sixteen. Joe's alcoholism was apparently caused, or at least exacerbated, by post-traumatic stress disorder that resulted from his tour of duty for the U.S. Army in Korea. The experience gave Joe such violent nightmares that Georgia warned family members never to touch Joe when he was sleeping, lest he wake up suddenly with his fists flying.

According to Georgia's sister, Virginia Smith, who wrote a memoir describing Larry's childhood, some of those arguments turned physical. "One summer day [Georgia] arrived at our farm sporting a beauty of a black eye and a cut, which had required stitches, above the eye," Smith wrote. "Although she was pregnant, Joey had hit her, breaking her glasses and forcing her to flee. The next day, Joey came to our farm, sincerely sorry for his actions. He always was regretful for any harm he caused, after he sobered up."

Much like Larry, Joe Bird was a quiet, remote person who didn't like being in large crowds. Even some of those closest to Larry didn't know Joe. "I would see Larry's dad at games, but he never sat," says Jan Condra, a former Springs Valley cheerleader whom Larry began dating during their senior year. "He would stand at the end of the gym by himself under one of the goals. I don't believe I ever spoke to him."

But Larry knew full well that his father, like nearly everyone in French Lick, was a huge Indiana University basketball fan. As Larry started putting up huge numbers on the basketball court his senior season at Springs Valley—he averaged 31 points and 21 rebounds in 1973–74—he began hearing from everyone in town that he should attend college in Bloomington. Not surprisingly, he was uncomfortable receiving all the attention. When Bird saw his name in a local newspaper, he complained to his new coach, Gary Holland, "Why can't we get Beezer's name in the paper some too?" (Holland had replaced Jim Jones, who had retired; James "Beezer" Carnes was Larry's best friend and teammate.)

His reclusiveness also made him a tough target for recruiters. One day, Denny Crum, the head coach at the University of Louisville, came to town and challenged Bird to a game of H-O-R-S-E. If Crum won, Bird would have to visit Louisville, about sixty miles away. Bird said okay. Then he beat Crum in about eight shots. Larry never did make the trip.

The school he most wanted to attend was Kentucky. Bird went with Holland and his parents on an official visit to Lexington, but Wildcats coach Joe B. Hall, who had been to Springs Valley to see Larry play, didn't offer him a scholarship. "People give Joe B. Hall hell about that, but I'm close friends with one of Joe's assistants, and he said when you talked with Larry Bird, he wouldn't talk to you; he wouldn't look at you," Bill Hodges says. "Ain't no way a Kentucky player can get by like that. They'd eat him alive."

Bird's eye-popping high school numbers eventually caught the attention of Indiana coach Bob Knight, who dispatched his assistant, Dave Bliss, to French Lick to see how good the kid really was. "He was wonderful to watch because he would pass the ball better than anybody on the floor, he would shoot the ball better than anybody on the floor, and he would try harder than anybody on the floor," Bliss says. Developing a relationship with Bird, on the other hand, wasn't easy. Aside from one occasion when Bird shared his preferred hobby of mushroom hunting ("I'd never heard of it. I'm a Protestant from upstate New York," Bliss says), most of Bliss's contact was with Jones and Holland.

Knight also attended several of Larry's games himself. During one conversation in Holland's office, Knight asked Larry which other schools he was considering. When Larry mentioned Indiana State as a possibility, Knight shot back, "If you're thinking about going to Indiana State, you shouldn't bother coming to Indiana."

It wasn't until the spring of 1974, when another player Knight was recruiting opted for the University of Cincinnati, that Indiana officially offered Bird a scholarship. Sensing that Bird still needed some prodding, Knight took the unusual step of asking three of his own players to drive to French Lick and meet Bird for lunch. John Laskowski, Kent Benson, and Steve Green made the trip and ate with Bird and Jones at a local Pizza Hut.

When they returned to Bloomington, Knight asked Laskowski how it went. "Well, Jim Jones seems like a really nice guy," Laskowski said. "But that Larry Bird, he didn't say a word."

Bird decided in April to sign with Indiana. That moment was a matter of great civic pride for his community, but those closest to Bird sensed his heart wasn't in it. "I know he respected Bob Knight, but I really think he went because other people pressured him to go," Beezer Carnes says. "He's the type of guy who doesn't like to let people down."

Bloomington is only fifty-six miles from French Lick, but for Bird it might as well have been a world away. When he arrived during the summer of 1974, he found himself rooming with Jim Wisman, a six-foot-three guard from Quincy, Illinois. Wisman's father was a mail carrier, and though his family was by no means wealthy, he seemed plenty well-to-do in Bird's eyes. "I made a mistake rooming Bird with Jim Wisman," Knight later said. "Bird had no clothes, and Wisman's closet was full. Wisman was real smart and could speak well. Bird was not, and couldn't, at age eighteen." Though Wisman generously told Larry he could wear his clothes whenever he wanted and even lent him money from time to time, Larry knew that couldn't last. On several occasions, he called home and told Georgia he wanted to leave, but she convinced him to stay.

When it came time to scrimmage with the older players, Larry thought he was treated badly by some of the team's veterans—especially Benson, who went out of his way to haze Bird and give him the full freshman treatment. "The philosophy in the old days was, until you prove you're ready to be on the team, then you're just a freshman," Laskowki says.

"A lot of times he was fairly unhappy with his performance [in the pickup games]," Wisman said. "Larry was much more relaxed when he could just go off and shoot. That's where he was really at home."

The start of classes only intensified Bird's feelings of isolation. Here he was, a poor, sheltered, intensely introverted teenager who had barely set foot outside his hometown of fewer than three thousand people, and he was stuck without any friends on a campus of more than thirty thousand undergraduates. He couldn't get over the fact that he had to walk several miles just to get to class. And, as he often said half-jokingly, "I ain't no genius in school."

If he thought he might get some emotional support from the coaches, that notion was quickly dispelled as well. One night, while walking down the street with Jan Condra, who had also enrolled at Indiana, at Larry's behest, and her sister, Larry looked up and saw Knight walking toward them. He stiffened and readied himself to speak to his head coach for the first time since arriving on campus. Knight walked toward Bird; Bird said hello—and Knight blew by without saying a word. "Larry didn't say anything, but I could tell with his demeanor that his feelings were hurt," Condra says. "Larry was used to people being a lot nicer to him. He didn't like Coach Knight's personality."

Knight would later regret treating Bird so coldly. "Larry Bird is one of my great mistakes," he said. "I was negligent in realizing what Bird needed at that time in his life."

The final straw came in late September when Larry received a bill for sixty dollars to cover the fee for a bowling class. Bird assumed he wouldn't have to pay the fee, and he sure as hell didn't have the sixty bucks. So he went to the basketball office, and, after being made to wait for what felt like a long time, he told assistant coach Bob Weltlich about the bill. Weltlich, in a manner that Larry considered abrupt, told Larry that it was his responsibility. End of meeting.

That was it. Larry immediately went back to his room and asked Georgia—again—if she would come pick him up. Once again, Georgia said no. Larry called his girlfriend and told her he was leaving. Then he packed up what few belongings he had and, leaving behind a small refrigerator he had brought with him from French Lick, headed out the door. When Wisman returned to find him packing, Larry said he was leaving and asked Wisman not to tell the coaches. Ignoring his roommate's pleas to reconsider, Larry headed out to Highway 37 and stuck his thumb in the air. Eventually, a man in a pickup truck pulled over to give him a lift out of town. It was left to one of Bird's uncles to call Knight and inform him that Larry had left and he wasn't coming back.

Georgia was so furious she didn't speak to Larry for weeks. For the next several months, he lived mostly at his grandmother's house. "Oh, I can be moody like Mom," he said. "One thing can make me mad for two days. Only she'll stay mad over one thing for two months." Two of Larry's uncles were also hard on him for leaving Bloomington. "They would give him the cold shoulder and tell him how disappointed they were in him," Condra says. "That was a time where he needed support from his family, and his uncles didn't give it to him."

Larry enrolled at Northwood Institute, a junior college in French Lick's neighboring town of West Baden, but it didn't take long for him to realize the competition there was weak. He quit after two weeks. "He was very unsettled," said Northwood's coach, Jack Johnson. "He had trouble attending class and was very undisciplined."

With no team to play for and no school to go to, Larry decided to take a job with the French Lick streets department. He would ask his good buddy and crewmate Beezer Carnes to pick him up at the crack of dawn so they could get there early. When Beezer would inevitably be late, Larry walked to work instead of waiting for him. "That's just the kind of work ethic he has," Carnes says. "Larry would get on a tractor and mow the grass. We'd collect garbage, dig ditches, clean out the trucks, paint curbs. He loved it. If he hadn't done what he did as a basketball player, I'd say he'd be the French Lick street commissioner right now."

In future years, as Larry Bird's celebrity burgeoned, his experience on the garbage truck would draw considerable interest, as well as a smattering of elitist derision. Larry, however, never saw it as beneath him. "I loved that job," he said in 1988. "It was outdoors, you were around your friends. Picking up brush, cleaning up. I felt like I was really accomplishing something. How many times are you riding around your town and you say to yourself, Why don't they fix that? Why don't they clean the streets up? And here I had the chance to do that. I had the chance to make my community look better."

"In French Lick, people respect people who will work, no matter what the job," says Chuck Akers, a close friend of Larry's and a former gym teacher at Springs Valley. "They don't look at work as degrading. They don't think any less of someone who works on a garbage truck than a guy who works at a bank." Bob Heaton, Bird's future teammate and roommate at Indiana State, has no problems envisioning Larry as the French Lick street commissioner. "Larry says working on that trash truck is some of his best times, and knowing Larry I'm sure it was fabulous," Heaton says. "No stress, working with his friends, being outside. Larry's favorite thing to do is cut grass. He always said nobody could cut grass better than him."

As much as Bird enjoyed his job, it could not feed his competitive jones the way basketball did. So at Akers's behest, Larry agreed to play for the AAU (Amateur Athletic Union) basketball team Akers had been playing for that was based out of Mitchell, Indiana. This was a much higher level of competition than Larry found at Northwood, yet he dominated those games just as he did in high school. His performances once again brought college recruiters out of the woodwork—Larry would spy a sharply dressed man in the stands and know instantly he was an outsider—but Larry brushed them off. He was having too much fun to think about going to school.

Playing for that AAU team also gave Bird a chance to travel. He loved the camaraderie of the road trips, especially since they gave him plenty of chances to pull off juvenile pranks. Akers remembered a time when Larry sat in his hotel room and called two other rooms pretending to be an attendant from the front desk. Larry "apologized" to the strangers as he informed them they would have to change rooms. "So he peeps out the door and he says, 'They're passing each other in the hall!' He was just a kid," Akers says. "He enjoyed traveling so much. We'd tell him, this is what college ball is like. You go on trips and you play in games."

Despite the embarrassment of having dropped out of Indiana, the fall and early winter of 1974–75 was a happy time in Larry's life. That bliss, alas, was shattered in February 1975, when Larry's father committed suicide. Joe Bird had become increasingly depressed and strapped for money. When a police officer showed up at his house looking for child support, Joe asked him to come back later that afternoon. Then he shot himself in the head with a shotgun. His suicide was big news in French Lick, but Larry rarely spoke of it, even among his closest friends. "Larry loved his dad a great deal, and he didn't like talking about it," Beezer says. "I didn't bring it up, either. That's just something that he dealt with himself. But believe me, he took it hard."

Just two months after Joe Bird took his life, Bill Hodges reported for his first day of work as an assistant coach at Indiana State. He met that morning with Bob King and the other assistants to discuss recruiting. As King went over Indiana State's current roster and a list of potential prospects, Hodges asked him, "Are you recruiting Larry Bird?"

King had heard of Bird and knew he had dropped out of Indiana University the previous September, but unlike Hodges he had never seen Bird play. "He's on our list," King said. "Is he good?"

"Oh yeah, he's good," Hodges said. "I bet he could start for us right away. Probably average about eighteen a game."

"You better go see him, then," King said.

The following day, Hodges and Stan Evans drove two hours south to French Lick. They didn't even know if Bird would be in town, so they planned to drive to Springs Valley High School and ask Larry's old coach, Gary Holland, to help them find him. Hodges intentionally didn't tell Holland they were coming. "When you need someone's help in recruiting," Hodges says, "you don't give them a chance to say no."

They found Holland in his office at the high school gymnasium, and the coach said he'd be glad to take them out to the small, single-level house on Washington Street where Larry lived. Hodges stood on the front porch and knocked on the door. When Georgia Bird answered, Hodges started to tell her who they were and why they were there, but Georgia cut him off. "Why do all you coaches keep bothering him?" she asked. "He doesn't want to go to college. He's not interested."

"Well, we think Indiana State might be a good place for him," Hodges said.

"He's not interested," Georgia repeated. She shut the door in his face.

Hodges looked over at Holland, who could only shrug. She wasn't usually like that, he said. Holland suggested they look for Bird at his grandmother's house. When they got there, however, nobody was home. Holland told them he would try to find Larry another time and promised to pass along the message. Evans suggested to Hodges that they leave. "Aw, hell, let's keep looking," Hodges said. "There can't be too many six-nine kids walking around this town."

They checked out a local pool hall, but Larry wasn't there. They stopped by the Shell station where a lot of the young folks in town hung out. Larry wasn't there, either. They drove around for a while until Hodges suddenly stopped and said, "There he is." There he was indeed, walking out of a laundromat beside his grandmother. He was carrying a basket of clothes.

Hodges quickly pulled the car up next to the laundromat, and he and Evans got out and introduced themselves. They told Larry they wanted to talk to him about coming to Indiana State. Larry demurred, saying he didn't have time to talk because he needed to install a fuel pump in his car. Larry spoke quietly and looked at the ground. Hodges thought Larry might have been a little embarrassed at how greasy his hands were.

The conversation might well have ended then and there had Larry's grandmother, Lizzie Kerns, not stepped in. "These nice men have come all this way to talk to you," she said. "The least you could do is hear what they have to say. Why don't you all come back to my house and you can visit there." Now, if there's one thing Larry Bird wasn't going to do, it was go against the wishes of his Granny Kerns. So they drove back to her house with the coaches following behind. When they got there, Larry told his grandmother that she should go into the house without him. He'd drive away and come back when the coaches were gone. But she wasn't having it. "We raised you better than that," she said. "You already told these men you'd talk to them."

Hodges and Evans followed them inside and took a seat in the living room while Granny Kerns milled about in the kitchen. Hodges did most of the talking. Having grown up in the small farming community of Zionsville in northern Indiana, he had a lot in common with Larry. They started by talking about Indiana basketball. Hodges told Bird he had played in high school against Rick Mount, a legendary Indiana ballplayer who went on to become an All-American at Purdue. Bird had played against Mount in an AAU game recently, so he knew all about him. They talked about other players around the state. Larry still wouldn't look at Hodges, but he started to relax and open up a bit. Hodges asked Larry what he had been doing. Larry told him about his work for the French Lick street department, including the garbage duty.

"Do you drive the truck?" Hodges asked.

"Nah, I just ride on the back," Larry replied with a smile.

Hodges was trying to figure out a way to steer the conversation back to Larry's recruitment without scaring him off. So he talked about his new job as an assistant coach at Indiana State and his need to find good players. Bird told Hodges he should recruit a kid in town named Kevin Carnes, the older brother of Larry's good buddy Beezer Carnes. Kevin had been the starting point guard on a team at Springs Valley that had won a sectional championship three years before. He was married and had a child, but he was still living in French Lick. "He would have been a really good player if he had gone to college," Larry said.

Hodges sensed an opening. "You know, Larry," he said, "someday they're gonna say the same thing about you if you don't go to school."

For the first time all day, Bird looked Hodges straight in the eye. He said nothing.

Some three decades later, Hodges still remembers every little detail from that first visit to French Lick. He remembers what Larry was wearing ("a white T-shirt and blue jeans"). He remembers what Granny Kerns's living room looked like ("hardwood floors, antique-ish country furniture, nothing fancy, but it was as clean as you can imagine"). He even remembers her hair color ("salt and pepper; she was a little itty-bitty lady") and what she served them ("iced tea, good and sweet"). Most of all, he remembers that moment when Larry Bird looked him straight in the eye for the first time and didn't say a word. "You can tell when you've sold somebody something," Hodges says. "I knew I had hit a home run. I figured it was time to go and let that soak in."

As Hodges started to wind down the visit, Evans became more involved in the conversation. He pressed Larry on whether he wanted to go to school and play basketball. As Larry continued to put them off, Evans grew impatient. "What are you going to do, work on a garbage truck the rest of your life?" he asked.

"I don't know, it's a pretty good job," Larry said. "I like it."

By now, Hodges knew he needed to get both of them out of there. He thanked Granny Kerns, suggested to Larry that he think about it, and said good-bye. When he and Evans got back into their car, Evans figured the visit had been for naught. "We're wasting our time with this kid," he said. "Anybody who'd rather work on a garbage truck than go to college isn't smart enough to play for us."

Had Hodges agreed with that assessment, it is likely that Larry Bird would never have played college basketball, much less in the NBA. Instead, Hodges kept up his pursuit, even though his experiences recruiting out of small Indiana rural communities had taught him the odds could be long. "A number of those kids just stay down there and wilt on the vine," Hodges says. "I'm not talking about French Lick. I'm talking about southern Indiana. A hell of a lot of good players never make it out of their town."

Another complication was that Larry couldn't come to Indiana State without an official release from Indiana University. Hodges got a form, filled it out, and addressed an envelope to the Indiana University basketball office. All he needed was Bird's signature. Hodges returned to French Lick a few days later, this time without Evans, who remained skeptical. "Here was a six-nine white kid who didn't show any interest in playing college basketball. How good could he be?" Evans says. "Kentucky passed over him. Bob Knight didn't show any effort to get him when he left Indiana. We needed players, and in my view one player who didn't want to come here was not the answer."

When Hodges stepped onto Georgia Bird's front porch this time, he got a much sweeter greeting. She told him Larry was home and immediately invited him inside. *This is different,* Hodges thought. What Hodges didn't realize was that Georgia Bird had wanted her son to go to Indiana State all along. "Larry was pressured into going to Indiana by people in town who wanted him to play in the Big Ten," she later recalled. "I was dying to say to Bobby Knight, 'Why don't you leave him alone, he doesn't want you,' but I never did. Then, when Coach Hodges came the next year, it was like an answer to a prayer, because I knew Larry had the talent but he wasn't using it. He was hanging around here, working for the town collecting garbage and painting park benches. But Larry wanted me to tell everybody he wasn't available, and I told Coach Hodges just that."

When Hodges came through the door and sat next to Larry in Georgia's living room, he showed Larry the release form. "How did you know I was thinking about coming?" Larry asked.

"I didn't," Hodges said. "But I know this is the best thing for you, and you're smart enough to make a good decision." Hodges explained that the release didn't commit Larry to coming to Indiana State; it just gave him the option. Larry signed.

After visiting for a while, Hodges told Larry he'd be back again soon. When he got up to leave, Larry followed him outside and said he had a question. If he came to Indiana State, could Hodges get him a summer job so he could go up there right away? Hodges assured him something could be worked out.

The next time Hodges came to town was on a day Bird was supposed to play for an independent team against a group of Indiana high school all-stars. Hodges drove into French Lick and found Larry putting up some hay. Despite several hours of rigorous work under a blistering sun, Larry went out that night and scored 43 points and grabbed 25 rebounds before fouling out.

Hodges had also learned that Tony Clark, one of Larry's former teammates at Springs Valley, was a sophomore at Indiana State. So he called Clark and asked if he'd go with him to watch one of Larry's AAU games. They went to the town of Mitchell, where Clark was amazed at how much his old friend had improved. "Oh, he looked good. He was six-nine, same passer as always, just phenomenal," Clark recalls. After a few more trips, Clark sensed that Hodges's pleasant persistence was starting to pay off. "Bill had a real good personality to fit Larry," Clark says. "He had that small-town understanding of what it took to motivate him. He definitely had a caring for Larry as an individual. He wanted Larry to get a degree, and it showed."

As Hodges pressed his case for Bird to visit Terre Haute, Larry kept trying to convince Hodges to recruit his buddy Kevin Carnes instead. So Hodges invited Larry to bring Kevin with him, and he would set up a scrimmage against the Indiana State varsity. Larry, who was always up for a challenge, readily agreed. So he grabbed Carnes and Mark Bird, Larry's brother, and the three of them headed for an overnight visit to Indiana State.

When the trio arrived at the gym, they were wearing blue jeans and tennis shoes. Hodges offered to get them some basketball gear, but they declined. They were used to playing in jeans, even if they were running outdoors in the dead of summer. Hodges offered a second time to get them shorts and basketball sneakers, but they again said that's okay; they'd just as soon play in their jeans.

So Hodges assigned them a couple of teammates and told them to have fun. Though he was technically forbidden by NCAA rules from watching, Hodges stood in a corner doorway and caught the action. He was astounded. The boys from French Lick absolutely drilled his varsity, game after game after game. Even Kevin Carnes, who had played on Larry's AAU team, was struck by how easily Bird dominated the competition. "When you're from a small community, you never know how you're going to compete against people like that," Kevin Carnes says. "I mean, I was amazed. We didn't lose a game that day. That's the first time I realized he wouldn't be out of his league if he played in college."

Hodges was convinced that Carnes was good enough to play for Indiana State, too. He introduced Carnes to Bob King and showed him the on-campus housing for married students. Carnes enjoyed the visit (aside from the moment when Larry threw ice-cold water on him when he was in the shower). During a stroll around campus, Larry, Kevin, and Mark came upon the track and staged an impromptu high-jumping contest. Still, Kevin was married with a child and felt that college wasn't for him.

Larry, on the other hand, was sold. He might not have been all that juiced about school, but he was very impressed that the Indiana

State players stayed in Terre Haute all summer. He loved the idea of going up against quality competition every single day, something he couldn't do in French Lick. It was also critical for him to know that, unlike in Bloomington, he wouldn't be a stranger in a strange land. Though Carnes wasn't joining him, his good friend Tony Clark was already there. And Hodges was recruiting another childhood chum and former Springs Valley teammate, Danny King, from Cumberland Junior College in Tennessee.

At the end of the visit, Larry told Hodges he needed to go back to French Lick for a couple of days to get his things together, but he had decided to come to Indiana State. He had been given a second chance at a life outside of French Lick, and he wanted to take it. If he couldn't make it work, he'd have to run home again, maybe this time for good.

4

On November 14, two weeks before the start of the 1978–79 season, Larry Bird and a few of his Indiana State teammates watched an exhibition game being aired on a fledgling national cable network called Home Box Office. The game featured the Michigan State Spartans against the same Soviet national team that would lose to the Sycamores in Terre Haute five days later. As Bird watched the Spartans dispatch the Soviets by 16 points, he told his buddies he believed Michigan State was going to win the NCAA championship.

The prediction did not sound far-fetched. Michigan State would begin the season ranked No. 7 in the Associated Press poll and quickly rose to No. 3 after winning its first three games over Central Michigan, California State–Fullerton (by just 3 points), and Western Michigan. That set up a major road date at thirteenth-ranked North Carolina. Magic Johnson said the game would be "for national attention, prestige and pride," but in a measure of the limited exposure college basketball received at the time, the game was not even televised back in Michigan, though it was available on radio. Jud Heathcote had been emphasizing rebounding throughout the preseason, yet he could see that his guys were playing on tired legs. "We kind of fizzled because we were tired of basketball," he says. "The Brazil trip really took a lot out of us."

The game was played in loud, sultry Carmichael Auditorium, where the Tar Heels had lost just thirteen times in their previous 125 games. The Spartans trailed for most of the game, but try as they did to come back, they were unable to match the intensity of their opponents or the crowd. Heathcote didn't help matters when he was whistled for a technical foul with 4:57 to go while arguing an official's call, leading to a 4-point play for North Carolina. Despite 8 turnovers from Magic Johnson (and a season-low 6 assists) and despite getting outrebounded by 3, the Spartans still had a chance to win in the final minute. But Jay Vincent missed an eight-foot jump shot with 5 seconds remaining to allow the Tar Heels to escape with a 70–69 win.

The missed shot was especially galling for Vincent, an earnest, sensitive young man who had worked hard since the end of the previous season to shed twenty-one pounds from his six-foot-eight frame. (Vincent was known to scarf down fast-food burgers and milk in the Spartans' locker room before practice, and Heathcote was constantly getting on him for being lazy.) "An eight-footer for Jay is something that he'll hit sixty percent of the time," Heathcote said. "This was just one of the forty." As for the Spartans' efforts under the boards, North Carolina forward Mike O'Koren came away unimpressed. "Michigan State doesn't block out well and there were a lot of open lanes for rebounding," he said.

Michigan State's record fell to 3–1, but the loss only dropped them from third to fifth in the next week's AP poll. "We got a tremendous lesson in rebounding at North Carolina," Heathcote said. "Maybe now our players will work harder on the things we've been harping on all season, defense and rebounding." If anything was going to snap the Spartans out of their early-season doldrums, it should have been their next contest against unranked Cincinnati. The game was going to be played in Detroit at the three-year-old Pontiac Silverdome. It was expected to draw around 28,000 spectators, which would make it the second-largest crowd ever to see a basketball game, next to the 52,693 who had watched UCLA lose to Houston in the Astrodome in 1968.

More than thirty-one thousand fans showed up. Their arrival created massive traffic jams, which forced officials to delay the start of the game by fifteen minutes. Once the people got settled, they were forced to suffer some more as their beloved Spartans put on a sloppy, desultory performance. Thanks to 15 points from its six-foot-nine center Pat Cummings, Cincinnati built a 31–24 halftime lead, causing a few Michigan State fans to boo the Spartans as they trotted to their locker room. When Cincinnati still led 37–28 early in the second half, it looked as if Michigan State might sleepwalk its way to a stunning defeat.

The Spartans rallied to win—not because of Magic Johnson, who finished with just 9 points, but because two of their role players, Ron Charles and Terry Donnelly, turned in clutch performances. Charles shed his Caribbean insouciance and fought his way through Cummings to grab 10 rebounds. Donnelly, the six-foot-two lefty who was usually the last option on offense, sank three timely jumpers in the second half. Michigan State woke up just in time to pull out a 63–52 win. "There's something missing right now and I don't know what it is," said Greg Kelser, who had a season-low 12 points. Added Johnson, "We just don't have the spirit and enthusiasm we had last season. I get fired up at times, but it's hard to get everyone else up."

The Spartans might have played with more enthusiasm if they had been able to get into their fast-break game. That was when Johnson and Kelser were at their best. Yet their scoring efforts were stymied by Cincinnati's zone defense as well as by Heathcote's conservative approach to offense. Like many coaches in the pre–shot clock era (the clock was not instituted in college basketball until 1985), Heathcote preferred that his teams slow the pace and control the tempo. If they established even a moderate lead in the last five minutes, he went straight to the delay game. Moreover, Heathcote was so quick to berate his players for every little mistake that they started to play tight. "It's hard to get relaxed and play loose if you have to constantly look over your shoulder," Kelser says.

Despite Michigan State's victory, the Cincinnati game was panned in the press as "rather dull and slow-paced," as Fred Stabley wrote in the *State Journal*. Another *State Journal* columnist, Bob Gross, sympathized with the thirty-one thousand spectators. "The big crowd had to be disappointed," he wrote. "It was bad enough just getting into the place, then to see two teams slosh it out."

As usual, the Spartans' toughest critic was the head coach himself. "We've played just one good half of basketball this season," Heathcote lamented, referring to the first half against Western Michigan. "We're not as good a team as we were when we played against the Russians or when we played in Brazil or even at the end of last season. And for as quick as we are, it would be hard for me to imagine any team slower than we were in the first half."

That Heathcote would render such a harsh verdict about a team that was 4–1 and ranked fifth in the nation surprised exactly no one. He was only in his third season in East Lansing, but he had solidified his reputation for being implacable, unsatisfiable, and at times downright unlikable.

It would be an understatement to say that Jud Heathcote was not a big name before Michigan State hired him in April 1976. His résumé consisted of fourteen years as a high school coach at West Valley High School in Spokane, Washington; seven years as an assistant coach at Washington State, his alma mater; and five years as the head coach at the University of Montana, where he led the Grizzlies to an 80–53 record. Heathcote's most noteworthy accomplishment had come during the second round of the 1975 NCAA tournament, when his Grizzlies took John Wooden's mighty UCLA Bruins to the wire before losing by 3 points. Since the tournament's early rounds were not televised nationally in those days, few people outside the West Coast knew about it. "I had never heard the name Jud Heathcote until they hired him," says Vern Payne, who at the time was an assistant coach under Heathcote's predecessor at Michigan State, Gus Ganakas.

Nor did Heathcote quite realize how deeply the basketball program had been scarred from the chain of events that had led to

Ganakas's dismissal. It began on January 4, 1975, when, during a team meeting the morning of a home game against second-ranked Indiana, Ganakas told his team that he was promoting a white player named Jeff Tropf to the starting lineup. Lindsay Hairston, the team captain, who was black, said he didn't think it was a good move. Ganakas replied that he was the coach, and the decision would stand.

Without warning, Hairston stood up and walked out of the locker room. He was followed by nine other players, all of them black. "In that era, that's how things were," says Edgar Wilson. He was one of the players who walked out but later said he disagreed with the decision. "If you didn't like something, you marched or you walked or you protested." Says Ganakas, "I was stunned. Then my assistants and I talked about it, and we decided we were going to play the game no matter what."

The coach instructed his staff to round up the players on Michigan State's junior varsity team so they could play against Indiana. An hour before tip-off, the varsity players who had walked out returned to the locker room to meet with Ganakas. Hairston tried to justify their action by complaining about their perceived unequal treatment compared to Michigan State's football team. He said the nine wanted to play, but Ganakas refused to let them. "I wanted to hear them say they're sorry, and I felt sorry for Jeff," Ganakas says. "When I told them they were suspended, they got up and walked out again."

Before the game started, Ganakas ran into Bob Knight in a hallway in Jenison Fieldhouse. Knight offered to have one of his black assistants talk to the players who had walked out, but Ganakas declined. When the game started, the jayvee Spartans actually hung with the Hoosiers during the first few minutes, forcing Knight to call time-out. Knight walked over to the Spartans' bench and told the coaches almost apologetically, "I gotta get these guys going." Thus fired up, the Hoosiers dealt the ersatz Spartans a humiliating 107–55 loss, the worst in Michigan State history.

The players begrudgingly apologized to Ganakas the next day, and the coach reinstated them. The episode set off a media firestorm, creating the impression that the Michigan State coach had lost control of his program. "Who's in Charge Anyway?" read one typical headline in the *Sporting News*. The next year, when the football program was hit with a three-year NCAA probation for violations that included the players' abuse of a credit card belonging to a booster, the school decided it was time to clean house. Ganakas was swept out in the spring of 1976 along with the football coach and the athletic director and was reassigned to another position in the athletic department.

Michigan State's new athletic director, Joe Kearney, was familiar with Jud Heathcote from their days coaching at competing high schools in Washington state. When Heathcote met with the university's interviewing committee in Chicago, he was peppered with questions about how he would have handled a walkout of his players. "I told them, if I ever got into a situation where my players did not do what I told them to do, I'm out of there. I would resign in a heartbeat," he says. "I guess that was the answer they wanted." Soon after he got to Lansing, Heathcote had lunch with three black businessmen who were university supporters. It didn't take long before Heathcote felt he had been invited to an interrogation, not a lunch. When one of the men repeatedly pressed Heathcote on whether he knew how to coach black players, Heathcote told the man he was going to run his program the way he wanted, and the lunch ended abruptly.

Meanwhile, Greg Kelser, who had shown great promise while averaging 11.7 points and 9.5 rebounds as a freshman, had decided to transfer. Dick Vitale, the University of Detroit coach who had recruited Kelser hard out of high school, was one of several coaches who tried to convince him to come to their school. The calls were so numerous that Kelser felt like he was being recruited all over again. Many of those coaches were quick to point out that Heathcote had coached very few black players at Montana. In the end, Kelser stayed at Michigan State, largely because the classy Ganakas convinced him it was the smart choice, but the notion of Heathcote's supposed inexperience coaching black players stayed with him.

After Heathcote arrived in East Lansing in the spring of 1976,

Kelser and his teammates liked him—at first. "It was the off-season and he would come to some of our pickup games. He wasn't critical at all," Kelser says. "He had this really dry, sarcastic sense of humor. He didn't spare anyone, including the other coaches. There were a lot of laughs around him."

And yet Heathcote's humor could be a little too sharp at times. Before the season began, he visited some of the dormitories on campus to try to generate interest in the program. When he visited Kelser's dorm, one of the residents asked him how the Spartans would compare to the University of Michigan that season. "Well," Heathcote replied, "the difference between us and Michigan is that they have Phil Hubbard and Ricky Green"—the Wolverines' returning All-Americans—"and we have Greg Kelser." Says Kelser, "Everybody got a big laugh, but I didn't think it was funny. In my mind, I was every bit as good as those guys."

Once practice started, however, Heathcote was through with the funny business. The differences between him and Ganakas could not have been more stark. Ganakas was cool and gentlemanly, not to mention a natty dresser. Heathcote had a wobbly limp due to an old football knee injury and a funny-looking, comb-over hairstyle. But more jarring was Heathcote's temperament. "All you had to do was make one mistake, one misstep, physically or mentally, and he was on you. I mean, *on* you," Kelser says. "To go from one extreme style to another like that was tough. I wasn't used to being coached from such a negative standpoint. Everything was negative, all day every day. Then you add to that the fact that we weren't a very good team his first year, and basketball was not fun anymore. It was something else."

"I never heard Coach Ganakas berate anyone," says Edgar Wilson, a senior forward on Heathcote's first team in 1976–77 who later worked for him as an assistant. "The thing we all had to learn was to get through all of that and get down to what he was actually communicating. If you did that, you were successful in his program."

The transition was equally difficult for Vern Payne, the only African American assistant coach and the only one from Ganakas's staff whom Heathcote had retained. "He and Gus were from different planets," Payne recalls. Payne was so unhappy those first few months that even before the season began, he decided he wanted to leave Michigan State. "I didn't tell anybody that except my wife," Payne says. "She said, if that's how you feel, you have to leave." When the season ended, he did just that, taking the job as the head coach at Wayne State in Detroit.

And yet when the players vented to Payne about Heathcote that first year, he stuck up for his boss. Kelser and Ron Charles both told Payne they wanted to transfer, but Payne talked them out of it because he was loyal to the university. He also could see that Heathcote knew basketball. "I'll stand up and tell anybody in the world, the man can coach," Payne says. "I told the kids, 'Don't listen to all the bullshit. Listen to those things he said that will help you be a better player and help us win.' That's what I told the kids. That's what I told myself."

Inevitably, the early tension was underscored by the issue of race. The players believed, with good reason, that Heathcote had been hired precisely *because* he was so different from Ganakas. To this day, Kelser maintains that Heathcote's domineering approach was rooted in negative stereotypes the coach held about black players, though he is quick to point out that he never heard Heathcote make any racially insensitive remarks. "He came in less than two years after that walkout," Kelser says. "It's no secret there was this feeling around that there needed to be some heavy discipline brought in. He was going to come with that anyway, so it was not a tough thing for him to do."

In this regard, Heathcote's biting sense of humor did not serve him well. He was a first-rate ballbuster, but while many of his wisecracks were genuinely funny, he tended to cut a little too close to the bone. For example, when Payne paid a visit to the Michigan State coaches' office after he had left for Wayne State, Heathcote jumped up and said he wanted Payne to meet his replacement. Then he opened a closet door and pointed to a shoeshine machine. "It was hard sometimes to separate Jud's humor from what he believes in his heart," Payne says. "From the first few weeks, I knew he had a ton to learn about differences with people. A ton." Heathcote says he does not recall this incident.

Heathcote's coaching style was especially trying for Bob Chapman, a six-foot-two guard from Saginaw, Michigan, who was a junior on Heathcote's first team. By his own admission, Chapman was just as bullheaded as the new coach, and he had been devastated by the firing of Ganakas, whom Chapman considered a father figure. The chemistry between Chapman and Heathcote was so combative that Chapman requested a meeting with the coach in his office and offered to quit the team. "I told him, 'It appears to me you'd like to have a team mostly full of guys who are white with just two or three blacks,'" Chapman says. "I said, 'I don't have a problem with that, but if that's your intent, then you better go get some white guys who can play.'"

Yet if the players felt they were victims of racial stereotyping, Heathcote could credibly make the same claim. Though Missoula, Montana, was obviously far less diverse than Lansing, Michigan—Heathcote recalled an occasion when a Grizzlies fan asked him how many "niggers" he planned on starting—he also points out that his last team at the University of Montana featured three black starters, including Micheal Ray Richardson, who went on to play eight years in the NBA. "People would ask me, 'Did you coach any black kids at Montana?' Like it was Alaska or Siberia," he says. "I wasn't aware that the blacks were on this side, the whites were on this side. I just tried to coach the team."

Even if some of his players disliked Heathcote personally, his basketball acumen was apparent from the start. He proved himself a keen tactician when he deployed a stall offense for Michigan State's game against the University of Michigan his first year. The Spartans lost by 4 points in overtime, but they had no right being that close to a national powerhouse that at the time was ranked No. 3 in the nation.

Heathcote was also a smart and diligent shooting coach. During one early workout his first season, he watched Terry Donnelly, whom he had never seen play in high school, launch a left-handed jump shot. "Stop!" he hollered. "What the hell kind of shot is that?" Heathcote told Donnelly that with his low, slow delivery he would never get his shot off in the Big Ten. He then spent weeks working individually with Donnelly breaking down his form as they rebuilt that jump shot from scratch. It was not long before Donnelly became one of Michigan State's most reliable outside shooters.

Moreover, no one could question Heathcote's integrity. Even when it was snowing and cold, he refused to give his players a ride because it was against NCAA rules. He wouldn't even lend them a quarter for the soda machine. If anything, Heathcote could be too honest. Dick Vitale learned that on the day he first met Heathcote. The University of Detroit coach had used his annual game against Michigan State to generate buzz for his program, but since most fans believed a Big Ten school should beat a team like Detroit, Michigan State had nothing to gain by continuing the series. Most coaches who inherited that kind of situation would find a way to politely weasel out of the commitment, but Heathcote was characteristically blunt. He had barely introduced himself to Vitale before telling him, "I just want you to know we are not going to be playing you any damn more."

There was a lighter side to Heathcote, but he was reluctant to let it show publicly. "So many don't know him," wrote Lynn Henning, a columnist for the *State Journal*, in January 1978. "If Jud's on the record he'll cut the levity and get down to basketball matters. The snickers will come after the mike's off and the notebooks have been put away. . . . But to the majority of MSU fans, Heathcote is still a bit of a mystery, or that red-faced guy down on the bench chewing at the officials like a Doberman."

His players often had no choice but to abide Heathcote's tirades, but there were some days when enough was enough. One such day occurred during the fall of 1977, when Heathcote used a practice to conduct a coaching clinic. He spent most of the session talking into a microphone, and the workout quickly devolved into a running commentary on all the mistakes his players were making. On this day,

Greg Kelser was the primary target. Kelser became so furious at the public humiliation that he had to resist the urge to walk out of practice. Afterward, he asked if he could meet with Heathcote one-on-one in his office. "What happened today can never happen again," Kelser told the coach. "I'm always respectful to you and I'm willing to take criticism, but you cannot talk like that to me in front of other people. I'm a man just like you." Heathcote didn't exactly apologize, but Kelser sensed he had earned a measure of respect.

Heathcote understood he was not the easiest coach to play for, but as he saw it his job was to win games, not friends. "I think the players had a hard time adjusting to my negative style," he says. "I'm not saying I had a happy team all the time, but I didn't have a mutiny, either."

There was one time, however, when he came close to having just that. It occurred after the Spartans' worst loss of the 1977–78 season, a 19-point drubbing at Purdue during which they committed 25 turnovers, including 9 by Earvin Johnson, who was then a freshman. Not surprisingly, the loss put Heathcote in a sour mood. On the bus ride back to East Lansing, when the players sat in the back as they usually did and listened to music on a boom box, Heathcote yelled from the front row, "Turn off that fucking music!"

For whatever reason, the players decided at that moment they had had enough of his tyrannical rule. They did as he said and turned off the music. Then they started singing. "Cut out that singing!" Heathcote yelled. They stopped singing—and started humming. After a few minutes of this minirebellion, assistant coach Don Monson walked to the back of the bus and said, "I'm just telling you guys, you better cut it out. He's about to blow." The players quieted down, but Kelser was feeling his blackness that night. He continued the protest by reciting part of Martin Luther King's "I Have a Dream" speech. Having made their little statement, the players figured that was the end of it. The next day, as they convened for their daily meeting before practice, Heathcote walked into the locker room and took off his coat. "If anybody in this room thinks he's tougher than me, stand up right now," he said.

Nobody moved.

"What happened on that bus last night will never happen again, ever," Heathcote continued. "So I'll ask you one more time. If anybody here thinks he's tougher than me, stand up right now."

Again, nobody moved. Point taken.

Thirty years later, Heathcote was asked what he would have done if one of the players had risen to accept his challenge. "Beat the shit out of him," he replied. "This goes back to when I was coaching in high school. I only had two suits to my name. We lose about the third game I coached, and the players are in the showers singing and dicking around. I run in the shower and I ruined my suit. I said, 'Hey, when you win, that's when you sing and dick around in the shower.' That incident at Michigan State was the same thing. I was challenging them. What do we stand for, guys? Are we a team here or are we a bunch of dicks?"

For all the trepidation that Magic Johnson felt about playing for Jud Heathcote, once he arrived on campus he found that Heathcote's yelling didn't bother him as much as he feared it would. Johnson wanted to win, too, and he knew a competitor when he saw one.

Still, there were plenty of times when just like everyone else Johnson bridled against Heathcote's methods, and he was more daring than any other player on the team when it came to challenging the coach's authority. "Earvin was where Jud met his Waterloo," says Lynn Henning, the former *State Journal* columnist. "He dominated every player he had ever coached, but Earvin was where the rubber met the road. Jud clearly knew where he had to draw the line, but he certainly took a different approach with [Johnson]."

For example, during a game in Johnson's freshman year against Purdue, Heathcote yanked him after he committed a few early turnovers. As Magic walked by the bench, he said, "I didn't come here to sit." Coming from another player, that type of comment might have prompted an outburst. Heathcote, however, said nothing and put Johnson back in the game a minute later.

"They would go back and forth all the time," Jay Vincent says. "One time during a game, Magic threw the ball away a couple of times. So Coach is yelling at him while Magic is dribbling the ball, and Magic stops dribbling and yells at Jud. This wasn't during a time-out, it wasn't a break, it was during the *game*. Magic just stopped, they yelled at each other, and then Magic kept playing."

The more contentious battles were usually reserved for practice. At one session in particular, Magic was arguing with Heathcote for repeatedly calling charging fouls on him. Eventually, Magic got so upset that he simply sat on the ball, bringing the practice to a virtual standstill. "He stared at Jud and Jud was staring at him. This went on for about ten minutes," Terry Donnelly recalls. "We were all dumbfounded. It was eyeball-to-eyeball, and it stopped practice. We all went to get water and waited to see who was going to break. Jud finally said practice was over and walked off the floor."

Off the court, Magic managed to push the envelope in subtle ways as well. Heathcote had a fetish for dress codes, and he had told the players to look respectable for their mandatory team breakfast. That policy quietly went out the window once Johnson started showing up in his sweats. "I don't know if Earvin did that on purpose, but he came like that, and nothing was said to him," says Darwin Payton, the team's student manager. "So the guys are like, Okay, we can dress like that now? And they did."

During the preseason trip to Brazil in the fall of 1978, Johnson also took it upon himself to enjoy a night on the town along with Kelser and Donnelly, even though Heathcote had imposed a strict 11 p.m. curfew. By the time the trio made it back to the hotel, it was around 2 a.m. They thought they had gotten off scot-free until their elevator door opened and they came face-to-face with Heathcote. The coach walked past them without saying anything. "I thought something would happen the next day, but there wasn't a word said about it," Donnelly says. "I wouldn't break curfew often, but if I was going to, I was going to do it with Greg and Earvin."

Still, it was hard to argue that Johnson hadn't earned at least some special treatment. Besides being the team's best player, he also played the smartest, practiced the hardest, and willingly bore all the burdens of leadership. Where other players might wither and sulk in the face of Heathcote's red-faced tirades, Johnson understood that the man acted that way only because he wanted to win. Though they weren't necessarily close friends, they nonetheless developed an understanding that didn't exist between the coach and any other player. "We came out of a restaurant one time during [the] trip to North Carolina," said Jim Adams, the team's radio broadcaster. "Earvin was walking down the street with his arm around Jud's shoulders. I was walking behind. I thought that no other player could get away with such a casual demeanor with a coach like Jud."

Yet if Heathcote had babied Earvin too much, he would have lost respect in the locker room. To Heathcote's credit, that didn't happen. "I don't think Coach compromised himself to coach Earvin at all," Kelser says. "I don't think he would have compromised himself to coach Bill Russell. But I will say this—I think he was smart enough to understand various temperaments that guys had. Earvin was not someone you could just berate and yell at constantly because he wasn't going to respond to that."

Jay Vincent agrees. "You can't tell me there's a coach anywhere who's not going to favor his top players," he says. "Coach picked his fights with Magic. The times he picked, he made sure."

One of those times came at halftime of the Far West Classic championship game against Indiana on December 30, 1978. The Spartans had taken six days off following their unimpressive win over Cincinnati, and they seemed to benefit from the rest during the first two days of the tournament, drubbing Washington State University by 46 points and beating Oregon State University by 8. But they returned to their uninspired ways against Indiana. Though the Spartans led 42–31 at halftime, they had allowed the Hoosiers' outstanding guard Mike Woodson to light up Heathcote's two-three matchup zone defense for 17 points in the half. When the Spartans got into their locker room, Heathcote lit into his players.

At one point, Heathcote focused his tirade on Johnson, and his star point guard tried to argue back. Heathcote exploded. "There's nobody here who's bigger than the goddamned program!" he yelled. He tore into Johnson for several more minutes. As he screamed, Johnson locked his eyes on the ground, a response that was equal parts chastened and defiant. "Earvin had his head down and wouldn't look at Jud. He was more or less saying, Fuck you," Mike Brkovich says. "Jud didn't get after him much, but Earvin wasn't playing well, and Jud was all over him."

The outburst had the desired effect, as Johnson went on to lead the Spartans to a strong second half and an easy 74–57 victory. More important, Johnson did not take the diatribe personally. After the game, he told Heathcote that the night before the tournament began he had called a team meeting at their hotel, where the players decided they wanted to win the tournament for their coach in honor of his homecoming to the Pacific Northwest. Moreover, since the three teams ranked ahead of them—Duke, UCLA, and Notre Dame—had all lost that week, Michigan State now had a clear shot at its first No. 1 ranking in eighty years.

The prospect of reaching No. 1 was going to make New Year's Eve even more festive once they got back home. Unfortunately, bad weather forced the team to spend that night in Denver. They made it as far as Minneapolis the next day, but once again they were snowed in. Before boarding their plane for Lansing on the morning of January 2, Heathcote called a team meeting and announced, "In case any of you in the room are interested, all of you are part of the number-one basketball team in America." The players cheered.

By the time they finally got back to Lansing that night, everyone was in a cranky mood from the long trip. They got even crankier as they stood by the luggage carousel for nearly an hour waiting for their bags. This was the last straw for Heathcote. It was a running joke on the team that the coach was so impatient that no matter where they went, as soon as they got there he couldn't wait to leave. Heathcote would even order his steak rare at restaurants because that meant it would take less time to cook. Now, with their seemingly endless travel ordeal still not ending, Heathcote wheeled on the student manager Darwin Payton, who was in charge of all the travel arrangements. "Darwin, where the hell are our bags?" he snapped.

"How am I supposed to know?" Payton replied. "I don't control the airplane."

Finally, Heathcote climbed onto the conveyor belt and disappeared through the flaps. A few minutes later, he was escorted, sans bags, back into the terminal by two security guards. It was all the players could do to keep from bursting out in hysterics.

Heathcote wasn't smiling right then, but many years later even he can chuckle at the memory. "Waiting when you shouldn't be waiting," he says, "was not one of my strong points."

5

As the month of December unfolded, the Indiana State Sycamores got an early glimpse of what it meant to have a little notoriety. On December 12, they took their 6–0 record and brand-new No. 20 ranking in the AP poll to Muncie, Indiana, to play Ball State University. The game drew what was believed to be the biggest crowd in school history, but Indiana State controlled the game throughout and won, 93–85. Bird had 31 points and 14 rebounds while Steve Reed, the steady point guard, dished out 10 assists. Ball State coach Steve Yoder was especially impressed with Carl Nicks, who had 22 points and 7 assists and was emerging as an offensive threat in his own right. "He's so physical, and has that quick first move," Yoder said. "I wish I could find someone who would lower his shoulder and go to the [rim] like that."

The Sycamores were even more impressive four days later against another in-state rival, Butler. When those two teams had played two years before, Bird tied his own Indiana State single-game scoring record by pouring in 47 points. This time, he did himself one better by scoring 48 in a 38-point rout. When the next week's AP poll came out, Indiana State moved up from No. 20 to No. 16. During their two-week holiday break, Indiana State moved up to No. 11 without even playing a game. Then on December 30 they easily beat Morris Harvey at home to improve to 9–0.

A lot of people may have been surprised at how well the Sycamores were playing, but Bird was not one of them. "Those magazines said all we would have would be me and I told people we would have a good team. Now they all want to run down here and jump on the bandwagon and get writeups," he told the *Terre Haute Tribune* in a rare published utterance. "I think New Mexico State, Drake and Southern Illinois are probably the top three [in the Missouri Valley Conference], but if we play like we can, we can handle all of them."

Facing skepticism was nothing new for Bird. Wherever he had been, he encountered doubts about whether he would get exposed when he moved on to the "next level." Even his coaches at Indiana State weren't sure how good he was after watching Bird obliterate the varsity players in practice during the 1975–76 season, when he sat out a year as a "redshirt" following his transfer from Indiana. As the team was about to take the floor for Bird's first exhibition game in his sophomore season in the fall of 1976, head coach Bob King turned to his assistant Stan Evans and said, "If he gets us fifteen points and ten rebounds, we'll have a heck of a find."

Bird didn't give them 15 and 10 that night. He gave them 31 and 15, along with 8 assists and 7 steals. "Even though we had seen the kid play the whole year, we had no clue," Evans says. "He was six-nine, one hundred eighty-five pounds, looked like he had never seen the sun. He looked emaciated. Seeing him practice against bad players was one thing. The question is, when you go against someone good, can you rise to the occasion? Well, Larry could, and he kept rising."

It didn't dawn on Bill Hodges how good Larry Bird really might be until Bird's sophomore year, when he played pickup games against Mel Daniels, a six-foot-nine center who had played for King at New Mexico from 1964 to 1967. Daniels had gone on to become a seven-time ABA all-star with the Indiana Pacers, and he frequently came to Terre Haute to play with King's guys. After one such session, Daniels walked into Hodges's office still sweaty from his workout and said, "That kid could play in the NBA right now."

"Come on," Hodges replied.

"I'm telling you, he's that good," Daniels said. "He's as good as anyone I've ever played against."

Hodges never forgot that moment. "You don't really know how good someone is until he plays against good competition," he says. "When Mel Daniels talks, you listen."

The main challenge for the coaches during Bird's redshirt year was just keeping him on campus. He had never been motivated by academics, and he was so frustrated by not being allowed to play that he often didn't bother attending the Sycamores' games. During the early part of his redshirt season, King often sat Bird down during practice because he was so good that King worried he was destroying the starters' confidence. One day, when King told Larry yet again to step out, he snapped. He stormed into the locker room, started gathering his things, and decided he was going back to French Lick. A minute later, King came into the locker room and explained his reasoning. Larry was appeased, but from then on King let him practice, the starters' egos be damned. "Bob quit caring about whether the first five lost," Hodges says. "He figured Larry Bird's a lot more important."

The episode was typical of the delicate balancing act the school had to walk during Bird's early months at Indiana State. "It was like holding your breath for a year," says Ed McKee, who was the sports information director. "The coaches kept telling me, 'Boy, this kid is something special,' but they wanted to keep it quiet because they didn't want Larry to bolt away. There was always the feeling of, will next year ever come?"

Fortunately for Indiana State, King was able to provide Bird with the nurturing presence he needed to get him through that first year. If King had been less patient, Larry could very well have left. Chuck Akers, Bird's former gym teacher and AAU teammate in French Lick, believed that even if Bird had stayed at Indiana, the school would have been a bad fit because Bob Knight was everything King wasn't. "Had Larry not left [Indiana] when he did, the first time Bob Knight cussed him out he would have been home," Akers said. "Larry needed a father figure, and Bob Knight's not fathering anybody."

Even as Bird became an All-American his junior year at Indiana State, many so-called experts wondered whether this big, white, lead-footed country kid would be effective when he got to the pros. After watching Larry play one night, Press Maravich, the former LSU coach who was working as a scout for the New Orleans Jazz, told Mike McCormick, a sportswriter in Terre Haute, that he thought Bird was too slow to play in the NBA. "I felt hopeless," McCormick says. "I thought this guy was a prospect."

Perhaps those outside observers would have felt otherwise had they understood the intense work ethic that fueled Bird's ascent. His passion for the game bordered on pathological. "When I was younger I played for the fun of it, like any other kid," Bird said. "I just don't know what kept me going and going and going. I remember we used to practice in the gym in high school. Then, on the way home, we'd stop and play on the playgrounds until eight o'clock. I played when I was cold and my body was aching and I was so tired . . . and I don't know why, I just kept playing and playing."

When Larry failed to show up for his high school team's postseason banquet his junior year, his coach, Jim Jones, left the event and found Larry shooting baskets by himself at his favorite court. Jones had to coax Bird to wash up and come to the dinner. Tony Clark, Bird's childhood friend and fellow Indiana State student, says, "I remember it would be raining, and he'd be up by the elementary school, just shooting in the rain. It was his release, I think. It didn't cost anything, and he found something that the more he worked at it, the better he got."

When he got to Indiana State, Larry would spend hours shooting after practice, sometimes with a friend who would rebound for him, oftentimes by himself. The only problem was finding him a place to work out. At first, intramural teams would kick him off the ISU arena floor. Then he found another gym in town where he could practice at night, but security ran him off. Finally, King enlisted the help of a man named Max Jones, who ran the Terre Haute Boys and Girls Club. Jones gave Larry a key to the building and showed him how to turn on the lights. The only thing he asked was that Larry accept responsibility for anyone he brought in there. "I'd come back from recruiting late at night and see the lights on in the Boys Club," Hodges says. "I knew Larry was over there shooting."

Those habits made quite an impression on his teammates. "We would scrimmage during the summer four days a week. Then we'd get Friday, Saturday, and Sunday off," Steve Reed says. "Larry would go down to the Boys Club on weekends and work on some facet of his game for hours. I'm thinking, this guy has to be nuts. Most of us are playing golf or waterskiing, particularly after you've been playing all week. But that's the type of dedication and competitiveness he had."

When the games came around, Bird showed he could accrue gaudy statistics without disrupting the flow of the team. He rarely dribbled more than once before taking a shot, and he was more likely to make the extra pass than force a bad shot. Though he had worked hard to extend his shooting range, the vast majority of his attempts came from within eight feet. He was, in other words, that rarest of phenomena—the unselfish superstar.

Consider the Sycamores' 1978 regular season home finale, when they routed Loyola. Bird reached 45 points with several minutes still remaining, leaving him just two points from tying Indiana State's single-game scoring record, which he had set the previous year. With the game's outcome long decided, King summoned Johnny Nelson, a five-foot-eight, 130-pound senior walk-on, into the game. Nelson's first shot attempt was short, and Bird got the rebound. The ten-thousand-plus fans at Hulman Center clamored for Bird to go for the record, but instead he threw the ball back to Nelson and set a pick for him. Nelson misfired again, Bird got the rebound, and he again dished it back to Nelson for another try. Nelson never did score, but neither did Bird. "Larry could have put that ball back up and set a

record but he got it back for me," Nelson said. "I will always appreciate that."

Nor was Larry ever the type to shy away from a fight. More often,
he was the guy looking for one. During his sophomore season, he
started a brouhaha with a group of mouthy fans before a game at Val-
paraiso. The following year, after Indiana State lost to Rutgers in the
second round of the NIT, Bird leveled a fan who had jumped on his
back in the postgame melee. The guy ended up on his back with a
bloody nose. Rick Shaw, the team's student manager, recalls thinking
that it looked like someone had poured ketchup all over the man's
face. Says Steve Reed, "The guy collapsed and security came out and
picked him up. I remember glancing at the guy's face and thinking,
Ugh, man, that was bad."

Once in a while, Larry would even turn his wrath on a teammate.
During the fall of his senior year, he and Leroy Staley, the six-foot-
five backup guard, got into a nasty scuffle during a pickup game, to
the point where they had to be pried apart by their teammates. "Larry
decked Leroy and then jumped on him. He was kicking him, claw-
ing, biting, everything," Carl Nicks recalls. "Larry was always ready
to fight. That was like recreation for him, especially when you got a
few beers in him." The day after that scuffle, Hodges called Staley
and Bird into his office to meet with him and Mel Daniels, now an
assistant coach, in an effort to smooth things over. "We got past it,"
Staley says. "It wasn't like Larry was going to get put off the team."
Bird grew to appreciate Staley's competitive streak, but the incident
underscored his confrontational nature. "Off the court, on the court,
that was Larry's way," says Bob Behnke, the team's trainer. "He wasn't
going to settle an argument with an intellectual debate."

There was no question that Bird was a singular talent, but as the
Sycamores kept winning game after game in the 1978–79 season, it
was becoming increasingly apparent that his supporting cast was better than anyone had realized. With Carl Nicks having established
himself as the number-two scorer, his backcourt mate, Steve Reed,
settled into his role as efficient setup man. He had followed up his

10-assist performance at Ball State by dishing out 11 against Butler University. Reed was a very good open shooter (he used to beat Bird regularly in games of H-O-R-S-E), and though he was gun-shy about scoring, he was an ideal complement to Bird, who could get him open shots when Bird was double-teamed. Two other starters, Brad Miley and Alex Gilbert, were also settling into their limited but important roles of defensive stopper and rebounder, respectively.

Even though Indiana State entered January with a 9–0 record and the No. 11 ranking in the AP poll, their hometown fans were not quite consumed by enthusiasm: on January 3, when Indiana State opened its Missouri Valley Conference season at home against Tulsa, there were more than one thousand empty seats in Hulman Center. In a game televised by HBO, whose broadcast team included Tommy Heinsohn, the former Celtics player and coach, Bird scored 27 points and grabbed 19 rebounds in a 101–89 win. Nicks added 26 points of his own, and even Miley, who was supposed to be a horrid shooter, chipped in a career-high 17 points. ("We fed Brad shooting pills before the game," Hodges quipped.) Bob Heaton, the sixth man who provided a healthy offensive spark when he substituted for Gilbert or Miley, chipped in 10 points as well. "We knew Bird was a great one, but we had no idea they had so much offensive power from so many players," Tulsa coach Jim King said. Heinsohn had the same reaction, telling a local reporter that "the fellows playing with Bird and Nicks are no slouches."

The win over Tulsa brought the Sycamores to 10–0. They followed that victory with easy wins over West Texas State on January 6, North Carolina A&T on January 9, and Bradley on January 13. "Bird's wanting to win rather than just score points is infectious," said Dick Versace, Bradley's first-year coach, after watching Bird amass 27 points, 18 rebounds, and 10 assists. The win over Versace's team improved the Sycamores' record to 13–0.

Two days later, Indiana State played at home against New Mexico State University. The Aggies were one of the teams who were picked in the preseason to finish ahead of the Sycamores in the Missouri Valley

Conference, and they gave Indiana State its toughest challenge of the season. With Bird hobbled by a sprained ankle he suffered right before halftime, the Aggies pushed out to a 6-point lead with 11:30 remaining on the clock. But Indiana State fought back, with Bird (24 points) and Nicks (20) once again leading the way, to take a 4-point lead at the 2:42 mark. The score was tied at 69–69 with 19 seconds remaining, when Bob Heaton was fouled on a shot attempt. He drained both free throws, and on the ensuing possession Bird stole the ball and fed Nicks for a layup to give the Sycamores a 73–69 win. Having dodged another bullet to improve to 14–0, they were feeling plenty confident and not a little lucky. "I'm not real superstitious, but I was thinking, there's a reason we're pulling these games out at the end when we should lose them," Nicks says. "I started buying into that. I think we all did. We started thinking, we are not going to lose a game."

Indiana State was now the only undefeated major college team in America. When the rankings came out that week, they found themselves at No. 5 in both the AP and UPI polls. Two AP voters had actually voted the Sycamores No. 1.

The unbeaten streak once again appeared in jeopardy at Wichita State University on January 18, when Bird picked up his third foul midway through the first half, forcing Hodges to bench him for the remainder of the period. But instead of folding, Bird's teammates outscored the Shockers 21–10 the remainder of the half, and Indiana State left with a 10-point win that improved their record to 15–0. "Psychologically our opponent doesn't think we're as effective without Bird," Hodges said. "We've got an awfully good ball club, and nobody knows that better than Larry. If he could sit on the bench and it would help the team, he'd be the first one to say take me out."

By this point, the pressure of remaining unbeaten and justifying the rankings should have been bearing down on the team. That didn't happen, partly because they were "a loose bunch," as Hodges put it. And nobody was looser than Bird. The star player was a first-rate cutup, with a fondness for juvenile pranks. If one of the guys fell asleep in the locker room or on the bus, Bird would dab some chewing tobacco on his lip and wait for him to wake up with a start. "I learned not to sleep around Larry," Brad Miley says. During bus rides, Bird liked to write crude words on fogged-up windows, and he was not above giving somebody a wedgie. Once, before leaving the locker room for pregame warm-ups, Bird grabbed Bob Behnke's son, Jimmy, and stuffed him in a locker—only Larry didn't realize the kid couldn't let himself out. The players returned a few minutes later and heard banging coming from inside the locker. When the locker door was opened, Jimmy Behnke popped out and yelled, "Larry Bird, I hate you!"

Even venerable old Bob King wasn't spared. King had a nervous habit of coughing every few minutes when he spoke to the team in the locker room. As King was giving a pregame talk during Bird's junior year, all the players, at Bird's behest, coughed each time King did. Once he realized what was going on, King couldn't help but laugh. On another occasion, Bird pulled a truly devilish prank on his French Lick buddy Tony Clark. Clark had just purchased a used car, and since he knew next to nothing about engines, he asked Bird to look it over. Bird checked under the hood and said, "It's a good car, but the muffler bearing is about to fall off." Clark took the car back to the dealership and tried to show the salesman the problem Bird had pointed out. "I don't know who told you to bring this thing back," the guy said, "but there's no such thing as a muffler bearing." When Clark relayed the story to Bird, he howled.

That fun-loving attitude helped prevent external pressures from poisoning the Sycamores' locker room. For example, before and after practice, Bird was always looking to challenge someone to a shooting contest—a teammate, a coach, a janitor, whoever was willing to take him on. If they were willing to put a few bucks on the line, all the better. In these competitions he often tried trick shots and talked plenty of trash when he pulled them off. One day as the team was leaving the court after practice, Bird picked up a ball and, standing about ten feet out of bounds, hurled it over a steel wire and straight into the basket. The guys immediately dropped their stuff and spent the next thirty minutes trying to duplicate the feat.

For all his shyness in the outside world, Bird could have a domi-neeering personality when the setting was familiar. That sometimes put Bill Hodges in an awkward position. As a rookie head coach who was still technically an interim replacement, Hodges was not in a po-sition to impose his authority the way Bob King did. For the most part, Bird accorded Hodges the respect he deserved, but when push came to shove, everyone understood who could push the hardest. "I love Bill, but in reality, it was Larry's team," Bob Behnke says. "I don't think Larry intentionally took advantage of that. It was just his nature. He never held back from telling you what he was thinking."

As an example, Behnke cites an instance where Hodges drew up a play during a time-out at the end of a close game at home. When the team took the court, Behnke heard Bird tell Carl Nicks that they didn't have enough time to run that play, so Nicks should just get him the ball and he'd take care of the rest. When asked about Behnke's recollection, Nicks says he remembers the sequence, though like Behnke he can't recall precisely what game it was. "To be honest with you, Larry said that a number of times," Nicks says. "Hodges understood that Larry was the type of guy that sometimes you just need to get out of his way. If I was the coach, I would have done the same thing. It worked out all right, didn't it?"

Indeed, in many ways Hodges's personality was a perfect fit for this team. He was a laid-back country boy who kept his even keel. While he was plenty handy with his Xs and Os, he was in uncharted waters just as his players were, so they banded together. "Hodges did a great job," Steve Reed says. "He kept us in the moment, so we didn't get anxious or scared when we got down. It was always two points at a time. He also really emphasized conditioning, so we al-ways felt if we were in the game at the end, we'd figure out a way to win." Even Stan Evans, the jilted assistant who is very disparaging about Hodges's coaching abilities, concedes that if he had gotten the job, the team would not have fared as well. "I would have screwed up a couple of games just by overcoaching," he says.

Hodges was also smart enough to recognize his own shortcomings as a coach. One of them was the ability to teach defense—at least compared to King, who had built his reputation as one of the most innovative defensive tacticians in the country. Whereas most coaches of his era instructed their players to force opposing ball handlers toward the middle of the court, King devised a scheme that pushed dribblers to the sides and corners. The advantage was that it enabled King's players to use the sidelines as an additional defender. The concept was so effective that Bob Knight later implemented it at Indiana.

Hodges, who had been regularly visiting with King at his house a couple times a week, was becoming frustrated that opponents were still managing to penetrate the middle of the court by throwing the ball over the top of the Sycamores' full-court press. The inability to prevent that from happening was partly why Indiana State's wins were closer than they needed to be. So one day, Hodges asked Sharel King, the coach's wife, if he could invite Bob to a practice. Sharel reluctantly agreed that Bob could stay for thirty minutes, but not a moment longer.

That's all the time King needed to diagnose the problem. "You've got no false influence," he told Hodges. The term described the token pressure a defender puts on the ball handler in the backcourt, forcing him to one side of the floor before he even crossed the half-court line. When the players made King's recommended adjustment, the improvement was instantaneous, and it sparked the team's impressive run through the month of January.

A 10-point win at Creighton University on January 20 made the Sycamores 16–0. When Indiana State defeated Southern Illinois— the consensus preseason favorite in the Missouri Valley—by 9 points at a jam-packed Hulman Center on January 22, Hodges paid his guys the ultimate compliment by saying that they had played "inspired defense." Now they were 17–0 and had moved up to No. 3 in both polls. They beat Creighton at home five days later to improve to 18–0. When the two teams that were ranked ahead of them, Notre Dame and North Carolina, each lost over the weekend, the Sycamores appeared poised to climb, amazingly, to the No. 1 ranking in America.

Yet a wall of skepticism remained. When the new polls came out on January 30, Notre Dame stayed at No. 1 while Indiana State was left at No. 2. In the AP poll, the Sycamores actually got more first-place votes than the Fighting Irish, but one person had left Indiana State off his ballot entirely and another voted them fifteenth, the lowest slot available. For all their accomplishments to date, the perception of the Sycamores was still that they were an unknown team in a second-rate conference who had never truly been tested.

Besides, this ragtag bunch couldn't possibly keep this undefeated thing going. Could they?

As January heralded the rise of Indiana State in the national polls, a much different story was playing out in East Lansing. Michigan State had begun 1979 as the No. 1 team in the nation following its win over Indiana in the championship of the Far West Classic. That was rarefied altitude for this program, and the Spartans were about to find out just how thin the air was up there.

After their long trip home from Portland, the Spartans picked up where they had left off, pummeling the University of Wisconsin by 29 points at Jenison Fieldhouse on January 4. Magic Johnson was at his very best, finishing with 21 points, 14 assists, and 13 rebounds. (The term "triple-double" had yet to make its way into the lexicon.) Johnson was equally proficient in the postgame locker room where he was, as Fred Stabley Jr. noted in the *State Journal*, "the center of attention . . . and with a microphone stuck in his face there are few better." The performance put Jud Heathcote in an unusually buoyant mood. Sitting in the coaches' locker room with a stat sheet in his lap, he cracked, "If I were an opposing coach and saw that big turkey bringing the ball down court every time, I think I'd vomit."

Johnson was certainly a unique weapon to take into these pivotal games, but now that he was beginning his second tour through the conference, he found that opponents were divining smarter schemes to defend him. During Magic's freshman year, not only had he ranked third in the Big Ten in scoring in conference games (19.8 average), but he had also led the conference in assists (6.8) and set a Michigan State single-season assist record with 222, largely because opposing teams were so unaccustomed to defending a six-foot-eight point guard. But as the season progressed, the other Big Ten coaches figured out that the weakest part of Johnson's game was his outside shooting. They also noted that aside from Johnson, the Spartans were short on dependable ball handlers. That kind of information was critical at a time when there was limited scouting of teams outside of the ones coaches were able to see in person. Now, as the Big Ten teams prepared for their games with Michigan State during Johnson's sophomore year, they did so with a better understanding of how best to exploit the Spartans' weaknesses.

Michigan State was also not used to being the most hunted team in the conference, and the team found it hard to match its opponents' intensity. The first hint of trouble came during a January 6 game against the University of Minnesota in Jenison Fieldhouse. The Golden Gophers, led by their six-foot-eleven junior center Kevin McHale, built a 42–29 lead with seventeen minutes to play. Heathcote responded by scrapping his usual two-three matchup zone, which was an innovative hybrid of zone and man-to-man, and switching to man-to-man in hopes that his players could apply more direct pressure on the Gophers' scorers. The gambit worked, but with Magic contributing just 9 points (along with 12 assists), the Spartans needed a career-high 19 points from Ron Charles to escape with a 69–62 win.

That victory set up a huge showdown on January 11 at the University of Illinois, which itself was undefeated (15–0) and ranked No. 3 by UPI and No. 4 by the AP. Like Michigan State, Illinois was undergoing a remarkable renaissance under its fourth-year coach, Lou Henson. The Illini had won just two Big Ten basketball titles in the previous twenty-seven years, but they boasted a formidable squad led by a pair of sophomore forwards, Eddie Johnson and Mark Smith. The anticipation for the game helped fuel a hoops excitement that was unusual for the Midwest, and for the Big Ten in particular. The conference had been so indifferent to basketball in the past that even when Ohio State University reached three consecutive NCAA championship games from 1960 to 1962, the school didn't even bother to put out a press brochure. "The publicity office was too busy taking care of football," said former coach Fred Taylor. Before the start of the 1977–78 season, Heathcote complained, "I don't think our conference publicizes basketball the way it should. There's no highlight film, no publication, no booklet."

Now the league was starting to catch on. For the 1978–79 season, basketball players for the first time were given the same training table privileges as football players. Traveling squads were bumped up from twelve to fifteen, and coaches were permitted to grant scholarships to transfer students who were sitting out a year while awaiting eligibility. The Michigan State–Illinois game was another important step in drumming up interest in Big Ten basketball. Even though a massive snowstorm hit central Illinois that day, a record crowd of 16,209, including Governor Jim Thompson, packed Assembly Hall on the university's campus in Champaign.

At the start, the fans were treated to compelling evidence of why the Spartans held the No. 1 ranking, as they hit their first ten shots to build a 20–9 lead over the home team. The Illini, however, were undeterred, responding with 14 unanswered points to give themselves a 4-point halftime lead. How gripping was the action? Toward the end of the first half, the public address announcer stated that a bomb threat had been phoned in to the arena. Nobody moved.

The lead seesawed back and forth for much of the second half, with Illinois eventually pushing out to a 51–46 lead and Michigan State answering to make it 55–55 heading into the final minute and a half. With one minute left, Magic tried to put the Spartans ahead, but his shot from five feet missed. Illinois held the ball for one last shot, but Illini guard Levi Cobb accidentally dribbled the ball off his foot. Magic dove to the floor and tried to wrestle the ball away from Cobb until the officials called for a jump ball. Cobb won the tap with fourteen seconds left and Illinois called time-out.

During the huddle, Heathcote told his players to pressure every potential shooter since he couldn't predict who would take the last attempt. The Spartans guarded the Illini zealously for the first few passes, but Eddie Johnson got an open look from eighteen feet as time was running out. The shot swished through with three ticks on the clock, dealing the Spartans a devastating 57–55 loss. Equally galling to Heathcote was the fact that his team had been outrebounded 50–22. The margin of defeat would have been much worse had Illinois not shot 39.7 percent from the floor compared to Michigan State's 51.9 percent. "Everybody was playing this game up like it meant the world," Johnson said. "Illinois has a very fine team, but we played poorly and still only lost by two points."

The Spartans looked to bounce back two days later at Purdue. Besides coming off the loss to Illinois, this was the opportunity for Michigan State to avenge its 19-point defeat in West Lafayette the year before. (That was the game that had led to the players' musical rebellion against Heathcote on the bus ride home.) Yet the Spartans came away unredeemed. Once again, Michigan State got beat on the boards (27–14) and lost on a crushing buzzer beater, this one coming on a twenty-five-foot desperation heave by Purdue forward Arnette Hallman. Even Purdue coach Lee Rose conceded that Hallman was the last person he wanted to take that shot in that situation. In less than forty-eight hours, Michigan State had gone from first in the nation to fourth in the Big Ten.

The Purdue loss was the latest example of the Spartans having suffered from their coach's excessive conservatism. When Rose sent the Boilermakers into a delay with more than five minutes remaining in the first half, the most effective response would have been for Heathcote to turn up the defensive pressure in an effort to get his team's running game going. Instead, he told his players to sit back and let Purdue hold the ball. "We were tired and Purdue had the momentum," he explained afterward. "I was happy to let them stall it out and go in at the half and regroup from only seven points down."

Moreover, Johnson, who had 8 points and 8 turnovers in the loss to Illinois, was just as bad against Purdue, finishing with just 9 points and 6 assists. "Our whole offense is built around Earvin having the ball and he's not playing very well right now," Heathcote said. The same could be said for his teammates. The casual demeanors of Jay Vincent and Ron Charles might have made for a harmonious locker room, but it was clearly hurting the team's efforts on the boards. Their opponents were playing with the nastiness you'd expect from athletes who were desperate to knock off the Big Ten's glamour boys, but the Spartans' big men were not showing that same urgency. As for outside scoring, Heathcote continued to be mystified by the lack of assertiveness from Mike Brkovich, the six-foot-four guard from Canada who had scored a grand total of 6 points in the Spartans' previous three games. Brkovich had as pure a stroke as Heathcote had ever seen, but he was too much of a perfectionist. That was evident after practice one day, when Brkovich sought out the coach to help him fix his shot. Brkovich drilled about ten straight jumpers before missing one. Then he turned to Heathcote and said plaintively, "See? Something is wrong."

When the No. 1 ranked team suddenly drops two straight games, it's only natural that the best player should come under the harshest scrutiny. Michigan State's loss to Purdue prompted Bill Gleason, a columnist for the *Chicago Sun-Times,* to pen a withering critique of Johnson's abilities. "He is a mediocre passer and ball handler," Gleason wrote. "He is a poor shooter and a poor defensive player. To hear the 'Golly! Gee!' analysts tell it, Johnson is 'another Oscar Robertson.' He isn't. Robertson could do everything. To compare Johnson with the 'Big O' is laughable. Johnson, right now, is not nearly the player Quinn Buckner was in his sophomore year at Indiana."

In the days before cable television and the Internet, a single scathing newspaper column could have a devastating impact. At his weekly press luncheon, Heathcote took exception to Gleason's analysis. "I think the story is a bum rap and written by a guy who never saw Earvin play," he said. "It's easy to criticize a guy who gets as much publicity as Earvin does. It's easy to think of Earvin Johnson as Superman."

Heathcote's response to the scrutiny was to close ranks. For the first time in his three years at Michigan State, he barred reporters from the team's locker room. He insisted that the new policy was the players' idea, and he said they would still be available outside the locker room after games. But no one doubted who had issued the edict.

With his team encountering the season's first bout of adversity, it was imperative for Heathcote to know what was going on inside his players' heads. One of the people he turned to for such insight was Darwin Payton, whose title as head student manager drastically understated his role. He was an avowed basketball junkie who understood the game well. He was also close friends with the players, especially the nucleus of Earvin Johnson, Greg Kelser, and Jay Vincent. As a senior, Payton had the maturity to size up situations, and since he wasn't a player he didn't fear telling Heathcote exactly what he thought.

Heathcote first came to appreciate this forthrightness early in his first year at Michigan State, when Payton was a sophomore. Heathcote had a habit from his previous coaching stints of calling his student managers "Management." One day he repeatedly barked "Management!" in an effort to get Payton's attention, but Payton ignored him. Finally, Jud said, "Darwin!"

"What?" Payton replied.

"Why didn't you answer me?" Heathcote demanded.

"Because my mother didn't name me Management."

From that day forward, Heathcote called him Darwin.

Eventually Heathcote started meeting with Payton in his office before games (or in his hotel room on the road) to take the pulse of his locker room. "Darwin was like another coach," Heathcote says. "All the players liked him, and they called him 'Dar-Baby.' He was invaluable. He might say, Coach, you were too hard on the guys today, or So-and-so is struggling with a class. I'd listen to him more than I'd listen to a player, because I was coaching the players. I wasn't coaching

Dar." Payton understood well his value to the team. "Some of the guys weren't as thick-skinned as others. They used to ask me, 'Dar-Baby, can you go tell Coach to lay off a little,'" he says. "I would go in there and say it without saying that someone actually told me that. I took my job seriously because those guys never treated me as a manager. They treated me like another player."

The heartbreaking losses at Illinois and Purdue dropped the Spartans to No. 6 in the AP poll. They rebounded by routing Indiana on January 18 by 24 points at home. Brkovich broke out of his offensive doldrums in that one to score a season-high 16 points, including 2 on a breakaway dunk midway through the second half. "I tell you, Mike can jump," said Kelser, one of the best leapers in the country. "I've been waiting a long time for Mike to get one of those off." Two days later, Brkovich played an even more pivotal role when the Spartans found themselves in another dogfight after blowing a 15-point half-time lead at home against the University of Iowa. It looked like the pressure was starting to take its toll on Heathcote, who picked up two technical fouls in the second half. (That did not elicit an automatic ejection back then.) Lynn Henning, the *State Journal* columnist who often took issue with Heathcote's hyperkinetic comportment on the sideline, upbraided the coach again for getting two T's in such an important game. "Technical fouls are the most unnecessary crime in basketball," Henning wrote. "They're misconduct penalties and a coach who preaches poise to his ballplayers should be setting the example. Heathcote isn't. It's not even an arguable point anymore. He's going berserk down there and it's becoming a sorry sight."

The Spartans had suffered from more than their fair share of bad luck, but this time the late break went their way when, with Iowa leading 65–63 and 3 seconds remaining, Hawkeyes guard Ronnie Lester was whistled for fouling Brkovich—a call that three decades later Iowa coach Lute Olson still insists was horrendous. The quiet, unassuming Brkovich stepped to the foul line under excruciating pressure. Though the NCAA tournament was still nearly two months away, the Spartans were keenly aware that no more than two teams would be admitted to the tournament from each conference. If Brkovich missed either free throw, it would drop the Spartans to 3–3 in the Big Ten, potentially ending their hopes of making the field.

Brkovich sank the first free throw, and Olson called time-out. During the huddle, Heathcote calmly went over what the team's strategy would be after Brkovich made the second free throw. In reality, with just 3 seconds remaining, there wasn't much strategy to discuss. Heathcote's real purpose was to convey the impression that it was a foregone conclusion that Brkovich would make the second free throw. With his confidence bolstered, Brkovich did make it, sending the game into overtime. Since the foul against Lester, Iowa's leading scorer, had been his fifth, the Hawkeyes were at a disadvantage in the extra session. Michigan State pulled out a dramatic 83–72 win. "That one-and-one that Brkovich hit against Iowa is the most pressure-packed feat I've ever seen a college kid execute," Lynn Henning says. "Without that, they probably don't even make the tournament."

The pair of wins bumped the Spartans up two places in the AP poll, to No. 4. Alas, they were back on the business end of yet another controversial call on January 26 in Ann Arbor, when Magic Johnson was called for a foul on Michigan freshman guard Keith Smith with the game tied and no time left on the clock. Heathcote tried to call a time-out to freeze Smith, but the officials said he couldn't do that because time had expired. He argued his case for over a minute, but to no avail. Finally, Smith stepped to the line and calmly sank his first attempt, giving Michigan a 49–48 win. The loss dropped the Spartans into a three-way tie for third place in the Big Ten with a 4–3 record, 3 games behind undefeated Ohio State. They were 11–4 overall.

Heathcote chased the referees off the court, still pleading his case. Reporters waited for twenty minutes outside the Spartans' locker room as they had been instructed, but when the players emerged they told the writers that Heathcote had forbidden them to give interviews.

When one scribe buttonholed Greg Kelser in the parking lot, he said, "We've lost four games by six points. There's nothing else to say."

"I just guess we're snakebit on the road," Heathcote said. "I'm not giving up, but our chances do not look good right now. We have three Big Ten losses and a lot of games ahead."

Having harbored visions of a national championship just two weeks before, the Spartans had sunk to a new low. And yet, as bad as things looked, they still hadn't hit rock bottom.

6

For a team that was so badly wounded, the Michigan State Spartans were getting what appeared to be the perfect salve: the lowly Northwestern University Wildcats. Traditionally the bottom-feeders of the Big Ten, the Wildcats had begun the 1978–79 season in typical fashion. By late January they sported a 4–12 record, including 0–7 in the conference. What's more, three of their forwards had been lost for the season for various reasons. Their dingy old gym, McGaw Hall, was not sold out for the game against the Spartans. The game on Saturday, January 27, would be one of the few involving Michigan State that was not going to be televised anywhere.

Jud Heathcote was concerned less with his next opponent than with the mind-set of his own players. "It's a must win for us if we have any hopes of ending up with a postseason berth," he said. "Northwestern has got to figure we're going to be down and this is a great chance to beat us. And the truth is, we are down. It's hard for the coaching staff and players to get over a loss like that [Michigan game]."

Presented with an opportunity to start turning their season around, the Spartans should have come out with great focus and intensity. Instead, they came out sluggish. Adding to the hazy feeling was the cloud of dust that had formed above the court, kicked into the air by the joggers running around the dirt track while Michigan State and Northwestern did battle. Heathcote sensed right away that his players were running on fumes, and with the score tied at 6–6 after four minutes of play, he made the unusual move of benching all his starters at once. The five-man substitution was no help, and one by one the first string came back in. Things got worse when Greg Kelser picked up his third foul at the ten-minute mark of the first half and Jay Vincent got his fourth just before intermission. The Spartans shot a woeful 10 for 27 from the field over the first half, and they trailed 39–29 at the break.

When the Spartans returned to the floor for the second half, they were greeted by an entirely different atmosphere. Word had spread around campus that the Wildcats had Magic Johnson and mighty Michigan State on the ropes. The stands, which had been half-filled for the first half, were now packed. A few band members and cheerleaders showed up to spur noise. And the Northwestern players responded with a devastating 10–0 run to open the second half. Heathcote once again tried a man-to-man defense, but the Wildcats continuously shredded it for easy buckets—reminding Heathcote why he played so much zone in the first place. At the other end of the floor, Northwestern coach Rich Falk packed his players in the paint and forced the Spartans to make jump shots. "If I was going to try and defend our team, that's what I would do," Heathcote said afterward. "We won't win many games by relying on our outside shooting."

Michigan State never got closer than 15 points, and the Spartans shot a season-low 32.8 percent for the game. This time, there were no controversial calls to complain about, no painful buzzer beaters to digest. There was only the humiliating final score of 83–65. Heathcote didn't even bother to explode in the locker room after the game. He was more resigned than irate, saying simply, "Fellas, we are not a very good basketball team right now."

Heathcote tried to put the best face on his team's collapse. "If I weren't the eternal optimist, I might figure the season is over," he said at his postgame press conference. "But we still have a plenty talented team that has to regroup and try to fight back." He also told the reporters his players were once again available for interviews in the locker room. "You can go down there and talk to them if you want to throw up," he said. There they found Magic Johnson, who had needed 22 shots to score his game-high 26 points. (He also had 10 assists and 10 rebounds.) "My stomach is turning about forty times a minute," Johnson said. "I've never been on a team that's lost five times in a season. I don't know how to react."

Even Falk seemed shocked by the turn of events. "I have too much respect for Michigan State and its players to believe that we could ever control a game with it like we did," he said. Asked if he thought Magic was the best player in the Big Ten, Falk came close to damning him with faint praise. "From a standpoint of being able to take over and dominate a game, yes he is. He's not a great shooter, but he does so many things well."

How could such a talented team play so poorly in such an important contest? "It was just a culmination of several weeks of losing," Terry Donnelly says. "Losing breeds problems internally. You start second-guessing each other. People start taking things personally. It just kind of snowballs."

The team didn't get back to East Lansing until late that night. When their bus rolled into the parking lot of Jenison Fieldhouse, they were greeted by Johnson's father, Earvin Sr., and by Charles Tucker. The two of them had been shooting baskets inside the gym while waiting for the team to return. Tucker and Earvin Sr. tried to cheer the guys up, but it wasn't easy.

Clearly, the Spartans had some serious soul searching to do, but fortunately they had a day off to regroup. Before practicing on Monday, Heathcote called a team meeting in hopes of clearing the air. The players and coaching staff gathered in the cramped coaches' lounge, and Heathcote asked his players to say what they thought was wrong. Kelser spoke first—"as I *always* did," he says—and set the tone by criticizing Heathcote directly. His chief complaint was that they had become too reliant on Magic to create scoring. Kelser emphasized it wasn't a matter of his ego being bruised, but rather that it made the offense stagnant and predictable. "I felt like the only good shot for me was a layup or a dunk," Kelser says. "I told him to go back to my sophomore year when I was scoring from everywhere and had the ball in my hands a lot. I was still capable of doing those things, but I had to feel free out there. If I made a mistake, I needed to feel like I wasn't going to endure coach's wrath every time."

Johnson echoed Kelser's complaints about being unable to play carefree. He also criticized Heathcote for putting the brakes on their running game. Jay Vincent chipped in with his own complaints, as did Ron Charles. Heathcote was especially surprised that Charles, the easygoing kid from the Virgin Islands whom everyone called "Bobo," felt unhappy. "We always thought you were like a rubber ball," Heathcote said. "Like we could throw you against the ball and you'd bounce right off." The players found Heathcote's analogy so amusing that for the remainder of the season, they called Charles "Rubber Ball."

Heathcote then went around the room and asked the other players if they wanted to chime in. One by one, they answered, "No gripe." ("I was a freshman. I wasn't saying shit," Rob Gonzalez says.) Kelser quickly cut in. "They *do* have a gripe," he said. "I know they feel the exact same way because we have talked about it amongst ourselves." Not surprisingly, Heathcote was unsympathetic to the notion that they weren't having enough fun. "Hey, if you want to have fun, go play intramural or church basketball," he said. "We're not out here for fun. We're here to win." Yet he also appeared to be listening to their concerns.

Eventually, Mike Longaker decided to have his say. As a six-foot-one junior walk-on who barely played in games, Longaker seemed an unlikely candidate to speak at such a tense moment. But he was also a brilliant premed student and Rhodes scholar candidate who carried a 3.9 grade-point average. Longaker used to memorize passages of books to show off his photographic memory, and he was also the designated academic tutor in the team's hotel. "And you'd better get [to his room] early or there would be a line of guys in the hall," said

Johnson, who had become especially good friends with Longaker. Rising to speak, Longaker picked up on the mantra the team had adopted during its preseason trip to Brazil: "potential." Before each game, Kelser led them on a spirited cheer to spell out the word. "We always talk about potential," Longaker said. "Well, there's a lot of talent in this room, but we're not playing near to our potential. And we better start doing it soon, or our season will be over."

Heathcote emphasized to his players that they needed to change their ways, too—especially on defense. He did not exactly promise a kinder, gentler regime, but the players sensed they had gotten through to the coach in a way they hadn't before. "It was a come-to-Jesus meeting," Terry Donnelly says. "I think Jud took it to heart. He really did. Jud's got an emotional side underneath everything. I think he listened to what we had to say and knew it wasn't fluff. I don't know that it changed him much, but he did listen." As a result of the exchange, says Vincent, "Coach backed off a little bit—a very, very little bit."

After the meeting, Heathcote also met privately with a few players, and as usual he sought out Darwin Payton's take on the situation. "Guys are too comfortable," the student manager told him. "The starting team feels that no matter what happens, nobody's going to take their job. Who's going to take Earvin's job, Coach? Who's going to take Greg's?"

Heathcote wasn't about to bench his two stars, but Payton's observation helped crystallize his belief that he needed to change the lineup. "When Earvin was a freshman, we snuck up on people," he says. "The coaches in the Big Ten aren't duds, you know. Suddenly, the next year they put a guy right in front of Earvin so we couldn't throw it to him. Now we have no fast break. We needed somebody else to throw it to [off a rebound], then we could hit Magic at midcourt, and we've got our fast break again."

Heathcote's solution was to move Gerald Busby, a six-foot-four freshman who had played a season-high twenty-six minutes against Northwestern, into the starting lineup to replace Donnelly. During practice that Monday following the team meeting, Busby wore a green jersey and worked with the starters. That night, however, he abruptly quit the team and returned to his home in Buchanan, Michigan. Busby was a soft-spoken kid who was raised as a Jehovah's Witness, and he had been disquieted by the profanity Heathcote unspooled daily. At first, assistant coach Bill Berry tried to talk Busby out of leaving, but the player held his ground. When Heathcote called Busby at home the next day, he accepted his decision but asked Busby to tell the press that he had left the team for nonbasketball reasons so it wouldn't reflect badly on the program. Heathcote would later tell reporters that Busby had "personal problems with his girl at home," but that was not the truth. "He never had anything good to say to me. It just got to be where it wasn't fun anymore," Busby says. "The thing I was thinking about from the time I got up in the morning was, I don't want to go to practice. . . . One day he rode Gregory so hard that he couldn't make a layup. I thought to myself, if he can do this to a senior, how is it going to be for me the next four years?"

With Busby gone, Heathcote tapped Mike Brkovich to replace Donnelly in the starting lineup. "It's not meant to be a slap at Terry, but we need more offense and Mike is a fine offensive player," he said. Heathcote also griped about the public criticism that he felt was suffocating his team during its time of crisis. "Now is the time our basketball players need the support and backing of our fans instead of the constant negativism we've been getting lately," he grumbled. "A lot of our players are approaching basketball like it's drudgery."

"The one thing we have to do is stay together," Greg Kelser said. "Our chances of winning or sharing the Big Ten title is not good right now, but our goal is getting into the NCAA tournament and we still have a chance to do that."

Ideally, the Spartans' next game would be against a weak opponent so they could get used to the lineup change and regain their confidence. Alas, the schedule would not provide that luxury. Big bad Ohio State, the first-place team in the Big Ten with a spotless

8–0 record, was coming to town on February 1. If ever the season was going to face a make-or-break moment, this was it.

Bill Hodges continued his regular visits at Bob King's house, and he called the head coach often to share what was happening with the team. Though King technically had the option to come back to coaching that season, by mid-January Hodges realized that wasn't going to happen. "He had a pretty good long-term memory, but he couldn't remember things that happened ten minutes ago," Hodges says. King's recovery was more halting than the public knew. When he listened to the Sycamores' first game on the radio at home, he turned to his wife, Sharel, and asked why he wasn't coaching. "I said, 'You're too sick to be there. We'll have to listen on the radio,'" Sharel says. "I think he forgot what happened." Because the surgeon had cut through a memory center in King's brain, Sharel had to go through scrapbooks with him to help piece together the parts of his life that had been lost in the fog.

King attended most of the Sycamores' home games, but he wasn't up for traveling. However, he made an exception for their game at New Mexico State on February 1. He had spent ten years as head coach at the University of New Mexico, so he had a lot of friends in the area. Besides, Las Cruces was always the team's favorite road trip of the year. They got to eat terrific Mexican food and visit the happening border town of Juárez.

King also knew he'd see a big-time college basketball game. The Aggies were in second place in the Missouri Valley Conference with a 6–2 record, and as their 4-point loss at Hulman Center two weeks earlier had demonstrated, they had the ability to hang with Indiana State, the nation's No. 2–ranked team, with an 18–0 record. Their fans were locked and loaded; a record crowd of 13,684 packed into the Pan American Center. The game would be televised in Terre Haute, with Indiana State's radio team of Bob Forbes and Joe MacIsaac providing the simultaneous TV call.

Right from the opening tap, New Mexico State's crowd was itching for a fight. With 7½ minutes to play in the first half and the Sycamores up by 7 points, Steve Reed fired a long pass to a streaking Bird. The pass went too far, and as Bird saved the ball from going out of bounds his momentum carried him into the bleachers. After he landed, a group of fans grabbed him and prevented him from returning to the floor. As the game action continued at the far end of the court, Bird flailed away in an effort to pry himself free. After several scary seconds, he broke loose with the help of some security guards. At that moment, he looked ready to take on everybody in the arena at once. On the air, MacIsaac said, "He's the last guy in this gymnasium that anybody wants to tangle with. I'll flat guarantee that."

After security escorted the offending fans out of the arena, Indiana State continued to build on its lead. The Sycamores had a 51–39 advantage at the intermission and owned a 15-point margin two minutes into the second half. The tide started to turn, however, when Carl Nicks picked up his fourth foul and had to go to the bench. Without his outside shooting to worry about, the Aggies were free to pack in their defense and limit Bird's touches. He was plenty active (he would finish the night with 37 points and 17 rebounds), but the Sycamores' offense became too one-dimensional. Meanwhile, at the other end of the floor, Aggies guard Chuck Goslin got ridiculously hot, at one point nailing three straight long jump shots in rapid fashion to help New Mexico State claw back to 65–62 with 9:53 to play.

Hodges sent Nicks back into the game, but the energetic guard was unable to get into the flow. He also hurt the team by missing three front ends of one-and-one free throw opportunities. The jam-packed arena got hotter and louder as the game remained tight into the final minutes. The Aggies were at last able to take an 80–79 lead on yet another Goslin jumper with just over two minutes left. When New Mexico State went into its delay game with under a minute to play, Nicks was forced to commit his fifth foul to stop the clock. Goslin hit the ensuing free throws, putting the Aggies up 82–79 with 37 seconds left.

Bird quickly responded with a fifteen-footer of his own, and then after Aggies forward Albert "Slab" Jones made one of two free throws to make it a 2-point game, Bird was fouled. That put him on the line for a one-and-one that could tie the game. Uncharacteristically, Bird's first free throw attempt was long, and New Mexico State guard Notie Pate snared the rebound. Bird immediately fouled Pate, his fifth of the game, and as he walked glumly to the Sycamores' bench and buttoned up his warm-up shirt, the crowd, sensing the upset was nigh, began chanting, "Eighteen-and-one! Eighteen-and-one!"

Pate, however, missed his free throw, leaving the score at 83–81. Steve Reed pulled up for a potential game-tying jumper, but he couldn't convert. New Mexico State's Greg Webb grabbed the rebound, Alex Gilbert fouled him with two seconds remaining (also his fifth foul), and the game appeared to be over. "Well, they could do it but it's very unlikely with just three seconds left and trailing by two," Forbes said to the fans back home. "So New Mexico State [is] very close to handing Indiana State its first loss of the season. A big victory, if they get it, for the Aggies." Forbes was so sure the cause was lost, he started packing up his radio equipment. All that remained on the table was his microphone.

Hodges called time-out, hoping to design some kind of miracle play that would get this thing into overtime. Only when he reached for his chalkboard, he couldn't find it. He exploded at the student manager, Rick Shaw, before gathering his guys. Danny King, a graduate assistant who grew up with Bird in French Lick, screamed in Bob Heaton's face, "Don't give up, Bob! Don't give up!" Heaton thought to himself, *Tell these other guys, man. Don't tell me.*

The players broke from the huddle and took their positions on the court. Only when Heaton got out there, he realized he didn't know where he was supposed to go. Either Hodges had forgotten to tell him or he hadn't been playing close enough attention. Meanwhile, near the Sycamores' bench, Slab Jones, seeing the Aggies' fans crowding around the edges of the court, warned Bird he should do his best to get out of there quickly. He didn't want Larry getting hurt in the mad rush.

Greg Webb stepped to the free throw line. If he made the shot, the Aggies would go up by 3, and the win would be sealed, since there was no 3-point line. Webb lofted the ball toward the basket . . . and it bounced harmlessly off the front rim. Brad Miley gathered the rebound, took one dribble, and pitched it ahead to Heaton, who was standing just behind the half-court line. Heaton planted both feet and chucked it toward the rim with two hands. "When the ball was halfway there to the basket, it looked like it was going to go over the backboard," he says.

It didn't. It hit the backboard and dropped through as time ran out. Overtime. One of the New Mexico State male cheerleaders who had been standing under the basket dropped his megaphone and flopped onto his back. Webb, whose errant free throw had preceded Heaton's bomb, also fell to his rear end right there on the court. "He made it! He made the shot! I don't believe it!" Forbes screamed. "I don't believe it! And it's tied! It's tied! He shot it from over the center line. I don't believe it. I don't believe this, but I have seen it."

Heaton's teammates sprinted onto the court and deliriously swarmed him. Hodges shared their elation—until he looked at his bench and saw Bird, Nicks, and Gilbert, all of whom had fouled out. *What the hell do we do now?* he wondered. He didn't have nearly as much to worry about as his counterpart, Aggies coach Ken Hayes, whose players returned to the court for the start of overtime looking positively dazed. "A high school team would have beaten them at that point. They were dumbfounded," Heaton says.

Forced to dig deeper into his bench than he had all season, Hodges inserted six-foot-nine junior center Eric Curry into the lineup for the opening tip and rotated in six-foot-six junior Rich Nemcek. When the Aggies committed two quick, careless turnovers, MacIsaac observed, "I'm not sure that shot hasn't got New Mexico State rattled. They just aren't moving the way they've been." In the overtime, the Sycamores got a twenty-foot jump shot from Heaton, a fifteen-foot bank shot from Leroy Staley, and a 3-point play when Brad Miley grabbed an offensive rebound, converted a layup, and was fouled. As they ran their delay offense to preserve a 1-point lead in the final minute, Bird stood on the sidelines and cheered madly. New Mexico State had to foul Reed to stop the clock, and he made one of two shots from the line to put the Sycamores up by a bucket. Webb had one last chance to tie it up for New Mexico State in the waning moments, but his jumper from the top of the key was off. Nemcek got the rebound for Indiana State and held the ball high for several seconds while the Aggies inexplicably failed to foul him.

The buzzer sounded, giving the Sycamores a stunning 91–89 win. They were still the only undefeated major college team in America.

Once again, the players rushed the court to celebrate. As they hoisted Hodges onto their shoulders, he reached down and embraced Bob King, who kissed Hodges on his cheek. Forbes was ebullient and exhausted on the air. "You can go a long time and see a lot of great basketball games," he said, "but it may be a long time before I'll ever see a game like that."

As he spoke to reporters afterward, Hodges sounded as if he still couldn't believe what had transpired. "I have to be honest. With three seconds to go and them shooting a free throw, I had to pray. I think we just saw a miracle." The rest of the team was picking up on that same theme. "I remember vividly thinking to myself, there's divine intervention here," Steve Reed says. "There's something about this year that is really special." Driving away from the arena that night, Sharel King listened to the radio and heard Aggies coach Ken Hayes remark that maybe Indiana State was a team of destiny. *Sounds pretty good to me,* she thought.

"If we had lost that game, we probably would have lost a couple more," Bird said years later. "That just kept us going."

Needless to say, the victory made the postgame meal all the more joyful. They went to a local Mexican restaurant and had a grand old time, even when Hodges ate some chili that was so spicy Sharel King had to give him honey to put out the fire in his mouth. As Bob Heaton's car pulled into the parking lot, Bird, who had arrived in a different car, pointed at his roommate, pumped his fist, and flashed a bright smile. "Larry didn't show a lot of emotion like that," Heaton says. "I mean, he was so excited. I think that was the most excited I've ever seen him."

The festive mood continued the next day, when they traveled to Oklahoma for their game against the University of Tulsa. They practiced at Oral Roberts University, and after the session was over the players started hoisting shots from the spot where Heaton had made his against New Mexico State. Naturally, Bird was the only one who sank a ball. "Shit, Heaton," he said, "that wasn't nuthin'." Later that night, they sat in the lobby of their hotel watching television, when ABC's national newscast replayed Heaton's heave. "Right there I was thinking, thousands of people just saw what I did. That was me on the TV," Heaton says. "That's when it kind of hit me."

Still high from their great escape in Las Cruces, the Sycamores dispatched the University of Tulsa 66–56 the next day to improve their record to 20–0, 10–0 in the Missouri Valley Conference. When that game ended, more than a thousand Indiana State students showed up at the house of university president Richard Landini. The president came outside to join them, whereupon the students tossed him, delighted, into a snowbank. The team flew home to Terre Haute the next day and were surprised to see Landini and several thousand fans waiting to greet them at Hulman Center for an impromptu pep rally.

Landini said the win over New Mexico State was "the mark of a very blessed team." A few days after the rally, he held a press conference to announce that Hodges had been signed to a three-year contract at an annual salary of $28,750 to be Indiana State's full-time head basketball coach. "He is relaxed and at peace with the world," Landini said. For Hodges, it was hard to imagine a more perfect week.

On the very same night that Indiana State was pulling off its miracle in Las Cruces, the Michigan State Spartans were making their last stand in East Lansing against Ohio State. Heathcote tried to use his trademark wit to defuse the situation. At a taping of his weekly television show following the Northwestern loss, he pointed out that he had received only one letter asking him to resign. "Unfortunately," he said, "it was signed by ten thousand people."

He remained committed to his lineup change, which would give Mike Brkovich, the trigger-shy Canadian, the first start of his career. Heathcote was also concerned about the state of mind of his core starters—especially Jay Vincent, who had been drawing heat for his desultory play of late. The last thing Heathcote wanted was for his starting center to lack confidence while going up against Herb Williams, Ohio State's formidable six-eleven center. When Vincent arrived at Jenison Fieldhouse for practice the day before the game, he found a note from Heathcote taped to his locker. "We know you're the best center in the Big Ten," the note read. "Go out and stop your critics."

Vincent responded by playing inspired basketball, scoring three early buckets and attacking the boards to help stake the Spartans to a 16–6 lead. Meanwhile, Greg Kelser decided to test Heathcote's promise to loosen the reins by shooting three long jumpers. That was not Kelser's strength, but fortunately each one went in. When he hit the third one from about twenty-three feet, the team's broadcaster, Tim Staudt, observed, "That's a mile away for anybody, let alone Kelser."

The Spartans rose to the occasion by playing some of their best basketball of the season in that first half. Their two-three zone choked off the passing lanes to Williams, just as it was designed to do. Heathcote had also taught them how to shift the zone to lock up an opponent's primary scorer, which in this case was Kelvin Ransey, the Buckeyes' jet-quick six-foot-one guard and second-leading scorer. Ransey was much more athletic than Johnson, but like most guards he was at a major size disadvantage trying to check Johnson at the other end of the floor. Johnson didn't need to be swifter or jump higher than his defender. He simply put Ransey on his back and zig-zagged his way repeatedly into the lane, where he would attempt his funny-looking push shot (oftentimes drawing a foul) or make an easy pass to a teammate. Johnson was also able to post up Ransey anytime he wanted to. He didn't drill long jumpers or score on spectacular dunks, and most of his assists were fairly routine. He was, first and foremost, an orchestrator, which is why Heathcote often said, "Earvin doesn't dominate a game as much as he controls it."

Remarkably, just as he promised his players, Heathcote evinced a much more casual demeanor on the sidelines than he had in the past. "Jud Heathcote is as calm tonight as I've seen him all year," Staudt observed. "He's just stayed on that bench like he's riveted to it." Even when the Spartans' bench was whistled for a technical foul, Staudt surmised that assistant coach Bill Berry was the offender because Heathcote hadn't left his seat.

The game took a dramatic turn with 2:23 remaining in the first half and the Spartans up by 9. When Ransey missed an attempt in the lane, Johnson went up for the rebound between two Ohio State players. He grabbed the ball with both hands, but as he came down his left foot got tangled between the legs of Buckeyes forward Jim Ellinghausen. That forced Johnson to land solely on his right foot. His ankle buckled, and Johnson hit the floor writhing in obvious pain.

The Jenison crowd, which a moment earlier had been at full throat, immediately grew hushed. Clint Thompson, the team's trainer, scampered onto the floor and knelt beside Johnson while Ron Charles and Greg Kelser leaned over in concern. When it became apparent that Magic wasn't getting up right away, Heathcote came over as well. After a few minutes of silence, Thompson helped Johnson onto his feet and off the court. They bypassed the team's bench and headed straight for the training room.

With their leader gone, the Spartans were left disoriented. The job of running the offense fell to Brkovich, but he was woefully unequipped and unprepared. Heathcote tried putting in a delay offense in hopes of getting them to halftime without further damage, but Brkovich lost the ball at half-court and had to foul Ransey on a breakaway layup. The Spartans still led by 34–27 at the break, but it was clear that without Magic they would have a hard time putting the Buckeyes away.

As Johnson's teammates walked down the hallway toward their locker room, they could see into the training room where Johnson was getting treatment. It didn't look good. The team's physician, David Hough, had examined Magic's ankle and saw that it was already beginning to swell up. He put a special boot on the ankle and ran cold water through the boot to keep the swelling down while maintaining pressure on the joint. At that point, the best they could do was buy some time. Thompson went into the main locker room and told Heathcote it was too early to tell whether Johnson would be able to return for the second half. Heathcote replied that if playing was going to jeopardize Earvin's health for the long term, Thompson should keep him out, even if Earvin wanted to come back. Heathcote and the other Spartans went back to the court for the second half assuming that Johnson would be out for the rest of the game and probably longer.

The second half began with another awkward turnover by Brkovich—Michigan State's ninth of the game—and Herb Williams scored on the ensuing possession to cut the lead to 34–29. "Michigan State has got to get some more ball handling and less intimidation on those guards," Staudt said. The Buckeyes went on a quick 6–2 spurt to pull to within 36–35.

A bank shot by Kelser pushed the lead back to 3, but shortly afterward he picked up his fourth foul with 15:31 to play. Heathcote had to take Kelser out, and Ohio State soon went ahead by a point. Back in the training room, Johnson listened to the game on the radio with tears in his eyes. He insisted to Thompson and Hough that he was okay to play, but they were skeptical. Eventually, they removed the boot and agreed to let him test his ankle. Thompson taped it tight, handed Johnson a basketball, and told him to dribble up and down the hallway. Johnson did as he was told, cutting back and forth to demonstrate he was well enough to play. Earvin was moving delicately for sure, but Hough figured that at that point he wasn't going to hurt himself any worse. The only question was whether he could tolerate the pain.

Hough and Thompson gave Johnson the go-ahead. Without hesitating, Earvin turned and jogged toward the court. He made his way down the hallway that fed into the narrow entryway between the bleachers on the north side of the arena. When the fans in that corner saw Johnson coming back out, they started to rise. Ohio State had possession on the opposite side of the floor, but when the other spectators heard the noise they turned to see what was going on. In a matter of seconds, as Johnson magically reappeared, all ten thousand–plus were on their feet.

Earvin took a seat on the bench. It was still not clear whether he was going to play or whether he had just come out to watch the second half. Thompson, who had trailed Johnson during his jaunt to the court, walked directly up to Heathcote, put both hands on his shoulders, and told him Earvin was good to go. Immediately, Heathcote turned around and sent Johnson to the scorer's table. As Earvin got up and removed his warm-up shirt, the walls of Jenison Fieldhouse shook.

Back on the court, Jay Vincent rebounded a Brkovich miss and scored to make it 46–43 in favor of Michigan State. The television broadcast cut to a shot of Johnson sprawled comfortably on the floor in front of the scorer's table. He had a big ol' smile on his face. Johnson reentered the game with 8:42 to play and Michigan State leading by 5. He continued to move gingerly, but since his game wasn't predicated on speed, he was still effective in directing the offense. He did most of his damage from the free throw line, where he sank five of his six attempts following his return. The last of those gave the Spartans a 62–59 lead with 1:05 to play. "I just thank the good Lord that free throws are made with hands and not ankles," Heathcote said later. After Ohio State's Jim Ellinghausen hit one of two foul shots to cut the Spartans' lead to 2, Kelser got the ball on the wing and slashed his way in for a layup. That put Michigan State up by 64–60 with 35 seconds to play.

With no shot clock or 3-point line, that lead should have been safe. Yet when Buckeyes guard Todd Penn hit a jumper to make it 64–62, Johnson tried to block out Ellinghausen underneath and was called for a foul, even though it was Johnson who ended up on his back. That sent Ellinghausen to the line for a one-and-one, and he made them both for a rare 4-point play. Donnelly's jump shot on the ensuing possession was off the mark, and the Spartans found themselves heading for yet another overtime.

The Spartans could have been deflated by having blown their chance to win in regulation, but they were still riding the emotions of Johnson's heroic return. Kelser scored on a 3-point play inside to open the extra session, and Michigan State never trailed again. Johnson scored his eighteenth and nineteenth points on a driving baseline layup with 3 minutes to play, and he later converted four consecutive free throws to give Michigan State a 77–70 lead with 1:16 remaining. After Ohio State guard Tony Hall missed two free throws, Brkovich sent the Jenison crowd into a frenzy by taking a fast-break feed from Donnelly and slamming the ball emphatically to give the Spartans a 9-point advantage. On the ensuing possession Brkovich, ever the perfectionist, fouled Ransey and was incensed about the call. A smiling Donnelly hugged him to calm him down. Herb Williams and Ransey scored a couple of baskets in the final seconds, but by that point it just didn't matter. Michigan State had the crucial win it needed, 84–79.

Besides putting them above .500 again in the Big Ten, the victory also handed first-place Ohio State its first loss, shrinking its lead over the Spartans to 3½ games. The Spartans had been through too much to have any illusions about the challenge they still faced, but they took obvious pride from having fought through the adversity. "Our kids went out to prove to people that they're still a good basketball team," Heathcote said. "They were tired of listening [to] and answering questions of what's wrong with the Spartans."

Naturally, the postgame conversation was dominated by Johnson's injury and his dramatic reemergence in the second half, which naturally led many observers to compare it to the night when Willis Reed returned from injury to spur the New York Knicks to victory in Game 7 of the 1970 NBA Finals. "The doctors and the trainers had already made up their minds that I wasn't going to play," Magic said. "But I told them that if we lost this game, there was no tomorrow." Asked about the ovation, Johnson smiled and said, "My ankle didn't feel quite so bad when the fans started cheering. It was beautiful."

The win over Ohio State was critical for Michigan State's pursuit of a Big Ten championship, but of course it was much more than that. As Lynn Henning wrote for the next day's *State Journal*, "So, kiddies of the future, get ready for many nights of fireplace stories from grandma and grandpa about the night Earvin Johnson hobbled out of the training room on one foot to save Michigan State. This is a tale that won't have to be embellished down through the years." Many years later, Magic Johnson was asked what that ovation really sounded like. As Henning predicted, he didn't have to embellish. "You couldn't hear anything," he said. "It was like your eardrums had popped. It kept going and going and going. That place never let the sound out. And when an NBA arena would get a little loud, I'd tell guys, This place is nothing. You should've heard Jenison."

7

Ed McKee, Indiana State's lanky, genial sports information director, sat in his small office that had once been a concession stand in Hulman Center and ticked off the media outlets who had contacted him in just the last few days. There was CBS radio, the *Providence Journal*, the *New York Post*. Some coal magazine had called, as did a woman from the National Solid Wastes Management Association. Apparently she had gotten word that the best college basketball player in America had once worked on a garbage truck, and she wanted to do a story for their newsletter. The Sycamores' still-undefeated season was presenting the school with an unprecedented opportunity to generate publicity. There was only one problem. "They all want to talk to Larry Bird," McKee said, "and Larry's not talking."

That put McKee in a tough bind. He didn't like denying requests to sportswriters any more than he liked bringing those requests to Bird and Bill Hodges in the first place. McKee also knew that nobody was going to try to force Larry to change his mind, including the school's president, Richard Landini. "People with my talents are a dime a dozen," Landini said. "People with Larry Bird's talents come along only once in a lifetime."

"The tail was really wagging the dog," McKee says. "Larry dictated what he wanted to do and what he didn't want to do. Bill wasn't going to rock the boat and neither was Landini. People were calling me at home at night wanting to set up an interview. I told them, 'You can come down here, but I can't promise I'm going to have any interview for you.'"

Bird's discomfort with outside attention had been apparent from his earliest days playing for Indiana State. When a group of fans printed up T-shirts midway through his sophomore season that read, "I'm a Bird Watcher," Bird told a local writer, "They shouldn't do that. They should put the whole team on there. Might hurt somebody's feelings." He also got upset during his junior season when he emerged from the shower after a game and found a dozen or more reporters waiting by his locker while they ignored the other players. When writers posed questions that had little to do with basketball, he made his displeasure clear. "Writers keep asking me about my girlfriend or what kind of car I have," he once complained. "Everyone wants to get so personal." At first, Larry's tight-lipped nature made him something of a curiosity to out-of-town reporters. After the Sycamores lost to Houston in the first round of the NIT in his sophomore year, Ish Haley of the *Dallas Morning News* wrote that Bird "looks like Ken (Hawk) Harrelson, controls the offensive boards like Paul Silas and talks like Harpo Marx."

No doubt Bird was concerned that the more painful details of his past would come to light, but there was another reason for his resistance to doing interviews: he didn't think he was any good at them. After Bird met with a handful of reporters following a win at Tulsa his junior year, he and assistant coach Stan Evans walked alone across the darkened court on their way to the team bus. Bird turned to Evans and quietly asked, "Did I sound stupid in there?"

Evans was taken aback. "No, Larry, you didn't sound stupid," he said. "You did fine."

"Everybody used him, but nobody would ever tell him how to

handle an interview," Evans says. "Nobody coached him on how to talk, how to anticipate a question. I think he really wanted that."

Naturally, the more Bird tried to hide his personal life from reporters, the more they had to know about it. In January 1978, *Sports Illustrated* dispatched its main college basketball writer, Larry Keith, to do a feature on Bird. The previous November, Bird had appeared on the magazine's cover posing with two Indiana State cheerleaders under the headline, "College Basketball's Secret Weapon." Bird was so stilted and uncommunicative during that photo shoot that the magazine's photographer Lane Stewart (who would shoot the top-hat-and-tails cover photo of Earvin Johnson the following year) spent the rest of his career citing the "Larry Bird Rule," which states that no matter how simple an idea may sound, the photographer should never fully count on the subject's ability to pull it off. There was no accompanying story inside the issue with Bird on the cover because it was a season preview. Now the magazine wanted to give Bird the full treatment, but Larry wanted nothing to do with it.

His response was to keep putting Keith off. At one point, he simply didn't show up for a scheduled appointment in the hotel room of the team's trainer, Bob Behnke. So Keith did what any good reporter would do in that situation: he rang up Georgia Bird in French Lick. She was more than happy to talk. When Keith approached Bird after his next game, Bird told him he didn't appreciate that Keith had called his mother. "I remember saying to him, 'We want to get to know you better as a person. It's not just about your statistics,'" Keith recalls. "Well, that was exactly the wrong thing to say. He didn't want people to get to know him as a person."

"You can't tell him nothing," Bird's junior year teammate Harry Morgan warned Keith. "He's got a head like a brick wall."

Bird's reticence with the media may have been a benign distraction during his first two years in Terre Haute, but as the Sycamores mushroomed into a full-blown media phenomenon during the 1978–79 season, the big-city media folks who came to town started to resent the silent treatment. Hodges, who inherited the promise Bird had gotten from Bob King, did his best to keep the distractions out of his locker room, but in the end there was only so much he could control.

Some members of the national press found Bird's Harpo Marx act charming, even alluring. David DuPree, a writer from the *Washington Post*, came to Terre Haute in late January knowing little about the Sycamores except, as he put it when asked by a local columnist, "the fact that their schedule was suspect." In his story, he labeled Bird an "enigma": "He is uncomfortable on airplanes, dislikes big cities and is wary of people he doesn't know. When he was still talking to the press, he preferred to discuss basketball and nothing else."

Henry Hecht of the *New York Post* took the characterization a step further. In an article headlined "Larry Bird, the Baffling Superstar," Hecht wrote that "Bird's silence—not your everyday, ordinary jock muteness, but utter withdrawal—adds a mythic, almost operatic quality to what might otherwise be mere talent."

"Maybe it added a little to the mystique of Larry Bird," Hodges said late that season. "The unattainable is what people really want."

Indiana State's locker room was open to the media after games, but Bird found all sorts of ways to duck the press. "I remember Larry going out the back door, the side door, not coming out of the locker room—and he wasn't forced to," Carl Nicks says. At halftime during road games, Ed McKee would issue a statement from his sports information office that read, "POSTGAME PROCEDURES: ISU LOCKER ROOM WILL BE CLOSED, BUT ISU SID ED MCKEE WILL BRING REQUESTED (WITH ONE EXCEPTION) TO THE HALLWAY." After one Indiana State road victory, a television reporter from St. Louis pleaded with McKee to get Bird for him, even claiming he would lose his job if Bird refused. McKee took the request to Larry but didn't exactly give him the hard sell. "I'll tell them I asked you and you said no," McKee said.

Bird felt so besieged that he started to get paranoid. He spied people he assumed were writers sitting near him at some of his favorite local hangouts and taking notes in the next booth. He touched on his disdain for the press during one of the few print interviews he gave that season. "You gotta be careful what you say around sportswriters," Bird told the Indiana State cross-country coach, who interviewed him for a publication called *Amateur Sports.* "A lot of them want to find out what goes on inside you, the private you. They don't want to know how good a basketball player you are. They don't even want to talk about basketball. They're interested in knowing who your girlfriend is, or they want to know . . . 'Why did you work on a garbage truck?' . . . I'm not saying all writers are like that, but there sure are a few who fit that image."

Bird did grant the occasional television or radio interview, figuring if his comments were being recorded, he couldn't be misquoted the way he believed he had been at that Missouri Valley Conference media day in November. McKee usually dispatched Rick Shaw, the student manager and assistant trainer, who had become friendly with Bird, to help those exchanges go as smoothly as possible: "I'd get with the reporter and say, 'The first thing you should say to him is, "I appreciate you doing this. It won't take much of your time."' It just seemed to work better if he heard them say thank you at the start."

Things started to get really sticky when another *Sports Illustrated* reporter, Bruce Newman, arrived in Terre Haute in late January. Since Indiana State had not been on national television (save for little-seen HBO), Newman had the opportunity to reveal for America what this team was all about. Calling the situation "the most pronounced fortress mentality I've ever run up against," Newman said of Bird, "I kind of like someone who tells the establishment, or people of some influence, to go to hell. I think that's good up to a point, but this is just foolish." The lack of access forced reporters to hunt elsewhere for information, which gave Bird and Indiana State less control over the stories. Newman happened to have a cousin who lived in Terre Haute, and they went out to dinner with one of her friends who worked in the county clerk's office. She mentioned that Bird had been slapped with a paternity suit from his ex-wife. "What made it weird to me was it was his ex-wife who was filing for paternity," Newman says.

Bird's failed marriage was another subject that he rarely discussed, even with his closest friends. He had married his high school girlfriend, Jan Condra, in November 1975, when he was sitting out at Indiana State as a redshirt. In October 1976, Jan filed for divorce on the eve of Larry's first basketball season. "We just got married too young," Condra says. "It was my decision to get divorced. There was so much stress with him playing basketball and me feeling like I always came last. I thought if I filed for divorce it might shock him into trying to change a little bit, but it didn't work out that way."

Even after the divorce, Larry and Jan kept seeing each other. One month later, she got pregnant, and by the following spring they broke up for good. "I was six months pregnant when he told me he had a girlfriend," Condra says. Their daughter, Corrie, was born in August 1977. According to Condra, the only time Larry saw his daughter while he was at Indiana State was a month after she was born, when Larry showed up at the apartment of a mutual friend whom Jan was visiting. "He started yelling at me for being there, but he did pick up Corrie and kissed her before he left," Condra says. Larry, however, insisted the child was not his, which prompted Jan to file the paternity suit in hopes it would force Larry to pay child support. In October 1979, a court in Terre Haute established through a blood test that Larry was the father and instructed him to set up a trust fund from which Corrie could withdraw money until she was twenty-one.

It wasn't until many years after he left Indiana State that Bird felt comfortable addressing publicly what had happened. "When I was a kid, I thought people who got divorced were the devil," Larry said in 1988, a year before he married Dinah Mattingly, the girlfriend he started seeing during Condra's pregnancy. "And then I go out and do it myself right away. Getting married was the worst mistake I ever made. Everything that ever happened to me, I've learned from it, but I'm still scarred by that. That scarred me for life."

Besides uncovering that unpleasant element of Bird's life, Bruce Newman also learned that Bird's father had committed suicide. When his story, headlined "Flying to the Top," appeared in the February 5, 1979, issue of *Sports Illustrated,* it marked the first time that fact had ever appeared in print. Bird's family in French Lick was furious at the disclosure. Larry's youngest brother, Eddie, cried when he read it.

Hodges was rankled by Newman's story as well. Newman had included a quote from Carl Nicks that hinted at jealousy over the star treatment Bird had been receiving in the press. "I don't understand why they don't want to ask me about me," Nicks had supposedly said. "I can play." Newman also wrote that Hodges "and many Indiana State players seem afraid of Bird." He cited how Hodges responded to a question from another reporter by saying, "I have no comment, because Larry and I have a good relationship, and I wouldn't want anything he reads in the paper to change that."

At a press luncheon on February 5, Hodges laced into Newman's piece, calling *Sports Illustrated* "second rate" and saying that his players would never talk to the magazine again. "You all know me," Hodges said. "Do you think I'm afraid of anyone? Do you think any of our basketball players are afraid of him? I think they look for the controversy. If they can't find it, they fabricate it." Hodges also said that Nicks was devastated when he saw his comment in the magazine. "Carl Nicks is the most giving and unselfish person anywhere. I thought Carl was going to cry when he read that article." (Even so, Nicks now concedes that Newman quoted him accurately. "It wasn't that I was jealous. I was just cocky, like hey, what about mine?" he says. "When you're feeling that way, hey, it comes out.")

Newman's story, however, was a veritable puff piece compared with the treatment Bird got from David Israel, a widely read columnist from the *Chicago Tribune.* The *Tribune* had sent a reporter to

Terre Haute to do a story on Bird, and like everyone else the reporter came away empty-handed. That prompted Israel to fire off a scathing column that was published on February 23 under the headline, "Tell Us, Larry Bird, Can You Bear the Silence?" "One of the best-known facts about this college basketball season is that Larry Bird, a pretty good player from some place called Indiana State, does not speak to reporters," Israel wrote. "This is excused because Bird is just a shy, white farmboy from the small town of French Lick, Ind. You have to wonder if this same unsociable conduct would be excused if Bird were a shy, black city kid from the housing projects of, say, Chicago. But I guess Larry Bird doesn't owe anything to his race, not even if basketball is giving him a chance to escape riding on the back of a garbage truck and make a few dollars." Israel also had choice words for Bill Hodges. Continuing to address Bird, he wrote, "Don't you think it is somehow sad and inappropriate that your coach, your superior, a man who is going to be working at Indiana State presumably long after you are gone, is so intimidated by you that he is afraid to speak his mind about you?"

Over the years, Israel never wavered from his initial take on the situation. "Hodges didn't do Bird any favors," he says. "Why the hell they put him in that bubble was beyond me. I think it did him a disservice and it did the school a disservice. He was going to spend the rest of his life talking to the press."

In fairness to Hodges, he was no more prepared to deal with the onslaught than Bird was. Hodges was just thirty-five years old himself. He had no previous head coaching experience. He didn't even have his own secretary. During those occasions when he was forced to choose between his superstar or some crabby sportswriter from a big city, it's hard to blame him for picking the side he did. "I had never dealt with the press. I wasn't ready for that. I was ready for the Xs and Os," he says. "They crucified me and Larry to some degree, but it forced them to talk to the other players, and that really made our team chemistry better."

The tension took the hardest toll on Ed McKee. It was bad

enough that he was unable to do his job as sports information director properly. In the Sycamores' locker room, he also came to be viewed as an instrument of the hated media. Taking their cue directly from Bird, the players ostracized McKee, making jokes at his expense and calling him "Horseface" behind his back. It got so bad that McKee avoided riding the team bus if he could. "For Larry and the team and the coaches, it became us versus them," McKee says. "I was them."

"Ed is a beautiful guy, a great guy, but Larry was really hard on him," says Bob Behnke, the trainer. "Larry would make nasty remarks behind Ed's back, and the guys would all laugh. It was kind of like, if Larry said it was supposed to be funny, it was funny. It wasn't fair to Ed because Ed was just doing his job."

If there was one media person who attracted more enmity from the Indiana State community than David Israel, it was NBC broadcaster Billy Packer. After coming away unimpressed by Bird's play at the World Invitational Tournament in Lexington the previous summer, Packer spent much of the season casting doubt as to whether Indiana State was really as perfect as its record indicated. He first voiced his suspicions during NBC's telecast of a Duke-Marquette game in December. When NBC was on hand for top-ranked Notre Dame's loss to No. 3 UCLA on February 11, play-by-play man Jim Simpson asked his partners, Packer and Al McGuire, whether Indiana State, which was ranked No. 2, should move up to the top spot in the polls. McGuire said yes, but Packer was quick to disagree. "I knew Al didn't know a player on Indiana State except for Bird, and he had never seen them play," Packer recalls. "I said, how can you make that statement? Who have they played? How can they be number one?"

The next day, a writer from the *Terre Haute Tribune* dubbed Packer "enemy number one" in Indiana State country (though the writer mistakenly identified him as "Billy Packard"). Vendors in town printed up anti-Packer T-shirts. A record store peddled a recording of a song called "Ode to Billy Packer." According to Packer, the reaction was so vitriolic he actually received death threats. Andy Amey, who covered the Sycamores for the *Tribune*, says that Packer "to this day couldn't walk into Terre Haute without getting harassed."

Packer was only echoing what most of the basketball cognoscenti were already thinking. Bob Ryan of the *Boston Globe* wrote a column for *Basketball Weekly* stating that the Sycamores' schedule was "just taxing enough not to be laughed at, but not hard enough to create the possibility of too many losses." Ryan added, "Indiana State is a nice team, but not a number one. . . . Alone among all major contenders, they need to stay unbeaten to keep the ranking. Why, then, should they be number one, even if in your head you feel they'd finish fourth in the Big Ten?"

Meanwhile, Indiana State's foes in the Missouri Valley Conference were coming up with ever more creative ways to knock them off. On February 10, the Sycamores traveled to Peoria, Illinois, to play Bradley. The Braves were led by their flamboyant and combative first-year coach Dick Versace, who earlier in the season had charged into the crowd at Tulsa to fight some fans who had thrown objects at his players. Knowing his team would be badly outmanned, Versace came up with a defense he called the "Bird Cage." It was a triangle-and-two, with both roving players assigned to Larry. "I kept thinking about how the guy accounts for fifty points just by stepping on the floor," Versace says. "I knew the other guys were going to get shots. We just had to hope they missed 'em." With five-foot-eleven guard Carl Maniscalco standing in front of Bird and six-foot-eight forward Harold McMath pressing against his back, the Braves were able to limit his touches throughout the game. True to form, Bird did not force the action. As Bradley remained within striking distance midway through the first half, Hodges called a time-out and started to draw up some plays that would get Bird the ball. "Hell," Bird said, "if they're gonna keep two guys on me, why don't I just stand in the corner and let these guys play four on three?"

Hodges agreed it was a good idea. Bird took only two shots the entire game, making one and adding a pair of free throws for a career-low 4 points. Meanwhile, Carl Nicks had 31 points, Steve Reed had a career-high 19, and Indiana State won, 91–72. "Defenses are defenses but [Versace] carried that a little bit too far," Bird said years later. "I mean, if I had the best team in the country come into my building, I think I'd come up with something a little better than that."

After the Sycamores knocked off West Texas State on February 12 to improve to 23–0 the same weekend that top-ranked Notre Dame lost to UCLA, they were finally voted No. 1 in the AP poll, though the coaches voting in the UPI poll left them at No. 2 behind UCLA, which had been ranked behind Indiana State at No. 3 the previous week. Despite their perfect record, the Sycamores were so lightly regarded in some quarters that six coaches voted them fourth or lower in the UPI poll and one voted them eighth. A week later, the Sycamores fell back to No. 2 in the AP's rankings—even though they hadn't lost. They got more first-place votes than top-ranked UCLA, but there were just enough voters, including one who ranked the Sycamores seventh, to cost them the top spot. "There's no way a team should be number two after getting almost twice as many first-place votes," Hodges said. The Terre Haute community's outrage reached farcical proportions when Indiana State's student body president wrote a letter to U.S. senator Birch Bayh demanding a federal investigation.

The biggest hurdle Indiana State faced in altering this perception was that it had not gotten any television exposure beyond its immediate area. But with the regular season nearing its close, that was about to change. America was finally going to get its first real look at Larry Bird. He was more than ready for his close-up.

It was a pretty safe bet that Michigan State would not come out flat for its rematch against Northwestern on February 3 at Jenison Fieldhouse. Though Johnson sat out most of the game because of the sprained ankle he had suffered during the match against Ohio State, the Spartans built a 16-point lead over the Wildcats in the second half. When Northwestern cut that lead to 7 points with less than 3 minutes to play, Johnson told Heathcote he thought he should check in. He didn't have to ask twice. Johnson had 4 points and a rebound the rest of the way, and the Spartans won, 61–50.

Johnson's absence for most of the game gave Greg Kelser the stage to himself, and he took advantage by scoring 18 points and grabbing 14 rebounds, both game highs. "Coach has given me the okay to start shooting more jump shots from outside and I think my whole game has started to loosen up," Kelser said. As the Spartans rolled through the second half of their Big Ten schedule, Kelser established himself more as Johnson's costar than his sidekick. Kelser could take himself a little too seriously (he asked that he be called "Gregory" instead of "Greg" at the start of his senior year), and there were times Heathcote detected a trace of jealousy that he wasn't garnering the accolades Magic did. (For example, Kelser would end his career without having ever been named the Big Ten's player of the week.) But Kelser was an intelligent, graceful athlete who played with quiet dignity—"a gentleman's gentleman," as the team's trainer, Clint Thompson, called him—and would end the season as an academic All-American. Though he had a narrow frame and a slight build, Kelser's incredible leaping ability and exquisite timing enabled him to become the best rebounder in school history. He also finished his career as the school's all-time leading scorer. Most of all, he was a great finisher on the fast break. The Magic-to-Kelser alley-oop became the Spartans' signature play during their stretch run.

Johnson's ankle must have healed in a hurry, because the day after the Northwestern win he was back in the starting lineup for a nonconference game against the University of Kansas. Normally, Heathcote would never schedule games two days in a row, but he agreed to play this one because it was going to be nationally televised by NBC, which sent its marquee trio of Dick Enberg, Al McGuire, and Billy Packer to East Lansing for the occasion. The Spartans should have been dog tired playing their third game in four days, but they were so fired up they played their best game of the season, crushing the Jayhawks, 85–61.

The lopsidedness of the game was a telling indication to Heathcote of just how potent his team could be if it reached the NCAA tournament. "We could play anybody outside of the league and destroy them," he says. "We played a different style than teams were used to. If they had time to scout us, that might have been different." The game also showed just how lethal the team's transition game was once Heathcote turned his guys loose. Even Mike Brkovich, who was developing into quite the dunker himself, threw down two thunderous slams, including one when he soared over Kansas's leading scorer, six-foot-two guard Darnell Valentine.

The two-three matchup zone was a big part of Michigan State's uniqueness, but mostly it lay in their six-foot-eight virtuoso point guard. As Johnson turned trick after trick, the NBC broadcasting team ran out of superlatives. "Here comes the Michigan State prestidigitator!" Enberg exclaimed early on. Johnson was unstoppable throughout the game despite some very real physical limitations. He made just three field goals and scored 12 points, but he added 11 assists and 10 rebounds. When he was on the move, he tended to look more ungainly than agile. "He ran like a hundred-year-old man, like he had bunions on his feet," says Edgar Wilson, who was a graduate assistant coach that season. "He couldn't jump, either. You might be able to beat him in a hundred-yard race, but if you raced to get to a ball ten feet away, he would beat you every time." Moreover, what Johnson lacked in speed, he made up for in efficiency. He committed his share of turnovers, but they usually stemmed from bad decision making, not because he was out of control. "Magic had limited speed, but in half a step, he was at full speed," Heathcote says. "And he could control himself at full speed. Most guys are out of control unless they're at three-quarters speed."

Once he got to where he wanted to go—and because of his size and ballhandling ability, he always got to where he wanted to go—he could unleash his greatest gift. Like all great passers, Johnson had the uncanny ability to find a teammate who didn't even realize he was open, then deliver the ball when it seemed impossible. If he could earn a few style points along the way, all the better. "Some players can get the ball to an open man for a shot, but Earvin can get the ball to the man for a basket. There's a difference," Heathcote said. For example, midway through the first half against Kansas, Johnson was dribbling above the foul line in the Spartans' half-court offense when he spotted Kelser cutting along the baseline. In a flash, he whipped the ball underhanded straight through the Jayhawks' half-court defense. It hit Kelser in the hands and he converted the easy layup.

At that point, McGuire spoke almost in a hushed tone. "I want to say something," he said. "I like to hold judgment a lot of times on players, but I gotta say, from what I've seen today and yesterday when I scouted him, Magic Johnson is probably the best passer I've ever seen in the history of college basketball."

"Ooh, the best you've ever seen?" Enberg said, sounding surprised.

"In my opinion, yes," McGuire replied. "Sometimes I thought [he played with] a little too much French pastry, but watching the first twelve minutes here, or first fifteen minutes, he's just unbelievable."

Johnson was a cult hero in East Lansing, but if anything the locals may have underestimated his appeal to a national audience. When Heathcote showed a Betamax videotape of the NBC broadcast to some local writers two weeks later, they were struck at how the broadcasters always called him "Magic Johnson." By one person's count, the trio used those words twenty-seven times in the first half alone. To his friends, family, teammates, and coaches, Johnson was always called Earvin. On the local telecasts, Tim Staudt called him Earvin, too, with a few references to the "Magic Man" thrown in.

As taken as NBC's team was with Johnson's abilities, they were even more in thrall to his personality. He played the game with rare, unbridled enthusiasm, beaming a luminescent smile any time he pulled off a great play. When Heathcote cleared his bench in the game's final minutes, NBC showed Johnson in the upper-right corner of the screen on the Michigan State bench, where he helped coach the reserves and yukked it up with Greg Kelser and Jay Vincent. "The love affair that Johnson has going with his teammates and everyone here in this area is really special," Enberg said.

It was indeed a joyful time for the entire program. As is often the case in sports, the Spartans' success on the court was a direct result of their closeness off of it. "We had a pretty close-knit team," Terry Donnelly says. "A lot of teams I know, they practice together, they eat together and then they all go their separate ways. With us, we went to restaurants together, we hung out together, we did a lot of things together. We were a neat team in that respect." Nobody on the team joined a campus fraternity, because they figured they were already a part of one. They also tried to draw the line against dating during the season, which fell under what they called the "Spartan rules." And when it came to breaking those rules, there was no question who the All-American was. "Earvin loved parties because parties draw women," says Darwin Payton, the student manager. "Earvin loves women. That's his only vice. He doesn't smoke. He doesn't drink. He doesn't gamble. I've never seen him drink a beer, but he was dating Michigan State girls when he was in high school."

After the rout over Kansas, Heathcote tweaked the lineup again, this time making it even smaller and swifter by reinserting Terry Donnelly as a starter and demoting Ron Charles to the bench. Meanwhile, the two-three matchup zone was becoming virtually insoluble. Other teams had used a matchup zone for years, but the genius in Heathcote's version lay in his ability to tweak the formation to neutralize an opponent's leading scorer. As the Spartans piled up win after win in February, some of the Big Ten's best players lay strewn behind them like roadkill. On February 8, Iowa's Ronnie Lester failed to reach double-figure scoring for the first time all year. On February 10, Ohio State's Herb Williams managed just 10 points. When the Spartans won at Indiana on February 15, the Hoosiers scored just 17 points in the second half. In the next game, they limited Michigan to merely 16 in the first half. On February 22, Purdue center Joe Barry Carroll, who came in as the league's leading scorer at 23.9 points per game, made only four field goals and finished with 10 points. Overall, the Spartans were holding their opponents to just 60.7 points per game, making theirs the sixth-stingiest defense in the nation. "Our zone is the best it's been all season, and it's getting better and better each time out," Heathcote said after the Michigan win.

"In our zone defense, [Heathcote] asks some guys to do the impossible," Kelser said. "Like the two guards have to cover three people. And if they flood one side, one guy has to cover two. Coach realizes that it's impossible, but we still have to try and do it, which makes our zone so effective." Another reason the zone was so effective was because Johnson played on the baseline, where he was able to grab defensive rebounds and initiate the fast break without needing an outlet pass. That meant the wings could leak out as soon as a shot went up. Oftentimes, Johnson would need only one or two dribbles—and sometimes none—before firing a pass downcourt like a quarterback operating in the pocket.

Michigan State's 73–67 win over Purdue on February 22 improved their record to 19–5, and, more important, to 11–4 in the Big Ten. Their chances of qualifying for the NCAA tournament had seemed remote just three weeks before, but after winning eight consecutive games (including the nonconference drubbing of Kansas), they were tied with Iowa for second place in the conference. The Spartans eagerly awaited Illinois for their final home game on February 24. Not only would it give them a chance to exact revenge for their heartbreaking defeat at the buzzer in Champaign in January, but the game also marked Kelser's final game in Jenison.

The game began with a sequence that typified the class that Kelser had shown throughout his career. As usual, he took the opening tip, and as usual he gave the Spartans the first possession. As

Kelser turned to run downcourt, he noticed that referee Charles Fouty had dropped his glasses. The gentleman's gentleman stopped running, picked up the glasses, and handed them to the official. During the game Kelser scored 24 points, including three dunks, to lead the Spartans to a 76–62 win that put them in a three-way tie for first place in the Big Ten with Ohio State and Iowa. After the game, Heathcote addressed the crowd and called Kelser "one of the greatest basketball players and individuals you'll ever know."

By the time the Spartans reached their regular season finale at Wisconsin on March 3, they had won nine straight to improve their conference record to 13–4 and clinch at least a tie for first place in the Big Ten. They were also ranked No. 4 in the AP poll. More important, because they swept Ohio State and Iowa, they owned the tiebreak advantage and were thus assured of getting the Big Ten's automatic bid to the NCAA tournament. A win over the Badgers would give them the league title outright for the second straight year, but they did not come out sharp. The Spartans trailed by 1 point at halftime, and Heathcote was not pleased. He railed in the locker room at their poor rebounding and asked someone to hand him a stat sheet to prove his point. Problem was, the box score indicated the two teams were even on the boards in the first half. "This can't be right," Heathcote said, momentarily flustered.

At that moment, Greg Lloyd, a little-used reserve guard who had butted heads with Heathcote all season, blurted out, "Stats don't lie." That was one of Heathcote's favorite expressions, but he was not in the mood to hear it tossed back at him right then. Heathcote turned to assistant coach Bill Berry and said, "You better get him out of here."

The Spartans hung tough in the second half, and when Johnson hit two free throws with 3 seconds left to make it 81–81, the game appeared to be headed to overtime. On the ensuing inbounds pass, however, Wisconsin guard Wes Matthews heaved a fifty-five-foot shot as the buzzer went off. Incredibly, it banked in, giving the Badgers an 83–81 win. "I didn't figure we had to check anybody from fifty-five feet away, but maybe this year we do," Heathcote said.

It wasn't the best way to end the regular season, but given all that had transpired the previous two months, perhaps it was fitting. "If I never see another long shot at the buzzer, it will be too soon," Kelser said. "I've seen enough for a lifetime this season."

8

On the fifteenth floor of the NBC headquarters at 30 Rockefeller Plaza in New York City, Rex Lardner, NBC Sports' programming chief, walked down the hallway to the corner office that belonged to the division's president, Chet Simmons. For weeks, Lardner had been reading about the under-the-radar team with its mysterious farm boy superstar who was winning every game and rising in the rankings. Al McGuire, the former Marquette coach who had become the network's primary college basketball analyst, was passing along raves from his peers in the coaching profession. Yet Lardner, like just about everyone outside of the state of Indiana, had never seen Larry Bird play. So he asked Simmons if he could add an Indiana State game to NBC's regular-season schedule. Simmons gave Lardner the go-ahead. Lardner called Ray Meyer, the coach at DePaul University, and asked for his blessing to let NBC drop a DePaul game so it could broadcast the Sycamores' regular season finale against Wichita State on February 25. Ever the gentleman, Meyer agreed.

For years NBC had been making a steadily increasing investment in college basketball, and by 1979 it was paying huge dividends. The network had built its reputation on the back of John Wooden's UCLA dynasty, which ended with Wooden's retirement in 1975. In 1969,

NBC first televised the NCAA championship game—which featured UCLA's star center, Lew Alcindor, who would later be known in his professional career as Kareem Abdul-Jabbar—and in 1975 it began televising regular season college basketball games as well. The network's programming staple was its Saturday doubleheader. The first game, usually involving UCLA or Notre Dame, was broadcast nationally, while the second window was devoted to two games that were aired regionally. The strategy reflected the prevailing sentiment that, for the most part, college basketball's appeal was more local than national, but the sport was clearly on the rise.

That ascent coincided with, and probably benefited from, a steep decline in the popularity of the National Basketball Association. In 1977, NBC added college games to its Sunday afternoon lineup so it could directly compete with NBA games that were airing on CBS. Twice that first season, the collegians beat the pros in the ratings, and by 1979 the overall Nielsen ratings for the college games were higher than those for the pros. The NBA's television appeal was so weak that CBS's affiliate in Atlanta didn't bother to show the games, even though Atlanta had an NBA franchise. "It would benefit us to run them if anybody watched, but our research showed that no one was watching," said the station's general manager. Even the NBA Finals weren't compelling enough to be aired live. They were shown, instead, via tape delay. Many theories were floated for the declining popularity of the pro game—the dearth of quality teams in major markets, the lack of a dynasty—but a common explanation was the one cited by (among others) TV writer William Leggett in the October 16, 1978, issue of *Sports Illustrated*: "Still others feel the growing preponderance of blacks on the court is a factor."

Fair or not, that perception damaged the league, which was already facing financial hardships despite having just absorbed four teams from the American Basketball Association, each of which paid $3.2 million to join the NBA. In 1969, the NBA had been 60 percent black, and seven of its top twenty scorers were white. Ten years later, it was 75 percent black and only two of the top twenty scorers were white. Seattle SuperSonics forward Paul Silas, who was president of the NBA Players Association, said in February 1979 that "it is a fact that white people in general look disfavorably upon blacks who are making astronomical amounts of money if it appears they are not working hard for that money." Another league executive was more blunt: "How can you sell a black sport to a white public?" In truth, that concern was probably overstated; after all, college basketball was also dominated by black players. But against this backdrop, Bird's race was one more reason behind NBC's decision to broadcast an Indiana State game.

The announcement of the Sycamores' forthcoming national television debut was met with great delight by the people of Terre Haute. The players, for their part, played up their roles as small-town cult heroes. A local car dealership filmed a promotional commercial for the team using the theme song from the movie *The Magnificent Seven*. The concept was a tribute to Indiana State's seven-man rotation, and the players wore blue ten-gallon cowboy hats for the spot. They kept the hats and wore them everywhere they went. Even the two black starters, Carl Nicks and Alex Gilbert, who presumably didn't see many horses while growing up in Chicago and East St. Louis, respectively, got into the act. "We all just kind of copied each other, wearing cowboy hats and boots and tight jeans," Nicks says. "We really liked to play up to that tough guy image."

The games at Hulman Center had become a real happening. Students were allowed to get in free, but since seating was on a first-come, first-served basis, they pitched tents and slept outside the arena several days in advance to get the best spots. The crowd also adopted the curious ritual of tossing sheets of toilet paper into the air throughout the games. It was not uncommon for play to be delayed so the maintenance crew could sweep away the debris. (The rolls in the public restrooms were pilfered long before tip-off.) When the games were over, the fans marked the inevitable win with a robust "Amen" chorus. Just three years before, the team had been fortunate to draw five thousand fans to home games. Now, Hulman Center had become the place to be in all of college basketball. "It was a nice feeling," Steve Reed says. "Whether you were in the McDonald's or a little restaurant, you're signing autographs all the time. I'm thinking, what did they want my autograph for? I'm just a country boy from Warsaw, Indiana."

The players had become such celebrities that one day several members of the St. Louis Cardinals baseball team visited Hulman as part of an off-season promotional tour called the "Cardinals Caravan." The group of big leaguers, which included the All-Star catcher Ted Simmons, visited Indiana State's locker room after the game and fawned over the players, especially Bird.

The little school that once had to ask newspapers to publish its scores was turning away credential requests due to a lack of space in the press box. The many NBA scouts who came into town had to be shoehorned into an overflow row of seats located on an upper concourse. One day, Ed McKee's student assistant, Craig McKee (no relation to Ed), got a call from a ticket manager saying that someone from the NBA had shown up for the game, but she was going to turn him away because there were no tickets left. "What's his name?" Craig asked.

After a pause, she replied, "He says his name is Jerry West."

Craig McKee was mortified that the legendary former NBA All-Star and current head coach of the Los Angeles Lakers was having trouble gaining admission. "Uh, please bring Mr. West in from out of the cold," he said, "and tell him I will find a seat for him."

If the players felt any pressure to live up to the hype, they sure didn't show it, partly because the team included a range of colorful characters who kept everyone from taking themselves too seriously. Just as Michigan State had Darwin Payton to make an invaluable contribution to team chemistry, the Sycamores had Rick Shaw, also a student manager who doubled as assistant trainer. Shaw was the guy the players went to if they needed an extra ticket for a game or a place at the training table for a high school buddy. He regaled them with his spot-on Richard Pryor imitations, he dressed up as Santa

Claus on Christmas, and he cracked them up by wearing a Steak 'n Shake hat on the team bus. Shaw was the one responsible for shepherding Larry Bird through the gauntlet of autograph seekers who swarmed him as he walked out of an arena. His greatest contribution, however, was his ability to perfectly duplicate Bird's signature. Bird would often walk into the locker room and dump into Shaw's lap a pile of stuff he had been asked to sign. In fact, Shaw was so good he learned to copy the signatures of every player on the team. One day many years later, Shaw was visiting an emergency room in a hospital in Terre Haute and he spotted an "autographed" photo of the 1978–79 Indiana State team on the wall. "I thought, Oh man, that's one I did," he says. "I had a knack for it."

When it came to colorful characters, nobody was more brightly hued than Tom Crowder, a six-foot-five senior forward from Cayuga, Indiana. Crowder had limited basketball skills, but he was an amazing leaper who once high-jumped six feet, eleven inches in a high school track meet. Three years before, he made the team as a walk-on by demonstrating he could kick the rim. Crowder rarely played, but he often revved up the crowd by performing his kick-the-rim trick as the team was leaving its pregame warm-ups for the locker room. Off the court, Crowder was an avid gun collector who invited teammates back to his dorm room so they could watch him feed a mouse to his pet boa constrictor. "Tom was so country, he made Larry look sophisticated," says Andy Amey, who covered the team for the *Terre Haute Tribune*. One day during a practice, Crowder dunked over a teammate and taunted him with a muscle pose, à la the Incredible Hulk. His buddies thought it was hilarious, so he repeated the pose during pregame meals. The players had also been making semiregular appearances on a local TV show for kids called *Captain Jack*, and Crowder's "Hulk" became a regular character. He would throw off his shirt and hop into his flex while the television screen turned green. As "The Hulk" craze metastasized, a group of Indiana State students organized a write-in campaign to vote Crowder into the Pizza Hut Basketball Classic, a prestigious postseason all-star game for seniors played in Las Vegas. By the time balloting was done, Crowder had received 143,918 votes, ranking him sixtieth nationally.

The team—its success and its personality—was a source of immense pride for a community that had spent too many decades playing in the shadow of Indiana, Purdue, and Illinois. "It brought the whole area together, not just Terre Haute," says Tom Reck, the former sports editor of the *Tribune*. "It became a Wabash Valley thing. We were *the* team. It was Indiana State over everyone else."

Bird appeared on *Captain Jack* along with the other players. During one segment, he wore a newspaper folded into a sailor's cap on his head while being interviewed by the Captain. (Asked to give his name, Larry cracked, "Brad Miley.") On another show, Captain Jack had asked each player to make him a drawing, and as the Captain leafed through the papers (which the viewers couldn't see), he was surprised to come upon one from Larry that wasn't exactly fit for young viewers. ("Let's just say the anatomy looked a little exaggerated," Miley says.) As befit someone who was pursuing his education degree, Larry had a particular fondness for kids. At the end of a home game late in the year, he was running toward the locker room and accidentally knocked over a nine-year-old boy who had come onto the court. Bird swooped up the youngster, brought him into the locker room, got him a program, and had the entire team sign it.

After another road game late in the year, Rick Shaw went to Bird and asked if he was ready to leave. Larry surprised the student manager by saying, "Yeah, but I'm gonna stop and sign some autographs on the way out." Shaw was pleasantly surprised. "We went over there and he signed for a while and talked to folks," he recalls. "He changed a little bit."

Even though Bird was the biggest celebrity Terre Haute had ever had, he still felt comfortable spending time at his favorite local haunts, Rafters and the Ballyhoo. (If there was one thing Larry enjoyed almost as much as playing basketball, it was drinking beer.) As opposed to the out-of-towners who constantly wanted to prod him, the locals surrounded him and protected him—and then left him alone. "I think Terre Haute became very similar to French Lick in that people respected his space," says Tony Clark, Larry's childhood buddy and fellow Indiana State student. "He was raised in French Lick, but this is where he grew up. This is where he really matured."

By the time NBC came to town for the final home game against Wichita State, the town of Terre Haute was in full rapture. The locals itched for a chance to come face-to-face with their nemesis Billy Packer but NBC, sensing the situation would be too contentious, decided not to send him. Instead, the game would be called by Al McGuire and Jim Simpson, the network's elegant play-by-play man. "I remember Jim Simpson was drinking white wine during the production meeting," Craig McKee says. "I thought that was *sooo* sophisticated. Drinking white wine in the middle of the afternoon." Simpson also surprised McKee by revealing that he was thinking about leaving NBC to join a new all-sports national cable network called ESPN, which was launching in the fall. McKee had never heard of it and thought Simpson was crazy to contemplate it.

The night before the game, a huge blizzard blew through the region, shutting down local traffic as well as the Indianapolis airport. When the Sycamores arrived at Hulman Center for their morning shootaround, they saw that several huge leaks had sprung through the roof. It looked as if the game might have to be canceled. The arena's maintenance crew enlisted the help of student volunteers, sending them back to the dorms to get mattresses that they could shove into the air vents to stanch the flow of water. Hours later, the workers were still mopping the floor as the players went through their pregame warm-ups. The blizzard made life miserable for the hundreds of students who had to camp out through the night, but they stayed out there nonetheless and got their prime seats.

When Simpson and McGuire arrived a couple hours before tip-off, they went through their usual pregame preparations. Normally, that would include speaking with all the players, but they were told in no uncertain terms that Bird did not want to speak with them because he didn't want too much attention to be focused on him at the expense of his teammates. But as the players were shooting around, Simpson looked up and saw McGuire talking to Bird at length. When Simpson asked McGuire how he got Bird to talk to him, McGuire replied, "I went to all the other guys and talked to them first. That way Larry knew I wasn't just singling him out."

When NBC finally hit the airwaves on Saturday afternoon, all the tension and excitement leading up to the game was released—largely in the form of thousands of sheets of toilet paper, which floated onto the court like so many snowflakes. "You're looking in on a very frantic Wabash Valley area," Simpson told viewers by way of introduction. "This is the first time the Indiana State Sycamores have been on national television, and are they ready. They think they're number one and they hope to prove it today."

In introducing McGuire, Simpson noted how much more popular McGuire, who had been saying all along that Indiana State deserved the No. 1 ranking, was in Terre Haute than Billy Packer. To underscore the point, NBC showed a picture of the T-shirt many people in the crowd were wearing, with the words to "Ode to Billy Packer" printed on the front. The lyrics read in part: "Don't come to our state / We'll haunt you / We'll taunt you / We'll make you a fool / Here's to Billy Packer / Don't come to our school!"

The game against Wichita State was not technically on national television—the southeast portion of the country was watching Kentucky play the University of South Carolina—but most of America finally got the chance to see what all the fuss was about. The game was more than seven minutes old before Bird attempted his first field goal, but once he did score (prompting another blizzard of toilet paper that delayed the action), he and his mates were off and running. Over the next two hours, Bird demonstrated the full range of his astounding versatility. He hit tough layups inside while fighting between defenders. He tossed in hook shots in the lane. He made turnaround bank shots from the wing and a handful of midrange pull-up jumpers. Most amazingly for a six-foot-nine center, he sank deep, high-arcing, feathery shots with defenders hanging all over him. He was also devastatingly effective from the foul line, where he made 83 percent of his attempts during the season.

Bird also revealed the diabolical competitive streak his teammates had come to know well. Midway through the first half, he had the ball deep in the left corner and faced his defender, Eric Kuhn, a six-foot-six freshman forward. Bird lifted the ball with two hands and placed it behind Kuhn's head. When Kuhn turned around to see where the ball went, Bird pulled it back and calmly nailed a twenty-three-footer. He was so pinned into the corner that the ball had to travel over the corner of the backboard before going in.

"Do you know how far away that is? That's in left field," McGuire marveled while watching the replay. "It seems the further out he is, the higher percentage there is that he puts the ball in."

Perhaps the most arresting aspect of Bird's performance that day, however, lay in what he didn't do. He didn't hog the ball. He didn't chuck up a ton of shots. He didn't dribble all over the court while his teammates stood and watched. When Wichita State double-covered him, which was often, he didn't force a bad shot. He simply passed. And he didn't do anything to disrupt the flow of the offense. Bird attempted thirty shots (including the ones where he was fouled) during the course of the game. On twenty of those attempts, he caught the ball and shot it without dribbling. Six times, he dribbled once before he shot. Three times, he dribbled twice. Only once, when he stole the ball on defense and dribbled the length of the court—left-handed, amazingly enough—did he take more than two dribbles before shooting.

Bird also showed the same innate gifts that Magic Johnson had when it came to passing, but since he was a center he operated from a different vantage point. Rather than fire no-look passes in transition,

Bird did most of his damage while crouched in the post, where he could thread pinpoint darts to his cutting teammates. Once he got into the lane, he was masterful at deft shovel passes through interior traffic. Bird was especially effective on the move because he could see openings emerging among all the shifting parts around him. For example, on one possession in the first half, Bird raced into the lane to chase down a long offensive rebound. He leaped to grab the ball and, before his feet hit the ground, he zipped a no-look pass to forward Brad Miley on the baseline.

Because Bird was white, played in the frontcourt, and was a gifted passer, many basketball observers compared him to the New York Knicks' star forward Bill Bradley. His future employer, Red Auerbach, saw a more apt analogy. "He's a big Cousy," Auerbach said, referring to Bob Cousy, the famed Celtics guard from the 1950s. "I never thought I'd compare anyone with Cousy, but Larry Bird has those great hands and great vision. He has a great concept of the game."

Indiana State led Wichita State 48–42 at halftime, and the Shockers managed to stay close for the first five minutes of the second half. From there, Bird and the Sycamores poured it on, breaking open the game with a 15–2 run and building a 20-point lead. As Simpson repeatedly talked up the story line of whether Indiana State was worthy of being ranked No. 1 in the nation, McGuire sounded convinced by what he was witnessing. "They're tough," he said. "You go on the road, win at New Mexico [State], win at Bradley, beat the Salukis down in Carbondale, Illinois. They beat Purdue by ten points. They beat Russia when Russia beat Purdue, Notre Dame, and Indiana in November. This is not a fluke. This is a ball club."

With about two and a half minutes left and the Sycamores holding a commanding lead, Hodges decided to remove Bird, who had scored 45 points. During the time-out, however, Mel Daniels, the former ABA all-star who had joined the staff as a full-time assistant, pointed out to Hodges that Bird was only 4 points shy of breaking the Indiana

State single-game scoring record that Bird himself had set. Hodges put him back in. A field goal and two free throws later, Bird had his record-setting 49 points (to go along with 19 rebounds), and Hodges took him out for good. After the game, Wichita State coach Gene Smithson told Hodges that he did not appreciate that move. "He was pissed, and you know he probably had a right to be," Hodges says.

As the closing seconds ticked away, NBC showed a picture of Bird sitting on the Sycamores' bench. The difference between that image and the one of Magic Johnson on the Michigan State bench three weeks before in the Spartans' rout of Kansas could not have been more stark. Bird wasn't smiling. He wasn't laughing with his teammates. He wasn't saying anything. He simply watched the game while gently thumbing his thin blond mustache. "Look at Larry," McGuire said. "Larry doesn't have any facial expression. He does all his talking between the lines."

And he had spoken loud and clear. The final score was Indiana State 109, Wichita State 84. The Sycamores were now 26–0. Two days later, they were voted No. 1 in both the AP and UPI polls for the first time all season. America had finally gotten a glimpse of Larry Bird, and he had made an impression in more ways than one. "All the next week I got lots of calls from my friends back in Denver who saw the game," Bob Heaton says. "They couldn't believe Larry Bird was a white guy."

Despite the tough loss at Wisconsin, the Michigan State Spartans were greeted by several hundred fans upon their return to Lansing's Capital City airport. Jud Heathcote wasn't a glass-is-half-full kind of guy, but even he was relatively sanguine about the setback in Madison. "I think if we had to win the game at Wisconsin, we would have," Heathcote said. "It was a tremendous comeback this season on the part of our players and few people realize all the emotions involved in our getting back to the top."

The Spartans had finished the season in a three-way tie for first place in the Big Ten with Iowa and Purdue, but they were awarded the league's automatic bid to the NCAA tournament because they held the advantage in the head-to-head tiebreaker. Since the Big Ten was not one of the thirteen conferences that conducted a postseason tournament to decide who went to the NCAAs, the Spartans could take the next week off to relax and regroup before setting off for their final push.

Heathcote didn't like the rule limiting conferences to sending two teams to the tournament, and if ever there was a case for eliminating that maximum, it was the Big Ten in 1978–79. Still, even having more than one team per conference was a relatively new concept. The NCAA had opened the bracket to teams other than conference champions just four years before, when the field grew to thirty-two teams—the first such expansion in twenty-two years. The NCAA's basketball committee expanded the tournament again before the 1979 tournament to include forty teams. Also for the first time, the committee was going to seed every team in the tournament, as opposed to just the top four in each region. The structural changes were a response to the way interest in this event was mushrooming. The committee wanted to make it feel like a true national championship.

With its undefeated regular season and No. 1 ranking, Indiana State knew it was guaranteed to be in the forty-team field via an at-large bid, but unlike Michigan State the Sycamores first had to grind their way through a conference tournament. As the regular season champs in the Missouri Valley Conference, Indiana State got to host the three-day tournament at Hulman Center, and they relished the chance to win the title in only their second full season as a member of the league.

In the first two rounds, the Sycamores beat West Texas State and Southern Illinois by 10 and 7 points, respectively, to earn a date with New Mexico State in the championship game. (After his team fell in the semifinals, Southern Illinois coach Joe Gottfried griped, "The of-

Earvin Johnson, the pride of Everett High School in Lansing, Michigan, with his coach, George Fox. (*George Fox photo*)

Larry Bird averaged 31 points and 21 rebounds as a senior at Springs Valley High School in French Lick, Indiana. (*Photograph courtesy of Jim Jones*)

Bird signed to play for Indiana University coach Bob Knight to please his community, but he dropped out of school and returned to French Lick before practice even began. (*Photograph courtesy of Jim Jones*)

Michigan State coach Jud Heathcote was never at a loss for words on the bench. (*Associated Press/MCP*)

Michigan State's student manager, Darwin Payton (*center, with boutonniere*), was an important source of insight and information for Coach Heathcote. (*Michigan State Athletic Communications*)

Indiana State head coach Bob King (*above, left*) was a father figure to Bird, but when he developed an aneurysm in his brain before the start of the 1978–79 season, he turned the reins over to his untested assistant, Bill Hodges (*above, right, next to Bird*). (*ISU Athletics Archives; Associated Press/Keating*)

Larry Bird on the cover of *Sports Illustrated*'s 1977 college basketball preview issue. He wouldn't stay a secret for long. (*Lane H. Stewart*/ Sports Illustrated)

A dapper Earvin Johnson soars on the cover of *Sports Illustrated*'s 1978 college basketball preview issue. (*Lane H. Stewart*/ Sports Illustrated)

Heathcote meets the press alongside Greg Kelser, Johnson, and Terry Donnelly. (*Michigan State Athletic Communications*)

Michigan State center Jay Vincent played in Magic's shadow in high school and college but still went on to play in the NBA. (*Michigan State Athletic Communications*)

Indiana State fans celebrate with their curious ritual of tossing sheets of toilet paper in the air. (*ISU Athletics Archives*)

During the Sycamores' magical run, Chicago native Carl Nicks was the team's second-best player. (*ISU Athletics Archives*)

Indiana State guard Steve Reed being guarded by his Michigan State counterpart, Mike Brkovich, in the championship game. (*ISU Athletics Archives*)

Brad Miley couldn't shoot a lick, but he was Indiana State's designated defensive stopper.
(*ISU Athletics Archives*)

Heathcote once said of Magic, "If I were an opposing coach and saw that big turkey bringing the ball down court, I think I'd vomit." (*Michigan State Athletic Communications*)

Bird was such a good passer that Celtics general manager Red Auerbach paid him the ultimate compliment by calling him "another [Bob] Cousy." (*Associated Press*)

Magic Johnson and Greg Kelser get interviewed by NBC's Billy Packer and Bryant Gumbel. *(Michigan State Athletic Communications)*

A star is born! Jamie "Shoes" Huffman gets some airtime from NBC's Dick Enberg and Al McGuire. *(Michigan State Athletic Communications)*

Magic and Bird were photographed together for the first time on Sunday, March 25, the day before the championship game. *(Associated Press/ Jerome McLendon)*

Kelser took advantage of Bird's inability to guard him on the perimeter. (*Michigan State Athletic Communications*)

Bird has what Magic wants . . . but not for long. (*James Drake/ Sports Illustrated/Getty Images*)

The Magic Man pulls off his final trick. (*Associated Press*)

Magic's dunk over Bob Heaton led to a critical four-point play late in the second half. (*Michigan State Athletic Communications*)

ficiating was not equal in the second half. Larry Bird is a great player, but I think he gets protection.") In the final against New Mexico State, Indiana State cruised to a 14-point halftime lead, but on its first defensive possession of the second half, Bird stuck out his left hand to deflect a New Mexico State pass and immediately seized his thumb in obvious pain. He winced again a minute later when he grabbed a defensive rebound, forcing Hodges to call a time-out and take Larry out of the game. Bird sat for six minutes on the bench while Behnke examined and wrapped his thumb, but New Mexico State shaved only 2 points off the Sycamores' lead while Bird was out. When Bird returned, he immediately sank two baskets, and Indiana State coasted to a 69–59 victory that ensured it would be just the sixteenth team in college basketball history to enter the NCAA tournament undefeated. When the team was presented with the championship trophy, Leroy Staley and Brad Miley held it aloft, walked across the court, which was strewn with sheets of toilet paper, and handed it to Bob King, who pumped his right fist as he received the trophy with his left hand. When it came time to cut down the nets, King, clad in a light-blue V-neck sweater and black tie, climbed the ladder and snipped the first strand.

The win also meant that Bill Hodges was the first rookie coach to go undefeated in the regular season since Lou Rossini went 23–0 at Columbia University in 1950–51. "I tell you, I'm a little bit numb right now," Hodges said during his postgame interview as his players continued cutting the net. "It's something I can't believe. I pinched myself a little while ago, but our guys really deserve it. They've worked hard. They do exactly as we ask them. I've got a great coaching staff. They wanted to do this for Coach King and they've done it." Hodges answered a few more questions until his players interrupted the interview by hoisting him onto their shoulders. "I'll see ya," Hodges said with a smile as they whisked him away.

When the players got back to their locker room after the game, they continued their celebration, tossing each other into the shower as well as anyone else who wandered by. Hodges got doused immediately. (He was so confident they would win he brought a sweatsuit to the arena so he could change into dry clothes.) The radio broadcaster, the equipment manager, and the trainer all got wet, too. A couple of the players ran into the hallway, grabbed a cheerleader, and threw her in for good measure. Even Richard Landini, the university president, and Senator Birch Bayh were victims. As the players were carrying Bayh to the showers, Brad Miley shouted, "Who is that fucker?"

But the elation would soon give way to grave concern. X-rays taken later that night revealed that Bird had fractured the tip of his left thumb on that deflection early in the second half. The injury would not keep him from playing in the NCAA tournament, but he would have to wear a thick wrap on the thumb, compromising his ability to grab the ball.

Hodges did not know the extent of Bird's injury until after the game was over, but he had another worry as he contemplated the specter of the NCAA tournament—namely, the requirement that every team open its locker room to reporters. The policy had recently been put into place largely because UCLA's John Wooden had never let the press into his locker rooms. "I don't like that policy," Hodges lamented. "It's kind of like letting someone into your bedroom."

No doubt Hodges was concerned about Bird, but Larry was becoming more media friendly than Hodges had realized. The day after the Sycamores won the Missouri Valley Conference tournament, Hodges and Bird flew to Atlanta so Bird could accept the Naismith Award as the national college player of the year. (Hodges was also the runaway choice for national coach of the year, though a few of the ballots had identified him as "Bill King," "Bob Hodges," and even "Bird's coach.") Hodges had warned Bird that if he was going to accept a trophy in a room full of reporters, he was going to have to answer questions.

Bird proved surprisingly relaxed. Accepting the award at the Atlanta Tipoff Club while wearing a white T-shirt and blue jeans, he began by saying, "You couldn't have picked a finer guy for this award." Asked about his injury, Bird confirmed that he fractured the tip of his left thumb. "That won't keep me from playing in the NCAA tournament. I know I can shoot," he said. "I realize I may not be as effective with this thumb as I might be otherwise, but anyone who thinks Indiana State is a one-man team is going to be in for a surprise."

The Naismith Award was just the first piece of hardware Bird was about to collect as the season was winding down. The affirmations that he was the best player in America had Red Auerbach concerned that other NBA teams were trying to convince Bird not to sign a contract with the Celtics and go back into the draft in June. Auerbach instructed his lawyer to send a telegram to NBA commissioner Larry O'Brien, asking him to make sure other teams "cease and desist from communicating with Larry Bird." "We are hearing rumors that some of the other teams in the league are tampering with Larry Bird," Auerbach said, "and we're not going to let them do that. No way. He's our exclusive property in the NBA at this moment, and we are the only team in the league that can deal with him."

Bird and Hodges were still in Atlanta on Sunday afternoon, March 4, when the NCAA's basketball committee was finalizing the bracket for the tournament. Once the selections were made, the committee members typically divided up the field and called all the schools to let them know where they were headed for the first round. There was no televised "Selection Show" to dramatize the announcement. For the most part, the committee did not even contact schools that were not invited. If nighttime came and a school had not gotten a call, it knew it hadn't made the cut.

In Terre Haute, President Landini and assistant athletic director Jerry Huntsman invited a small group of reporters into Huntsman's office to await the big call. It was supposed to come by 3:30, but they waited for two interminable hours and still hadn't heard anything.

When the phone did ring, it was Hodges calling from Atlanta or some other person wanting to know if they had heard yet. "It would seem everybody in the country but us has been called," Huntsman told one caller.

After a while, one of the reporters said to Landini, "We'll want a comment from you if Indiana State is not included in the forty-team field."

"I would have plenty to say but I'm not sure you could print it," Landini replied.

Finally, when Huntsman learned that the Associated Press had reported that the Sycamores had been tapped as the number one seed in the Midwest region, he called the NCAA headquarters in Shawnee Mission, Kansas, and got confirmation. The whole exercise was supposed to be a formality, but for a school playing in its first-ever NCAA tournament, it was a thrilling moment all the same.

Michigan State, meanwhile, garnered the number-two seed in the Mideast region. This was a tough draw. Not only did the committee put the Spartans on track to meet a glamorous Notre Dame team in the regional final, but it potentially matched them against the University of Detroit in their first game, assuming the Titans, who were ranked No. 17 in the Associated Press poll, could get by unranked Lamar University in the opening round. (The top six seeds in each region got a first-round bye.) Heathcote did not like the idea of having to face his in-state rival. "I can think of a number of opponents I'd rather play in the first round than Detroit," he said. "It could create a psychological situation that could work in their favor."

Michigan State was ranked three spots behind Indiana State in the AP poll, but there was no question who was entering the tournament with higher expectations. Larry Donald, for one, projected the Sycamores as the eighth-best team in the field in *Basketball Times*. "I keep trying to imagine what ISU would do against, say, a big, physical team like Notre Dame. And the answer is always the same," Donald wrote. His assessment of the Sycamores: "Nice team. Great story. Super player. But not NCAA champions." The conventional wisdom was neatly summed up by Bruce Newman in *Sports Illustrated*: "Indiana State may be the first team ever to come into the tournament top-ranked in both polls, undefeated in 29 games and still sneaking up on people."

9

As Indiana State set off for the school's first NCAA tournament, the condition of Larry Bird's left thumb was the primary topic of conversation. The team's doctor determined that he had suffered a triple hairline fracture, not enough to sideline him but still a painful injury. Bird had been practicing throughout the week with a splint on his hand, but NCAA rules prevented him from wearing the splint during a game. Instead, he would have to make do with a thick piece of rubber and heavy tape. "All he has to do is touch it and he's going to be in great pain," Brad Miley said. "I just hope someone doesn't go pounding on his hand just to get him out of the game."

Larry's thumb may have been causing him pain, but he wasn't hurting for suggestions on how to fix it. The most unusual idea was dialed in to the Indiana State athletic department by Dick Gregory, the well-known comedian and political activist. Gregory, who had been on the track team at Southern Illinois with Indiana State's gymnastics coach, offered Bird a special herbal recipe that Gregory said had once numbed the pain of a broken toe. He also said he had given the recipe to Muhammad Ali after he had his jaw broken in a fight against Ken Norton. Bird declined to try the herbal elixir, and Hodges also ruled out the quick-fix idea of injecting his thumb with novocaine. "We aren't going to take a chance with Larry's future to win a basketball game," Hodges said.

In advance of the team's first NCAA tournament game on Sunday, March 11, in Lawrence, Kansas, President Landini agreed to close down the university on Friday, the last day of classes before spring break, so students would have a chance to get to the game. The school also arranged for ten buses to transport fans for the nine-hour trip. (Some waited in line for tickets for over twelve hours.) When the contingent of school employees arrived at the team's hotel, they gathered in the lobby and had themselves a party. "We had a lot of [hard liquor] there, but almost nobody drank it. Everybody drank beer," recalls John Newton, who worked directly under Landini. "Larry drank beer, so everybody drank beer. Everybody wanted to be the good ol' boys." The players, meanwhile, traveled in their usual good ol' boy attire: cowboy hats, blue jeans, and T-shirts. "They dressed very casually, and Larry set the tone," Ed McKee says. "They even let their hair grow. I was embarrassed that our university was made to look that way."

The beginning of the NCAA tournament would finally give the Sycamores and their fans their face-to-face meeting with Billy Packer, who was calling the game for NBC alongside Jim Simpson. Hodges had taken a liking to Packer, who wrote him a letter several weeks earlier congratulating him on the season, though Packer did not endear himself to the Sycamore faithful by spelling Larry's last name "Byrd." Packer had also been openly critical of the decision by the U.S. Basketball Writers Association to name North Carolina coach Dean Smith its national coach of the year. "[Hodges] should be the unanimous college coach of the year," Packer told reporters in Kansas. "I don't see how anyone else should be considered."

Hodges enjoyed meeting Packer for the first time, but the Indiana State players didn't exactly make him feel welcome. As they began practice the day before the game, Bird spotted Packer standing under a basket and suggested to his teammates that they all throw basketballs at him. He counted to three, and they fired. It was supposedly all in good fun but, says Packer, "They were really pissed."

Packer was also a good sport when faced with the inevitable razzing from Indiana State's fans. When one man brought him a sign calling Packer a turkey, Packer signed it for him and good-naturedly posed for a picture. Still, he remained skeptical about the team's chances to make a run deep into the tournament. When a reporter from Terre Haute asked him about Indiana State's chances of winning it all, Packer countered by asking the writer who among the Sycamores besides Bird had been recruited by a Big Ten school? (The answer, of course, was nobody.) Packer predicted that the University of Texas, not Indiana State, would come out of the Midwest region and that North Carolina would win the national championship.

For their inaugural NCAA tournament game following their first-round bye, the Sycamores faced the Virginia Tech Gobblers, who had blitzed Jacksonville University by 17 points in the opening round. (Virginia Tech changed its nickname to the Hokies in 1982.) During a team meeting on the morning of the game, Hodges started to diagram some adjustments in their half-court offense that would keep Bird on one side of the floor, which would allow him to catch the ball with his right, uninjured hand. Bird, however, assured Hodges that he shouldn't change anything. Bird repeated the same instruction to the point guard, Steve Reed, who had made a concerted effort to pass to Larry's right hand during practices.

Once the game began, the Sycamores were uncharacteristically sloppy and unpoised. For the first time all season, they were letting the external pressures affect them on the court. "I was more nervous before that game than I was about any game all year," Hodges says. "I felt like if we could get by that first game, we'd be okay, but boy, we came out tight." Bird, clearly bothered by the wrap on his left hand, did not grab his first rebound until seven minutes had gone. He also committed three unforced turnovers early on. Carl Nicks, whose full-throttle approach led him to play out of control under normal circumstances, was also heedlessly forcing the action. Since the Gobblers were a small, quick team that preferred to play in transition, the miscues played right into their hands. Midway through the first half, Virginia Tech led, 18–14.

Hodges called time-out and decided to switch to a two-three zone defense. This was an unusual break from their normal man-to-man, but Hodges felt it would slow down the tempo of the game and allow his players to get into an offensive rhythm. "Bill was really, really good at making game-time adjustments," says assistant coach Terry Thimlar. "He understood our guys and handled them well."

The move paid off. After the Sycamores scored 4 quick points, Leroy Staley, the reserve guard, missed a long jumper from the left wing during a half-court possession. Since Virginia Tech was double-teaming Bird in the post, that left Alex Gilbert, Indiana State's best leaper, alone under the basket. When Staley's miss caromed off the back rim, Gilbert jumped high into the air, grabbed the ball with his left hand, and flushed it emphatically, giving Indiana State a 20–18 lead. "That was a clinic in leaping right there!" Packer exclaimed.

The dunk lit a fire under the players as well as their fans, who had been nervously muted in the early going. "They have a great group of followers here from Indiana State," Packer said as the throng rose to its feet. "They're all over town and have really made their presence felt. I'm sure that's one of the reasons this team has done so well. They've really got people behind them."

"And they all know Billy Packer is in town, believe me," Simpson said.

"We've had fun," Packer replied.

Gilbert's dunk jolted the Sycamores back into a relaxed mind-set. Hodges switched back to man-to-man, and Indiana State methodically scored 14 more unanswered points to complete a 20–0 run. Virginia Tech was never in the game after that. The most remarkable aspect about the spurt was that Bird did not contribute a single field goal. Though Bird would finish with 22 points, 13 rebounds, and 7 assists, the game, which Indiana State won 86–69, showcased the value of role players like Gilbert (12 points) and Miley, the defensive specialist who blanketed Dale Solomon, Virginia Tech's talented six-foot-eight freshman center. Solomon had scored 24 points in the Gobblers' win over Jacksonville, but managed just 12 against Miley.

"I just want everybody to understand we don't have no one-man team," said Nicks, who also had 22 points. "We proved that today."

In the closing minutes of the game, NBC showed a picture of Bird sitting on the Indiana State bench as the trainer Bob Behnke cut into the bandage around his left thumb. Bird winced badly as Behnke pulled off the wrap. "He has a kind of toughness in him that no other athlete has had in my eighteen years of work," Behnke said after the game. "He plays with problems that would cause the average player to just sit and watch the game." Virginia Tech coach Charlie Moir was duly impressed. "They are for real," he said. "I thought we contained [Bird], but he is an unselfish player. He passed up shots he could have taken."

After the game, as per NCAA policy, the Sycamores opened their locker room to the press. Bird, however, was nowhere to be found, and Hodges had no reason to believe he would have anything to say during the following week's Midwest regional games in Cincinnati. "Unless Larry decides to," Hodges said, "he won't be talking to the press."

Earvin Johnson was talking to the press.

"The thing that has surprised me most during my career here, other than our winning the Big Ten title by three games last year, was all the publicity and notoriety Michigan State has gotten throughout the country," he told a gathering of reporters two days before the Spartans' first NCAA tournament game. "We get letters every day from places like New York City, Los Angeles and Dallas. They know about us everywhere." Johnson also continued to field queries about whether he was going to turn pro at the end of the season. "I've had a lot of free advice the past couple of years," he said. "I'm still wide open and I won't be making any decision until after Michigan State's season is completed."

The Spartans were scheduled to begin the tournament in Murfreesboro, Tennessee, on the home court of Middle Tennessee State University. Jud Heathcote got there a day ahead of his players so he could watch the first-round game between Lamar and Detroit. The Spartans were going to play the winner, and after fretting about the psychological advantage Detroit might have against his team, Heathcote watched Detroit get upset by the Cardinals 95–87, which, naturally, made him fret even more. "We spent all week preparing for Detroit and getting our players ready for the game because I was convinced Detroit would win," he lamented. "So Lamar goes out and wins, and we have to prepare to play them." In truth, Heathcote came away believing Michigan State was much, much better than Lamar. He confided this to his assistants but instructed them not to pass it along to the players.

At least Heathcote would be going up against a team he had seen. Billy Tubbs, Lamar's colorful, wise-cracking coach, said he had never watched the Spartans play aside from a few glimpses on television. "I'd like to tell you a little about Michigan State, but I don't know very much at all," Tubbs said the day before the game in his thick, southern drawl. "I don't even know what the hell a matchup zone is, and I know my players don't, either." Tubbs didn't appear to have on much of a game face. He was still hungover from his long night spent celebrating his team's upset of Detroit. "Don't let anybody ever tell you that Murfreesboro is dry," Tubbs said while holding his throbbing head. "Man, I'm still looking for that dump truck that hit me."

If Michigan State was in danger of being too complacent, Tubbs took care of that when he declared, in a half-joking reference to his team's win over Detroit, "We're aiming to take care of the whole state of Michigan." And if *that* didn't fire up the Spartans, the Cardinals did it for them during pregame warm-ups. The Lamar players talked trash directly to Heathcote, reminding him that he said he didn't think they would beat Detroit and making fun of his funky comb-over hairdo. Most of the Michigan State players were still in the locker room, but Darwin Payton was sitting next to Heathcote and reported what he heard back to the troops. "We may have had issues with Jud, but nobody was going to talk that way to our coach," Payton says.

Adding insult to insult, when Lamar came out for its final warm-up before the opening tip, the players circled the Spartans while holding their fingers in the air before returning to their side of the floor. During NBC's pregame segment, Al McGuire stood beside Dick Enberg and recounted for viewers what the Lamar players had done. "We're in for a lot of fun," McGuire predicted.

Well, one team was in for some fun. Lamar had averaged more than 88 points per game, and as Tubbs cranked up his full-court pressure in hopes of creating an up-and-down contest, the Spartans were happy to play along. Johnson was as usual a whirling dervish in the open floor, beating defenders with behind-the-back dribbles and setting up his teammates with one pretty no-look feed after another. Greg Kelser was the main beneficiary, scoring 14 points in the first half as Michigan State took a commanding 46–27 lead at the break. "The same thing holds true with Johnson as it does with Larry Bird," McGuire said on the telecast. "You'd prefer to have 'em take a shot than pass. If they pass, it's ninety percent they're going to get a basket. If they shoot, it's only fifty."

The performance was further vindication of Heathcote's decision to go to a smaller lineup following the Northwestern debacle and deploy a less structured offense in an effort to kick the running game into high gear. "We used to have these big cards with the offensive plays on them, and the assistant coach would hold them up over his head," Terry Donnelly says. "We didn't see the cards as much once we got on a roll. We were able to freelance more. I think that was another way for Jud to release us a little bit more and let Earvin run the team."

Lynn Henning, the former *State Journal* columnist, says, "Jud never wanted it to be known that he had to back off, but he backed off and let those guys have their freedom. The freedom translated into victories."

The only low point for Michigan State came during halftime, when Jay Vincent developed a pain in his foot that was so sharp he couldn't walk. Vincent had injured the fat pad under his big toe in the loss at Wisconsin, and in his attempt to play through the pain he compensated by running on the outside of his foot, which only made matters worse. He spent the entire second half on the bench with ice packs taped to his foot, and after the game he left the arena on crutches.

Once Michigan State's lead reached 28 points late in the second half, Heathcote cleared his bench. That's when the game turned from a laugher into a farce. With a little over two minutes left, Jamie Huffman, a sophomore guard who had seen action in just five games all season, went up for an offensive rebound and lost his left shoe. While Lamar dribbled toward its basket and the Spartans ran back on defense, Huffman was stranded in the opposite corner trying to get his shoe back on. This was a problem because (a) Huffman tied his shoelaces extra tight; (b) he cut his fingernails extra short; and (c) his coach was screaming at him to get his ass down the floor. After about thirty seconds, Al McGuire noticed that Lamar was playing four on five. "We got a guy down here with his shoe off, Dick," he said. "He's been down for about thirty seconds waiting for the team to come back down."

Lamar scored, Michigan State went into its offense, and poor Huffman still couldn't get his shoe on. "They've been playing four on five!" Enberg said cheerfully. "No one even notices it. The poor guy's in a slump. His teammates don't even notice it." Mike Longaker, the brainiac walk-on, missed a shot, Lamar got the rebound, and Huffman was still shoeless. Now McGuire was in hysterics. "He's still there! He can't get it on! He's nervous. He hasn't tied his shoe yet." Finally, Huffman got the laces undone, put on his shoe, and rejoined the game. "Here he comes!" McGuire rejoiced. "The game is saved!"

Enberg checked the Michigan State roster and reported that the player's name was Jamie Huffman. "For the rest of your life," McGuire said, "you're going to be known as 'Shoes.'"

Said Enberg, "Attaboy. Shoes Huffman. Coined by the coach himself."

Grateful for a piece of entertainment to liven up a game turned dull, Enberg and McGuire exulted when Huffman scored on a driving layup for his first basket of the season. Mercifully, the game soon ended with Michigan State winning, 95–64. Kelser finished with a season-high 31 points to go along with 14 rebounds, while Magic, who broke his own school single-season assist record in the first half, contributed 13 points, 17 rebounds, and 10 assists. As Tubbs passed Heathcote on his way to the postgame press conference, Heathcote heard him complaining to his assistants about the report he had received from an outside scouting service describing the Spartans as a "walk-it-up team." "The guy who wrote that report scouted us against Indiana," Heathcote says. "Well, Bob Knight would rather not have one offensive rebound than let you get a fast break, so against them we had to walk the ball up. That's why the Big Ten coaches were always much better prepared to play us than the teams we played in the NCAA. No one else quite understood what Magic did."

"That's what you call a good ole country butt-whipping," Tubbs said after the game. "I told our guys to watch Johnson and they did. They said in the dressing room at halftime he's playing a hell of a game."

As Johnson waited next to Enberg and McGuire to begin a postgame interview, NBC unfortunately cut away from its coverage in Murfreesboro to show the final minutes of the University of Toledo's 74–72 upset of Iowa in Bloomington, Indiana. Enberg stood next to the sweaty Johnson for ten minutes, then fifteen, waiting for the cue from New York to begin. Finally, word came through Enberg's earpiece that they had run out of time and there would be no interview at all. When Enberg apologized profusely, Johnson slapped him on the back. "That's okay, Mr. Enberg," he said. "We'll be seeing a lot of you guys the next couple of weeks." Johnson turned and jogged toward the locker room. Enberg could only shake his head. "He was only nineteen, but he had such presence," Enberg says. "He really was the Pied Piper of college basketball."

Before heading to Cincinnati for the Midwest regional, Larry Bird and Bill Hodges took a quick detour to Chicago, where they again accepted awards for national player of the year and coach of the year, this time from the Associated Press. Once again, Bird was surprisingly comfortable among the reporters—perhaps too comfortable. With his broken left thumb wrapped in a thick bandage, Bird accepted the Adolph Rupp Trophy, looked up at the gathering, and asked, "Is David Israel here?" Told that the columnist who had excoriated him in the *Chicago Tribune* wasn't present, Bird said, "That's too bad. I always wanted to see what a real live prick looked like."

Finally given the chance to ask Bird a few questions, the writers spent much of the session asking why he hadn't been answering them all season. "Playing college basketball is supposed to be fun, but if I had to spend an hour or so every day talking to reporters, I wouldn't have had time for much else," Bird said. "If I let Carl Nicks and others talk to the press, it helps them. Now they get the publicity they deserve. I can handle the press. I can talk. But when they say something bad and put me down, it hurts my family." Bird was also asked about the widely held belief that he was going to be a "great white hope" for an NBA that seemed to be starving for one. "I'm not a racist, but there aren't many whites left because there are so many good, great black players," he said. "I hope I can hold myself up with them. I know they're waiting for me."

Indiana State's opponent in the Midwest semifinal on Thursday, March 15, was the University of Oklahoma. The game gave Bird the chance to reunite with Sooners coach Dave Bliss, who had recruited Bird to Indiana in 1974 as an assistant for Bob Knight. It wasn't much of a reunion: the two didn't speak to each other before, during, or after the game. "I remember seeing him and kind of wondering if he even remembered me," Bliss says. "Larry is such a competitor that even if he saw you he might look right through you. If he wasn't going to remember me, then I wasn't going to remember him."

Bird opened the game by draining a pretty rainbow jumper and then buried a variety of shots throughout the first half. The Sooners stayed close for a while, but Indiana State got a spark late in the first half from Leroy Staley. The six-foot-five guard came off the bench at the 4:56 mark with the team trailing by 3 points and immediately sank a basket off an offensive rebound and a pair of free throws to give the Sycamores a 34–33 lead. They never trailed again.

Staley's contribution came as part of the substitution pattern Hodges had deployed so successfully from the first game of the season. Brad Miley, the six-foot-eight forward whose quick feet made him a stellar defender, and Alex Gilbert, the six-foot-eight jumping jack from East St. Louis, would start the game. When Hodges needed more offense, he would bring in Staley and Bob Heaton. He would shuttle his players throughout the game (leaving Bird and Carl Nicks in as much as possible), but during the final few minutes Hodges usually had Heaton and Staley in the game because they were also better free throw shooters than the two starters. (Gilbert shot an unsightly 27 percent from the line that season.)

Staley's tip-in of a Bird miss gave Indiana State a 45–37 lead at halftime. For much of the second half, the Sycamores demonstrated that they were more than just a single superstar. When Nicks found Miley for a layup with a terrific no-look pass to put the Sycamores up by 8, NBC announcer Gary Thompson said, "Boy, this is a splendid passing club." When Oklahoma's leading scorer and rebounder Al Beal scored to cut Indiana State's lead to 47–41, Gilbert answered with a layup off a pretty feed from Bird, after which Nicks buried a seventeen-foot jumper to push the lead to 10 points. After an Oklahoma basket, Gilbert scored again and was fouled by Beal while going for an offensive rebound. Though Gilbert's free throw barely scratched the rim, the foul was Beal's fourth. When Beal was whistled for his fifth and final foul with 10:44 still remaining, the Sooners' best hope for a comeback slipped away. "We are not a catch-up team," Bliss said later. "We are a stay-ahead team. We got behind, hurried our shots and played right into their hands."

Indiana State sailed to a convincing 93–72 victory, thanks to the well-balanced attack that included 20 points from Nicks, 12 from Gilbert, and 9 each from Heaton and Staley. Bird, meanwhile, was his ordinary, spectacular self: 29 points, 15 rebounds, 5 assists. The game had drawn a record crowd of 17,252 to Cincinnati's Riverfront

Coliseum, the largest crowd ever to watch a college basketball game in the state of Ohio. Two of the most interested observers were Red Auerbach, the Boston Celtics' general manager, and Dave Cowens, the team's head coach. After the game, the two of them visited briefly with Bird and suggested he join the Celtics immediately after Indiana State's season ended. Bird, however, told them he wanted to finish out the year and get his degree.

The Sycamores' record now stood at 31–0, and they were one game away from an improbable trip to the national semifinals in Salt Lake City. "Let me tell you, Larry Bird is a hell of a basketball player," Bliss said. "Until you've played against him you can't judge him. His shooting, as good as it is, isn't going to win as many games for Indiana State as his passing will. They are a very good team. With Larry Bird, they are a great team."

In the Midwest Regional final on Saturday, March 17, Indiana State would face another great team with a hell of a player: the University of Arkansas, which was ranked No. 5 in the AP poll, and Sidney Moncrief, a six-foot-four senior guard who had finished second to Bird in the AP's player of the year balloting. (Earvin Johnson was third.) Coached by Eddie Sutton, a forty-three-year-old disciple of the legendary coach Henry Iba, the Razorbacks had been to the Final Four the year before and would be by far the best team the Sycamores had played all year.

Which is not to say the Sycamores were excessively uptight. At their morning shootaround, Hodges told Bryant Gumbel, the up-and-coming broadcaster who would be hosting NBC's coverage, that he had a player who could kick the rim. When Gumbel said he didn't believe him, Hodges summoned Tom Crowder to perform his trick. "I had never seen anything like that in my life," Gumbel says.

Unlike the previous round, which was shown only to parts of the country, all four regional finals were going to be televised nationally.

Indiana State and the University of Arkansas played in the early game on Saturday afternoon, and Riverfront Coliseum was filled with the kind of pitched electricity that a big game like this warranted. The Sycamores brought along their frenzied, toilet-paper-tossing throng of fans, but Arkansas had a massive following of its own, most of whom were wearing red Hogs hats. More than a few of the Arkansas fans were wearing T-shirts that read, "Where the hell is Terre Haute?"

They would find out soon enough. In a contest that was taut and competitive from the start, Bird produced one of his finest showings of the year. He had 17 points in the first half alone, and the Razorbacks led by just 2 points at the break, 39–37. During halftime, Hodges told his players he was going to put on the full-court press in the second half. Waiting until the second half to make that kind of move was a clever tactic that Hodges learned from Bob King. It was effective because it diminished the other coach's ability to adjust to the switch.

Hodges's strategy worked perfectly. A few minutes into the second half, the Sycamores went into their press, immediately forced multiple turnovers, and took their first lead of the game at 55–53. Arkansas still had no answer for Bird. At one point, Bird spun away from two straight double teams and hit near-impossible fallaway jumpers from deep in the right corner. "Alan Zahn just looked over this way and shrugged his shoulders," Packer said of the Arkansas player defending Bird. "He's doing a good job defensively. Bird just is taking it to him." Bird also made sure to let the Razorbacks know how helpless they were against him. "He was really giving it to their center, [Steve] Schall," Brad Miley says. "He was talking to him while he was making spinning twenty-footers. They always said he was one of the legendary trash talkers in the NBA, but I don't remember him ever doing that until that game."

Early in the second half, Bird made as pretty a pass as he had made all season. Driving into the lane from the right wing, he jumped into the air and, with his back completely turned toward the basket, flipped the ball with his left hand over his left shoulder straight into the hands of Miley, who converted the easy layup. Bird then stripped the ball from Arkansas forward Scott Hastings on the next possession, leading to an Alex Gilbert basket in transition. The Indiana State fans leapt to their feet. "He's bringing down the house now," Packer said.

Finally, Sutton had to make his own adjustment. He decided to assign Sidney Moncrief to guard Bird, All-American on All-American. "Moncrief on Bird now!" Packer exclaimed. "This is gonna really be something. They're taking the ultimate gamble here." Though he was giving up a good five inches, Moncrief did a fair job keeping Bird under control the rest of the way. Problem was, when Bird was under the basket, Moncrief had to play in front of him, which meant he needed help from one or two other Razorbacks to guard Bird's back. That left Bird's teammates available for open jumpers and uncontested rebounds. Just as they had done all season, the other Sycamores took full advantage. Carl Nicks scored 12 points in the second half, Bob Heaton came off the bench to nail an outside jumper, and Miley scored twice on tip-ins with nobody blocking him out. Meanwhile, at the other end of the floor, Moncrief answered with an array of slashing drives and nifty pull-up jumpers, some of which came after two or three shot fakes. The action was exhilarating and fast-paced, prompting Packer to say to Simpson, "Jim, you really don't want this game to end, do you?"

With 1:08 to play and the game tied 71–71, Arkansas had the ball, and Sutton called time-out. He told his players to work the ball around for a while and call another time out with about 15 seconds remaining. Shortly after they began their possession, however, Nicks hopped forward to defend Razorbacks point guard U. S. Reed and accidentally tripped Reed with his left foot. It was clearly a foul, but the official made no call. When Reed stood up with the ball, he was whistled for traveling, giving Indiana State the ball with 1:02 to play.

Now it was Bill Hodges's turn to manage the final possession. He too instructed his players to work down the clock, then called time-out with 18 seconds remaining. Hodges drew up a play to get Bird the ball, but he told Bird that if he was double- or triple-teamed he should try to find an open man. Before they broke the huddle, Bird told his teammates to be ready to catch the ball. He sensed that Arkansas was going to do whatever was necessary to make sure somebody else took the final shot.

Sure enough, on Indiana State's final possession, Bird touched the ball only once. He took a pass from Steve Reed on the right wing and immediately threw it to Heaton at the top of the key. Heaton passed to Nicks on the right wing. Nicks looked for Bird in the post, but Larry was double-covered, so Nicks swung it across the court to Reed. As the clock ticked down to 7 seconds, Reed pulled up for what looked to be an open shot, but instead dumped the ball to Heaton in the lane. Heaton gathered the ball, took one dribble, and lofted the ball, oddly enough, with his left hand. The ball hit the front of the rim, the left side, the right side, the front again . . . and dropped through. The final 2 seconds expired before Arkansas could throw the ball inbounds. The game was over. Indiana State had won, 73–71. Incredibly, they were still undefeated. And they were going to Salt Lake City.

Hundreds of blue-clad fans rushed the floor. Bird raced the length of the court, and the players piled onto one another. Amid the bedlam, Hodges forgot to shake Sutton's hand. Simpson shouted into his microphone, "He made it! Heaton's second time! He did it! Game is over! Game is over! Bob Heaton keeps Indiana State undefeated and on to the Final Four!" Recalling Heaton's miracle bomb over New Mexico State earlier in the season, Packer told Simpson, "It's destiny for these guys, Jim! He made a fifty-footer to win another ball game for 'em!"

Craig McKee, the student who was working in the sports information office, somehow fought his way through the crowd to bring Bird over to Bryant Gumbel for the postgame interview. At first, Bird head-faked McKee and disappeared into the masses. Eventually, he made his way back to where Gumbel and Packer were standing with Hodges. "All right, Jim," Gumbel said, "I'm in the middle of this with Larry Bird. Another outstanding game. Larry, how good does it feel? You're going to the Final Four."

"It's great," Bird said breathlessly above the din. "I don't know what to say. We're here and we finally made it."

That the final basket had once again been converted by Heaton made the whole sequence of events all the more unbelievable. "I sort of lost the ball in the shuffle," Heaton said after the game. "I was going to take it up with my right hand, but I was afraid of getting blocked. So I just sort of threw it up with my left. I was hoping somebody would tip it in." Ironically, when Heaton was eleven years old, he got his left arm caught in a tractor at his family's small farm and cut it badly. His grandfather stopped the engine just in time. "If he wasn't there, I would probably not have a left arm," Heaton says. "As it turned out, I used the left arm to hit that shot."

"This was the greatest basketball game I have ever been associated with, at least at this level," Sutton said. "It's too bad it wasn't a football game so that it could have ended in a tie." Sutton added that he thought Nicks had fouled U. S. Reed on Arkansas's final possession and said that "at times I do think the officials protect Bird." But more than anything else, he chastised himself for waiting so long to switch Moncrief onto Bird. "Hey, they're a heck of a team," he said. "I've been voting them number one for several weeks now. Until somebody beats them, I'd say they deserve that rating."

By this time Packer, who had just seen Bird play live twice in two weeks, was understanding just how special a player he was. "Bird grew on me," Packer says. "He was slow and couldn't jump, but I saw the son of a gun can really pass, and he's tough and nasty. Then I started to appreciate that he really understood how to play, because his supporting cast really had no business at this level."

The Sycamores, however, were long since through worrying about outside opinions. "I've never talked with this team about how others feel or where we were rated because I felt that might take away from our focus," Hodges said. He also expressed some anger at a column in the local paper that had compared him to Al McGuire in an unflattering way. "Accept us as we are," Hodges said. "Let us be the way we are. Don't expect us to be something we are not. We're going to do our thing our way. I'm here to get a job done. I'm not Al McGuire. I don't drink black Russians. I drink Tab. And if anyone doesn't like it, then tough bippy."

Tough bippy? It was not an ordinary battle cry, but then again, this was no ordinary team.

When the Spartans returned to East Lansing following their pummeling of Lamar University, they discovered their campus had been swept by a wave of "Shoes" mania. Huffman hadn't realized the extent to which Enberg and McGuire had fixated on his unfortunate incident, but when he walked into his dormitory he was greeted by a big banner that read, "Welcome home, Shoes." Everywhere he went, people called out his new nickname, which was apparently second only in popularity to Earvin Johnson's. "All the guys on my floor were like, Man, you're a celebrity," Huffman says. "When I'd go places, everybody would want my autograph. It was crazy. My social life definitely picked up, too. I was pretty shy and quiet, but all of a sudden I was going out with some pretty good-looking girls."

On the flip side, as the week wore on, it became apparent that the injury to Jay Vincent's foot was more serious than Jud Heathcote had initially realized. A second X-ray revealed that Vincent had suffered a stress fracture. He tried to practice on Thursday in Indianapolis, the site of the Mideast Regional semifinals and final, but he had to stop immediately and left the court limping badly. Heathcote said there was a slim hope Vincent could play over the weekend, but most likely he was done for the remainder of the tournament.

Heathcote was also unhappy at an article that Mick McCabe had written in the *Detroit Free Press* following the win over Lamar. The article marked the first time that someone had reported the details of the team meeting that had taken place after the loss at Northwestern. McCabe's story included a quote from Johnson saying, "We told the coaches to stay off our backs and we would play harder." When McCabe approached Heathcote at the team's hotel in Indianapolis, Heathcote let him have it. "He wasn't screaming, but he was really pissed. He said the whole thing was bullshit," McCabe says. "Lynn [Henning] was happy because it meant he wasn't the only one Jud was pissed at."

Michigan State's opponent in the Mideast Regional semifinal, Louisiana State University, was also a man short. Its leading scorer, sophomore forward DeWayne Scales, had been suspended by coach Dale Brown for having improper contact with an agent. But Vincent's injury was still a huge problem for the Spartans because it struck at their primary vulnerability: lack of depth. Without Vincent, Heathcote had to move Ron Charles, who normally played forward, into the starting center spot, leaving six-foot-seven freshman forward Rob Gonzalez, whose playing time had increased the previous few weeks, as the only serviceable reserve. Charles admitted that he had been "down in the dumps" since his demotion from the starting lineup in early February, but on the bus ride to Market Square Arena for the regional semifinal game against LSU on Friday, March 16, he got an unexpected boost. The Michigan State players were listening to a Lakeside song called "It's All the Way Live." They changed it to "It's All the Way Bobo" and serenaded Charles throughout the ride. "They were getting me fired up," Charles said.

In the early going, Kelser was the one on fire. He had consecutive steals for breakaway dunks in the first few minutes to help stake Michigan State to a 13–5 lead. With LSU obviously rattled, the Spartans pushed out to a 36–19 halftime advantage, thanks partly to Charles, who turned in the best performance of his career, finishing with 18 points and 14 rebounds. Kelser was later plagued by foul trouble (he picked up his fifth foul with 3:38 to play), and Magic had a bad shooting night (5 for 16 from the floor, though he did go 14 for 15 from the foul line to finish with 24 points), but though the Tigers got to within 12 points with 13 minutes to play, the outcome of the game was never in doubt. Michigan State came away with an easy 87–71 win to reach the Mideast Regional final. "It was probably my best all-around game," Charles said. "A game like this makes me feel awfully good, because I showed I can play in the middle."

With each successive step, Michigan State was introducing another television audience to its wildly entertaining style of basketball. It was also introducing its charismatic point guard to another gaggle of enthralled national writers. It was hard to tell who enjoyed the exchanges more. After the LSU game, Johnson remained in his uniform and chatted endlessly in the Spartans' locker room with a group of writers that included Mike Lupica, a columnist for the *New York Daily News*. Johnson laughed and told stories as he punctuated his points with a tape cutter. The conversation went on so long that the rest of the players had boarded the bus and Johnson was still yapping. Finally, Heathcote came over and asked him to wrap it up. "Just a couple of more questions, okay?" Johnson asked. When the writers made their way to the door in deference to Heathcote's request, Magic shrugged and said, "Well, I guess that's it then."

The win over LSU set up the biggest game of the tournament to that point: Michigan State against Notre Dame for the Mideast Regional championship and a trip to Salt Lake City. The Fighting Irish were a high-powered team with six future NBA players, including forwards Kelly Tripucka and Bill Laimbeer. They were also the nation's most well-known team thanks to the six games they had played on NBC that season. Notre Dame coach Digger Phelps had a long history with Eddie Einhorn, the visionary television executive whose groundbreaking TVS network had sold its syndicated college basketball package to NBC in 1975. Notre Dame was on NBC so often that many people suggested the network's initials really stood for Notre Dame Broadcasting Company. "We all got sick of watching Notre Dame," Terry Donnelly says. "Their games were always on TV. We figured, here's our chance to put Michigan State on the map."

One of the reasons Notre Dame was a formidable opponent was that the Fighting Irish had a player in Bill Hanzlik who seemed to have the necessary attributes to contain Johnson. At six-foot-seven, Hanzlik was one of the few guards in the country who could match up with Magic in terms of size. What's more, he was mobile and had deep shooting range, which could give Johnson problems on defense.

"Earvin has got to show me that he can shoot and will shoot from the outside, or else I'll try to prevent him from penetrating and play the passing lanes," Hanzlik said. Greg Kelser offered a better method for taking out Magic: "If I had to guard Earvin, I'd say something about his mother at the start of the game and hope he'd take a swing at me."

From Notre Dame's perspective, there was a downside to all that television exposure: it gave Heathcote the chance to watch them play multiple times. This was no small advantage considering that scouting and preparation were Heathcote's forte. One thing he noticed was that Phelps never put a man back on defense for the opening tap. This was partly because the Irish had a big, athletic forward in Orlando Woolridge, who rarely lost the tap. Kelser, however, also rarely lost the tap. Not only was Kelser a great jumper, but he knew how to turn his body and jump into his opponent to gain an edge without committing a foul.

Because Heathcote was by nature a conservative coach, he usually had Kelser tip the ball behind him so the team could set up its half-court offense. The day before the Notre Dame game, however, he told his guys he had another idea. "Can you win the tip?" he asked Kelser at practice. Kelser assured him he could. So Heathcote designed a play for Kelser to tip the ball ahead to Johnson, who would immediately throw a bounce pass to a streaking Mike Brkovich for a layup. It was the same play that had given the Spartans a quick 2–0 lead over Kentucky in the Mideast Regional final the year before. They rehearsed the play several times during practice before the Notre Dame game.

That night, the team went out for dinner. During the regular season, Heathcote strictly controlled what the players could order, but once the postseason came he told them they could get whatever they wanted, regardless of price. "The guys lost their minds," Darwin Payton says. "They were ordering desserts they never heard of. During that whole tournament, Jud flipped the script and became more relaxed. We were all like, He's got a heart! Did he go see the Wizard?"

"I sensed we had to have a relaxed atmosphere," Heathcote says.

"The buildup for that game could have made us tight as a drum." When Heathcote walked into the locker room before the game on Sunday, March 18, Magic, who as usual was in charge of the music, flipped off the stereo. "What are you doing?" Heathcote asked. Magic replied that he was turning off the music so they could hear the coach speak. "You don't need to hear anything from me," Heathcote said. "You all know what to do. Just go out there and kick their ass." A few minutes later, the players huddled around Heathcote to get ready to take the floor. As he gave them his final thoughts, they heard his voice catch. "You could tell he was emotional," Brkovich says. "It was an important game for him."

During pregame warm-ups, both Johnson and Kelser told Brkovich to be sure he dunked the ball emphatically on the opening tap play. The play worked exactly as Heathcote had drawn it up. Kelser beat Woolridge to the ball and tipped it forward. Johnson reached up with both hands and batted the ball blindly over his head. It bounced on the floor once, and in one motion Brkovich scooped it up and slammed it home.

Continuing to throw caution to the wind, Heathcote sicced his full-court press on the Fighting Irish. Once again, they were caught off guard, and Terry Donnelly stole the inbounds pass. (Danny Nee, a Notre Dame assistant, would later tell Heathcote that he had never before heard Phelps twice say "Oh, fuck!" so early in a game.) The Spartans came away empty on the possession when Johnson threw the ball away, but the tone had been set.

Hanzlik was feeling a little chippy early on. When he took a charge on Johnson, he taunted him by intentionally mangling his name, saying, "Not today, Irwin." But the Irish didn't have much to brag about after that as America was treated to a vintage display of Michigan State basketball. Once again, Johnson rarely shot the ball—he didn't convert his first field goal until there was 4:30 left in the first half—but he ran the offense beautifully. He repeatedly set up his teammates, including Brkovich, who displayed a rare aggressiveness in scoring 9 of the team's first 11 points. With the Spartans leading 11–8, Magic caught a pass from Rob Gonzalez, and in a flash he fired a pass to Kelser for a baseline dunk. "He didn't catch the ball. He just changed direction of the ball," Al McGuire observed.

A few minutes later, Johnson stole the ball from inside the two-three zone and shoveled it to Donnelly, who lofted it downcourt in an effort to get it back to Magic. Johnson ran down the ball, took one dribble, and flipped a beautiful no-look pass behind him—skipping slightly into the air for extra flair—and into Kelser's hands for another easy dunk. Dick Enberg was enraptured: "Earvin 'Magic' Johnson directing the Spartan ballet company from East Lansing, Michigan, into a seven-point lead."

Meanwhile, Heathcote's two-three zone was choking off Notre Dame's supposedly superior inside game, forcing the Irish into taking long jump shots. Notre Dame hung tough—the Spartans led 34–23 at halftime—but the Irish were clearly overmatched. "I could see in the first three or four minutes of the game that we were better than they were," says Kelser, who scored 18 points in the first half. "We saw those guys on TV so much, they seemed larger than they really were, but I could tell we were quicker and more athletic, and that would eventually take its toll. I remember my confidence growing each time up and down the floor because I was getting the shots I wanted."

Many of those shots came off deft alley-oop feeds from Magic. "That's our offense," Terry Donnelly said. "One passes and the other one dunks." The dunk, which had been made illegal in college basketball in 1967, had been reinstated just three years before. Now Johnson and Kelser were becoming the first high-profile duo in college to make the alley-oop a staple of their arsenal. They liked to boast that they had a mysterious telekinetic connection—"We just have a little eye contact before the pass. I know it's coming and he knows I'll get it," Kelser said—but Heathcote called that "bullshit." "Those were set plays," he says.

Set plays or not, the Spartans were in an amazing rhythm on both ends of the floor, enabling them to maintain a double-digit lead early in the second half. The only thing that could derail them was foul trouble. Sure enough, Ron Charles picked up his fourth with more than 13 minutes still remaining. At that point, Heathcote surprised everyone by inserting Jay Vincent into the game. The Spartans' fans rose and cheered as Vincent walked gingerly onto the court. He was clearly affected by his broken foot, yet a few possessions later he found himself being closely guarded by Bill Laimbeer at the top of the key. Vincent instinctively gave Laimbeer a head-and-shoulders fake, and when Laimbeer jumped up to block him, Vincent drove around him to the basket with one dribble and dropped in a soft layup off the glass. The play was worth only 2 points but it gave the Spartans an immeasurable emotional lift. "He jumped on somebody who had a broken foot," Vincent says. "I really couldn't move, but I did a fake, and he went for it."

The Spartans continued to put on their clinic for the remainder of the game. With more than 8 minutes left, Heathcote installed his "75" offense, a delay tactic that called for them to work the ball around until they got a 75 percent shot, which usually meant a layup. The Spartans were so well schooled in the offense that all Notre Dame could do was commit fouls. Most of them were on Johnson, an 84 percent free throw shooter who converted seven of his eight attempts. When Enberg wondered why Johnson didn't demonstrate the same proficiency on his outside shot, Al McGuire smartly replied, "I've never known anyone to be a great free throw shooter and not be able to hit from the outside. I just think he doesn't take enough shots."

Since this was the last regional final of the weekend, Enberg and McGuire spent the last few minutes of the game sizing up the quartet that would be assembling the following weekend in Salt Lake City. All four were great stories; Ray Meyer, DePaul's sixty-five-year-old coach, was going to his first Final Four, while the University of Pennsylvania had become the first Ivy League team to get there since Bill Bradley took Princeton to the Final Four in 1965. But two teams—specifically, two players—were already looming large. "Should Michigan State win here, that tournament would feature maybe the two best-passing big men in college basketball history," Enberg said to McGuire. "Have there ever been two better men than Larry Bird and Earvin Johnson? You've called them the two best you've ever seen."

"Yeah, they're both Bob Cousys," McGuire replied. "The difference is, it's easier for Larry Bird to pass because he normally has two men on him. So there's a man open. It's difficult for Magic Johnson to pass because there's only one man on him, and everybody else on the court is being covered by another man. Yet he still hits them."

Michigan State completed an 80–68 win over Notre Dame behind Kelser's season-high 34 points and 13 rebounds. Johnson finished with 19 points, 13 assists, and 5 rebounds. Enberg and McGuire openly rooted for "Shoes" Huffman to enter the game during the final minute. Heathcote sent Huffman to the scorer's table, but the clock ran out before he could check in. As the last 30 seconds ticked away, Heathcote shook hands with everyone on the Spartans' bench, pumped both his fists in the air, and flashed a bright, wide smile. "That was one of the few times I'd seen Jud smile on the basketball court," Donnelly says. When the buzzer sounded, the players tackled each other on the court, then formed a tight circle and sang the "Potential" song that had become their mantra.

"This is a tribute to a great bunch who made a superb comeback this season," Heathcote said. "We have a team approach to the game but we still have two superstars in Earvin and Gregory. The rest are support players and they are playing well right now." Notre Dame guard Rich Branning admitted the Irish were on their heels from start to finish. "Right off the bat when they got the tip, made the dunk, and then stole the ball, I knew we were in trouble," he said. "We knew they like to throw the lob pass to [Kelser], but there's not much you can do when he jumps eleven feet and puts his head a foot above the rim."

"It's a credit to Jud that his team is as disciplined and organized as it is but yet his players have the freedom to be themselves," said Digger Phelps. "Michigan State has spurts where it can be devastating, totally dominating. And I've never seen a player like Earvin."

Having won its three games in the tournament by an average margin of nearly 20 points, and having handed each of those teams its worst loss of the season, the Spartans had every reason to be brimming with confidence as they looked ahead to their game against Penn in the national semifinals. "I've dreamed of winning a national championship for a long time and when it struck me that we now have a chance it was too much," Johnson said. "If we're on top of our game, ain't nobody in the world can beat Michigan State."

A reporter asked Johnson if he would like to play Larry Bird and Indiana State in Salt Lake City. "I sure would because that would mean we'd be in the finals," he said. "It would be a challenge, and I love challenges."

10

Indiana State will meet DePaul in Saturday's semifinal round in Salt Lake City, with Michigan State going against Penn. The winners will meet Monday night for the national championship. Unless the gods of hoopdom truly have something against us, they will give us an Indiana State–Michigan State final.

Pretty please.

—Dave Kindred, *The Washington Post*, March 20, 1979

So it was that the college basketball world descended upon conservative, picturesque Salt Lake City, Utah, on the final weekend in March 1979. The city, and its modestly sized Special Events Center at the University of Utah (capacity: fifteen thousand), was hardly a harbinger of the metropolized, domed spectacle the Final Four would soon become. But as the weekend got under way, there was a palpable sense in the mountain air that something very, very big was about to happen, providing the gods of hoopdom did their part.

The compelling story lines at the 1979 Final Four were not limited to the specter of a Bird vs. Magic showdown. Another big focus of interest was Ray Meyer, DePaul's venerable, sixty-five-year-old coach, who had just been elected for enshrinement at the Naismith

Memorial Basketball Hall of Fame in Springfield, Massachusetts. Meyer was in his thirty-seventh year at DePaul and hadn't been to the semifinals of the NCAA tournament since 1943, when his Blue Demons squad featured a gangly but agile young center named George Mikan. The field for that tournament consisted of just eight teams, and the semifinalists did not convene at one site. (The "final four" format didn't begin until 1952.) By 1979, Meyer was considered to be a living legend, but as the sun was setting on his career many openly wondered whether the old man would ever make it back to the game's grandest stage.

After reaching the Midwest Regional final in 1978, the Blue Demons had been strengthened by the addition of a talented Chicago native named Mark Aguirre, a chubby six-foot-six center with soft hands who led all freshman scorers during the 1978–79 season with a 24.1 average. DePaul's placement as the No. 2 seed in the West Region landed it in a matchup with top-seeded UCLA in the regional final at the Marriott Center in Provo, Utah. After DePaul built a 17-point lead over the Bruins at halftime, a dance troupe from nearby Brigham Young University took the floor and entertained the crowd. The dancers were still performing when the UCLA team emerged from its locker room for the second half. Upon seeing the players, the Bruins' band fired up the school fight song, drowning out the dance music. The arena was filled mostly with local citizens, and they lustily booed the UCLA band for its rudeness. For the remainder of the game, those fans cheered for DePaul as if they had lived in the Windy City their whole lives. Partly buoyed by the partisan crowd, DePaul hung on for a 95–91 win.

The victory left Al McGuire, sitting courtside for NBC, in tears. There was little doubt as to who would be the sentimental favorite in Salt Lake City. "This is the greatest thing that's ever happened to me," Meyer said. "I don't care if we win another game because all I ever said was that I wanted to make the Final Four."

DePaul's win over UCLA was considered an upset, but for shock value the Blue Demons had nothing on the University of Pennsylvania

Quakers. Seeded ninth in the East Region, Penn, which had won its eighth Ivy League title in ten years, pulled off a slew of shockers to get to the tournament's final weekend. In their first two games in Raleigh, North Carolina, the Quakers knocked off an Iona team led by Jeff Ruland, and two days later they stunned No. 3 North Carolina with a score of 72–71. On that same day, Duke University, ranked No. 6 in the AP poll, was also upset by St. John's. Not for nothing is that day still referred to as "Black Sunday" on Tobacco Road.

The East Regionals were held the following week at Greensboro Coliseum, also in North Carolina. The games were technically sold out, but since Duke and North Carolina were not playing, the arena was half empty both days, illustrating how much room the NCAA tournament still had to grow. After knocking off No. 8 Syracuse in the regional semifinals ("Penn didn't surprise me. I'm not from North Carolina," sniffed the young Syracuse coach, Jim Boeheim), the Quakers edged St. John's 64–62 to reach the national semifinals.

When the Quakers returned home to Philadelphia after beating St. John's, they were welcomed at the airport by hundreds of fans, including the university president and provost. They were so besieged by the media at practice on Tuesday, March 20, that they had to retreat to their locker room and figure out set times for press conferences. Meanwhile, they couldn't even work out on their usual practice floor because the Palestra was hosting an indoor tennis tournament that week. On the day they left for Salt Lake City, the school held a huge pep rally that began with a march through the heart of campus and ended with nearly ten thousand fans gathering in Franklin Field, the football stadium. When coach Bob Weinauer took the stage, he stepped to the microphone and yelled, "Where's Princeton now?"

It was a wonderful few days, but hardly the best way to prepare for the challenge that lay ahead. "We were doing so much that week, having dinners, luncheons," says James Salters, who was a junior guard on the team. "If you're really looking at the finest basketball, being ready to play, that was not the finest scene for us."

Thus, NBC had many reasons to be excited about the possibilities set to unfurl in Salt Lake City. All four regional finals from the previous weekend had set new records for Nielsen ratings, led by the 12.3 generated by the Michigan State–Notre Dame game (compared to 10.8 the year before in the same window). The network sent a camera crew early in the week to Chicago, where Meyer was more than happy to give them whatever access they wanted. "We were all Ray Meyered up," says Don McGuire, NBC's main features producer. "We had a bunch of stuff showing him sweeping the gym. We interviewed half a dozen priests who all had great Ray Meyer stories."

With so many terrific story lines on hand, there was almost no scenario that would be a disappointment. But if NBC really wanted to hit a home run, there was no doubt which would make the best climax. As Bob Ryan wrote for that week's issue of *Basketball Times,* "If Indiana State with Larry Bird meets Michigan State with Earvin Johnson in the finals and the result isn't the biggest TV rating ever, for a college basketball game, then either we, the press, aren't doing our jobs or this country's sports fans are beyond salvation."

As the family members, employees, and boosters of the Indiana State basketball program settled into their seats, a familiar voice came over the intercom of the sleek chartered jet. "It's good to see all you fair-weather friends on board," Larry Bird cracked. "Where y'all been all year?"

Bird being Bird, he tossed in a few more bawdy jokes, even though his mother, Georgia, was one of the passengers. A few of the other players picked up where he left off and made wisecracks into the intercom as well. "Larry paved the way," Steve Reed says. "We were having fun."

The team had already had quite the eventful day. After wrapping up their final practice, their bus was given a police escort to the airport. Several thousand fans gathered at Hulman Field to see them off. The next day, a photo ran in the *Terre Haute Tribune* showing

Bob Heaton and Tom Crowder boarding the jet wearing their trade-mark cowboy hats. The caption identified them simply as "Miracle Man" and "The Hulk." Mere names would no longer do.

The Sycamores were indeed heading for the big time, and nobody was going to be bigger than Bird. The day after their triumph over Arkansas, Bird and Hodges traveled to New York City to collect yet another pair of trophies for national player of the year and coach of the year, this time bestowed by the National Association of Basketball Coaches. After accepting the award and thanking his teammates, Bird revealed that he had aggravated the triple fracture in his left thumb during the postgame melee after the win over Arkansas. "Some fan grabbed it. I don't think he knew what he was doing," Bird said. "I dropped him to his knees with a punch to the mouth. It was just a re-action. I think I convinced him. It hurts a little, but it won't have no effect on the outcome." Bird went on to say, apparently without irony, that if he couldn't reach a contract with the Celtics, he would like to play pro ball in New York. "That's where everything is at. The media is here, TV, there's more people," he said. "I belong in New York."

When he returned to Terre Haute, it was all Bird could do to get away from distractions. He was enjoying a relatively quiet afternoon at home with Heaton, his roommate, when Heaton's high school coach showed up with his family to wish them luck. Bird greeted the visitors warmly, and as they got ready to leave he leaned down and kissed the coach's young daughter on the cheek. "That was a gesture I would never have expected from Larry," says Craig McKee, the stu-dent sports information assistant, who had been at the house work-ing with Heaton on a class project. "He knew these were important people in Bob's life. For all the coldness he usually showed, he was capable of a generosity of spirit that would come out of nowhere sometimes."

Jud Heathcote, on the other hand, was not doling out kisses that week. He was so concerned about outside influences that for the first time since he was a coach he closed his team's practice that week in Jenison Fieldhouse. "Each practice we've been attracting 200 or 300 fans in the stands and as soon as practice is officially over, they swarm the floor," Heathcote said. "The support the fans have given has been tremendous but the kids are tired right now."

Since Michigan State was on spring break, Heathcote decided to take his team out to Salt Lake City on Wednesday, a day earlier than the other teams, both to get acclimated to the altitude and to get them away from the craziness at home. When they arrived, he took them to a local gym and put them through one of their toughest practices of the postseason. "It was in some little, dank, dusty gym, and we were going at it," Kelser says. "I think that was his way of getting us back, grounded and centered. No one was applauding us out there. It was only us."

The early arrival also gave the Spartans a chance to enjoy some quiet time together. On Thursday night, Heathcote took them for a gourmet dinner at Snowbird, a high-end ski resort that was owned by a Michigan State alumnus. Most of the players had never been skiing, much less dined in such an elegant setting. "We drove up to the base of the mountain in the bus, and you had to ride this elevator through the mountain to get to the top of the ski lodge. It was terrific," Terry Donnelly says. Once they reached the top, they were treated to a picturesque view of the sun setting behind the snow-kissed Wasatch mountains. "They told us that President Carter had just eaten there a couple of days before," Darwin Payton recalls. "It was like we were the show. We were the main event."

The evening took on a slightly wistful air as the realization sunk in that the end of the season was nigh. "We knew our time together was growing short. We were really trying to soak that in and savor all of it," Kelser says. "I was the only senior on the team, so I may have felt that more than everybody else, but we knew it could be Earvin's last year, too."

Heathcote decided that he was going to make his players off-limits to the press aside from what was required by the NCAA. This stemmed partly from his discomfort at how so many people were holding up his team as the favorite. When Joe Falls wrote an article stating as much in the *Detroit News,* Heathcote said, "We have a number of columnists in our area who think we're going to win the national title. We hope they're right, but I don't think that's the kind of column we want our players to read." Lynn Henning, as usual, was eager to give the coach a tweak. "Heathcote has often complained because he feels the press hasn't given him or his program enough credit," Henning wrote. "Now, he takes exception to articles paying him and his players the ultimate compliment."

Be that as it may, the other teams could have used a few more barriers of their own that weekend. While Michigan State stayed at a hotel near the airport, the Sycamores lodged at the Hotel Utah, which was located in the heart of Salt Lake City, across the street from the world headquarters of the Mormon church. Hundreds of Indiana State supporters stayed at that same hotel, as did the Michigan State band, whose members thought nothing of playing their instruments late into the night, robbing the Indiana State players of some badly needed sleep. "I remember the fans were outside our hotel yelling and screaming and keeping us awake," Bill Hodges says. "And the press ran the doggone tournament. They told you where you could go. I had to go so many meetings and press conferences that I couldn't even have dinner with the team."

That may partly explain why Hodges came off as so reserved to outsiders, though compared with Heathcote anybody would seem like a wallflower. "Hodges was painfully shy," NBC's Don McGuire recalls. "He wanted to help you, but he just didn't know how to do it. It was probably good news for him that in those days, there wasn't the kind of attention he would have gotten today." Larry Keith, who covered the 1979 Final Four for *Sports Illustrated,* remembers that Hodges "was not a fun person. He was thrown into the breach with no preparation, and as I recall he was not well-suited to the task. He was not comfortable in the national spotlight and he did not enjoy it."

Nonetheless, Hodges's players did their best to have a ball. The highlight came one night when they went to dinner, and Bird accidentally spit a glob of tobacco juice on Tom Crowder's brand-new, styling white bell-bottom pants. The guys laughed for hours as Crowder repeatedly cried, "Can you be-*leeve* he did that?"

For the other visitors, however, there wasn't a ton of fun to be had in Salt Lake City. The capital was officially "dry," meaning alcohol was difficult to acquire. As part of its opening press session Wednesday night, the NCAA offered a five-minute presentation on how visitors could get drinks, which usually involved paying a membership fee to join local private clubs. "In many respects, it was a fairly colorless week," Henning says. "I'm not sure Salt Lake City was a whole lot different than it would have been any other time. They weren't indifferent by any means, and people were aware that the nation had descended on the community. But you just felt like it wasn't a big deal that the Final Four was in town."

Bird, alas, had nothing to say at the Friday press conferences, but he and his teammates let it all hang out at the open practices that afternoon. A few of the guys even played a game of H-O-R-S-E with Billy Packer. "He was a good shot. He was definitely hanging with us," Heaton says. After Crowder performed his must-see, kick-the-rim trick for the fans, their full workout got under way. "We always started off with a full-court ballhandling drill," assistant coach Terry Thimlar recalls. "So we go into this drill, and you could hear the oohs and aahs of the crowd. It was almost like people were surprised that our guys were so skilled. It was a really good feeling that they could see we were legitimate, not just a team that had won a bunch of games against teams that weren't very good."

Much of the chatter about the DePaul–Indiana State matchup naturally centered around the question of how the Blue Demons would defend Larry Bird. The task was going to be made more difficult by the fact that six-foot-six senior forward Curtis Watkins, DePaul's best defender and the man who was going to be assigned to check Bird, had injured his left knee late in the win over UCLA. While most teams tried varying strategies involving junk defenses and double teams, Meyer was going to try a more basic approach. "We're not going to gang up on the man," Meyer said. "There's no way to stop him. We will let Bird get his points and try to stop everybody else."

Michigan State also had a lingering injury concern in Jay Vincent. Heathcote said that Vincent's broken foot had been improving and he might see some playing time, but he definitely wouldn't start. Beyond that, Heathcote's main concern was the possibility his players would get complacent. All week long, he talked to them about how good Penn was, but they were skeptical. "Coach," Johnson kept saying, "they're in the Ivy League."

"Well," Heathcote would reply, "they did beat North Carolina and Syracuse and St. John's. So they must be pretty good."

"Yeah, but . . . they're in the *Ivy* League."

The extra day in Salt Lake City also helped the Spartans get adjusted, literally, to the atmosphere. The Penn players had scoffed when Weinauer told them they might struggle in the thin air, but after their first practice they lined up to take a breath from an oxygen tank behind their bench.

The Quakers had a quick, athletic team headlined by their leading scorer, six-foot-seven senior forward Tony Price. Weinauer observed with some annoyance that almost every story about his team referred to them as "intelligent." "It's nice to be an intelligent team, but all the intelligence in the world won't win basketball games," he said. "We also have a heck of a lot of talent." Then again, maybe the Penn players weren't as intelligent as people thought. Instead of giving the Spartans their due, the Quakers seemed to go out of their way to antagonize their opponents. "To me, Michigan State is nothing but a bunch of dudes playing basketball just like we are," Price said. "We're the type of team that plays exciting basketball, too, but we like to take advantage of other teams trying to show off and doing things they shouldn't be doing." Price went on to say that he was going to force Kelser to shoot from the outside because he didn't want Kelser to get a bunch of dunks on national TV like he did against Notre Dame. Price's teammate Tim Smith said with considerable bravado that he would employ the same strategy against Earvin Johnson. "He's not a very good shot from fifteen to twenty feet," Smith said. "Johnson is a great player without a doubt, but I've seen a lot of his moves a million times on the schoolyard. He executes them well, but I know what to do against them."

Even Coach Weinauer gave Michigan State some bulletin board material. "They have two superstars, but I think we have more overall talent and overall speed," he said. "They won't be able to run on us like they did on Notre Dame."

Perhaps Heathcote knew what he was doing when he closed off his players from the press. Toward the end of the public workout on Friday, the Spartans staged an impromptu dunking show for the fans, most of whom were clad in Michigan State green-and-white. As they soared in for one acrobatic jam after another, the Quakers, who were scheduled to take the floor next, watched from the tunnel. Among the people sitting courtside was the former Columbia University coach Jack Rohan, who was writing a scouting report for the *New York Times*. Rohan's ghostwriter on the project was Malcolm Moran, a recently hired *Times* staffer. Gesturing over to where the Penn players stood, Rohan leaned over and told Moran, "If I was their coach, I'd get them out of there. They don't need to be watching this."

The semifinals had created so much interest that the NCAA had to turn away nearly a hundred credential requests from media organizations because there was no more room in the Special Events Center when the Final Four got under way on Saturday, March 24. (One of the writers who did get onto press row was David Israel. He had to change seats, however, because the Indiana State fans kept pelting him with objects, including, naturally, a roll of toilet paper.) Penn coach Bob Weinauer, meanwhile, had a problem of his own: he had never seen the Spartans play, on television or in person. The only material he had to study was a game film he had acquired from North Carolina coach Dean Smith of the Tar Heels' 1-point win over the Spartans back on December 16 in Chapel Hill. Considering how much of a different team the Spartans now were, that film was not much help.

Weinauer was right when he said that Penn had excellent overall team quickness, and with so many ball handlers and shooters the Quakers were well equipped to go up against the Spartans' zone. In fact, during the first 10 minutes of the game, they penetrated Heathcote's matchup zone as well as any team had all year. Center Matt White got inside of Greg Kelser for a point-blank layup. Two possessions later, he found space on the baseline and took a nice feed from senior guard Bobby Willis. Tony Price got a layup off an inbounds pass. A minute later, Price found Willis on a weakside cut for another bank shot from close range. On another possession, when White was pressured in the post, he dumped the ball off to freshman forward Vincent Ross, who was wide open on the opposite block.

Good shots, all. Problem was, the Quakers missed every one.

Whether they were spooked by the size and quickness of Michigan State's frontline players or were simply paralyzed by the circumstances, the Quakers played like a shell of the team that had taken the NCAA tournament by storm. As they sank deeper and deeper into offensive ineptitude, the Spartans capitalized with remarkable efficiency. Four different players contributed to a 9–0 run that pushed the Spartans to an early 13–4 lead and forced Weinauer to call time-out. After Willis knocked down a jumper to cut the lead to 7, Michigan State broke the Quakers' spirits by scoring 19 unanswered points. The stunning spurt gave the Spartans a 32–6 lead with 7:19 to play in the first half. About the only thing that could stop the Spartans was the flying toilet paper that came from the Indiana State cheering section, forcing officials briefly to halt the action.

Magic Johnson began the game looking for his offense more than usual. With the six-foot-four Tim Smith guarding him, Johnson got the ball inside to take advantage of his size, then stepped out to the perimeter to nail four consecutive long-range shots. "I thought he took particular care to square up and take good jump shots," says Bob Ryan, the *Boston Globe* columnist and contributor to *Basketball*

Weekly. "Normally he didn't care about his shooting percentages. He'd take flyers and floaters and flips. When I watched him during that Penn game, my thinking was he wanted to show the pro scouts that he could shoot the ball."

Magic also proved—again—that he was a ballhandling wizard. Late in the first half, he got a defensive rebound, took two dribbles with his left hand away from a pair of Penn defenders, and then flipped the ball behind his back to split the double team. As NBC showed a replay of the move, Dick Enberg marveled, "You forget, and maybe people are watching Johnson for the first time—ladies and gentlemen, that man is six feet, eight inches tall. That's not a six-one, six-two man handling the ball so deftly. He's a basketball giant who handles it like a little guard."

Just when it seemed as if nothing could go wrong for the Spartans, they endured a scary moment late in the first half. Johnson fed Terry Donnelly for a breakaway layup, but as the lefty guard was converting the basket, Penn's Tony Price undercut him in an attempt to draw the charge. Donnelly landed flat on his back and writhed on the floor in pain. When he finally got up, Donnelly went straight into the locker room with a badly bruised lower back. He returned to the bench before the end of the half but never reentered the game.

Aside from that, the contest was a breeze for the Spartans. With their lead reaching ridiculous proportions late in the first half, Greg Kelser, who was taking a breather on the bench, turned to the writers sitting behind him and said, "We're doing it to them, aren't we?" When the half finally ended, Michigan State owned a 50–17 lead. "It's just unbelievable we could have this kind of score when you get down to the final four teams in the United States," Enberg said. The Spartans had shot 63.3 percent in the first 20 minutes while the Quakers shot 16.7 percent. In the locker room, Heathcote didn't even try to pretend they might lose. His only concern was his players' decorum. "Hey, let's not try to embarrass anybody out there," he told them. "And let's be sure not to embarrass ourselves."

Michigan State outscored Penn by only 1 point in the second half and walked away with a 101–67 win. Though the victory had come much easier than anyone expected, Donnelly's fall, combined with Vincent's lingering foot problem (he played just 9 minutes), gave Heathcote reason to be concerned as he looked ahead to the Monday night final. "We'll have a couple of players who will be below par but hopefully they'll play well," he said.

After the game, Billy Packer asked Johnson about the way he dominated Penn guard Tim Smith inside. "Well, all year really I've been going inside," Johnson said. "With a six-four man on me, he said he was gonna stop me from getting the ball so—"

"He told you that?" Packer interjected.

"No, I read it in the paper. So I thought I would go inside and see what he could do with me. I had about four inches on him so it paid off."

Johnson finished with 29 points on 9 for 10 shooting to go along with 10 assists and 10 rebounds. Kelser added 28 points, 9 rebounds, and 4 blocks. "We saw where Price said he was going to make Gregory a perimeter player because he didn't want him slam-dunking on national TV," Johnson said. "That's fine with us because Gregory can shoot. And I think I can shoot, too. If I'm straight up and looking at the basket, I'm a good shooter."

Penn's coach was soundly convinced of the abilities of Michigan State's two superstars. "Earvin Johnson and Gregory Kelser are two of the most outstanding, dominating basketball players I have ever come across in my coaching career," Weinauer said. "We tried to minimize their abilities to our team prior to the game to prevent them from thinking they were superhuman."

For Johnson, the only real downside of the night was that his mother wasn't there to watch him play. Because Christine Johnson was a Seventh-Day Adventist, she spent that Saturday evening in the hotel room, not watching television or listening to the radio. "She won't even know who won until we get back to the room," Earvin Sr. said. "But she'll be there Monday night, you can count on that."

The only question was which team she'd watch her son go up

against. Johnson said after the game that the Spartans would be ready regardless of their opponent, but the Michigan State fans, like everyone else, had a clear preference. They made that known late in the first half when, with the Spartans leading Penn 46–14, a chant rang out from the green-and-white section of the Special Events Center: "We want the Bird! We want the Bird!"

The Indiana State fans rose and gave their riposte: "You'll get the Bird! You'll get the Bird!"

And the "bird" is just what they flipped them.

Ray Meyer was standing in DePaul's locker room getting ready to go over his scouting report on Indiana State. As he began, he was interrupted by his son, Joey, who was an assistant on his staff. Joey politely suggested that he not give away his secret plan with a dozen or so media people standing in the back of the room at the coach's invitation. "Hey guys, Joey doesn't think it's such a good idea for you to be in here for this," Meyer said. "Would you mind stepping out for a little bit?"

If the Blue Demons were going to hand Indiana State its first loss of the season, they were going to have to do it with only five players. The subs on DePaul's bench were so mediocre that the coach rarely used them; the reserves had scored a total of 163 points all season, roughly 5 points per game. Meyer justified this by saying he liked to have his best players on the floor at all times, but that was a convenient and unconvincing explanation.

DePaul's lack of depth would be even more of a liability considering that the man Meyer assigned to cover Bird straight up, Curtis Watkins, was playing with his injured left leg wrapped in thick tape from midcalf to midthigh. Nobody had been able to contain Bird single-handedly in three years, but Meyer was now asking Watkins to give it a try at less than full strength. Sensing a clear advantage, Bird played aggressively from the start—and he put on quite a show. His first bucket came on a turnaround bank shot that put Indiana State up 4–2. Within the next few minutes, he followed his own miss, drained a seventeen-footer (which prompted Al McGuire to call him "probably the best who's ever played from that distance at his height"), hit a pull-up jumper over Watkins, converted a left-handed layup off a feed from Brad Miley, and swished a rainbow twenty-footer from deep in the right corner. Even so, DePaul stayed close. Midway through the first half, Indiana State led 20–18, and Bird had 12 of those points.

By this time, the Michigan State players had showered and dressed, and they were watching the game from inside the arena. It was their first chance to see Bird play in person. "He got instant respect from every guy on the team," Mike Brkovich says. Kelser could see that Bird was the best player on the floor, but he also believed that DePaul was not defending him properly. "They let him have too much freedom out there," Kelser says. "I don't think any of us really cared who we played, because we thought we could beat either team. But I remember thinking to myself, it certainly would be nice to knock off an undefeated team."

Billy Packer agreed with Kelser's assessment of Meyer's game plan. Meyer switched to a zone defense late in the first half, but that just allowed Bird more chances to get open looks. When Bird drained a wide-open shot from twenty feet, Packer said, "If you're Ray Meyer over there, you've gotta start saying to yourself, 'Hey, we're gonna have to start denying the pass.' He's getting out there and touching it from eighteen feet."

The good news for DePaul—and NBC—was that the Blue Demons continued to answer Bird shot for shot. Mark Aguirre played like a nervous freshman at the start, but once he settled down, the plump power forward made a few baskets. ("He's six-foot-seven, but with the size of his rear end he plays about six-ten!" McGuire cracked.) DePaul guard Gary Garland, who was called the "Music Man" because his aunt was the singer Dionne Warwick, added 10 points in the first half. A leaner from Bird in the waning seconds of the first half gave him 23 points, and it staked Indiana State to a 45–42 lead going into the locker room.

It was a great 20 minutes of basketball: Indiana State had shot 75 percent from the floor, DePaul had shot 60 percent, and the score had been tied fifteen times.

Before the start of the second half, Meyer complained to the refs about what he perceived to be favorable treatment for Bird. "You front him and you get a foul automatically. This is ridiculous," he said. Meyer's complaint failed to prevent Indiana State from pushing out to an 11-point lead after 3½ minutes, and it looked as if the game could turn into another runaway. DePaul climbed all the way back, however, helped by a flurry of careless Indiana State turnovers. (The Sycamores would finish the game with twenty-two miscues, with Bird contributing a season-high eleven.) The Blue Demons took a 73–71 lead with 4:59 remaining, but Meyer made a mistake by sending his team into its delay offense, which ended with guard Clyde Bradshaw throwing the ball out of bounds off of Curtis Watkins's leg. On the next possession, Bird fed "Miracle Man" Bob Heaton for a layup, and the game was tied once again.

After a free throw from Garland put DePaul up 74–73 with 1:37 to play, it was up to Heaton—naturally—to give the Sycamores the lead for good. He took a pretty feed from a penetrating Carl Nicks and converted it for a layup to put Indiana State up by one with 50 seconds to play. DePaul had one last chance to win, but after working the ball around endlessly the Blue Demons could do no better than a fallaway nineteen-foot heave from Aguirre with 4 seconds remaining. "When Aguirre got the ball in the corner, I knew he would try to go one-on-one," said Brad Miley, who was assigned to guard the freshman. "I thought it was his most fluid shot of the game. I thought he made it. Guess he was a little off balance."

Aguirre missed badly. Leroy Staley grabbed the rebound, was immediately fouled, and made one of two free throws to allow Indiana State to escape with a 76–74 win. "I'm emotionally drained," Hodges said. "The whole season has been like a dream. Sometimes I want to pinch myself. I am thankful that Coach King gave me the opportunity, and I'm also thankful that I didn't do anything to mess the kids up." Asked if Heaton was his designated game-winning shooter, Hodges smiled and said, "I can't take any credit for Heaton's touch for making clutch baskets. I think God is on his side or something."

Ray Meyer voiced frustration that his team was so unable to stop Bird. "I don't know how many times I told our kids to guard their man and not worry about Bird. But we kept turning our heads numerous times, and he got them easy shots," Meyer said. "We have no regrets. My goal always had been to make it to the Final Four. Our goal now is to make it to the finals. We'll be back."

Part of the reason for Meyer's optimism was that he believed he was about to sign another talented Chicago schoolboy, a speedy six-foot point guard named Isiah Thomas. Indiana coach Bob Knight was also recruiting Thomas but, said Meyer, "IU will not get Thomas. The boy's mother happens to like the old man." (Indiana, of course, did get Thomas, and the old man never made it back to the Final Four.)

Playing the most important game of his life, Bird had been at his absolute best. He finished with 35 points (on 16 for 19 shooting) and 16 rebounds. After the game, he tried to pull his disappearing act with the press, but a direct plea from Wayne Duke, the Big Ten commissioner and chairman of the NCAA men's basketball committee, convinced him to meet briefly with reporters. The first thing he was asked was what goes through his mind when he is in the proverbial "zone," as he clearly was during that first half. "Usually I just feel sorry for the guy who's guarding me," Bird said, eliciting a few chuckles. "I felt so good I was begging for the ball. I couldn't grip the ball as well as usual, and I made more mistakes than I usually do. If I had known I would make eleven turnovers I would have thought we would lose."

As for the hype about his forthcoming duel with Magic Johnson, Bird wasn't buying it. "Me and Earvin Johnson don't go matching up," he said. "We're different kinds of players. He's a passer and I'm a scorer." Pressed again on the question, Bird replied, "Well, I guess this is what the writers all dream about, two guys like us in here." Someone asked if he would talk about his future in the pros. "No, I gotta go see my mother," he replied, abruptly ending the Q&A.

The gods of hoopdom had been cooperative. Larry Bird and the Indiana State Sycamores were now one win away from becoming the most unlikely NCAA champion in history. And yet, to many people, they still remained a mystery that had not been fully unraveled. "They advanced to the championship game as the most unknown undefeated team in the country," Malcolm Moran wrote for the next day's *New York Times*. "They are also the only one."

11

The Michigan State players had left the Indiana State–DePaul game at halftime, so by the time the Sycamores wrapped up the win the Spartans were resting comfortably in their hotel rooms out by the airport. The Sycamores, on the other hand, didn't return to the Hotel Utah until late that night, when the place was so teeming with revelers that the local fire marshals had to hold people out. Bird retired to his room and hung out with a few of his good friends. "Larry seemed unusually tired," says Tony Clark, his pal from French Lick. "It was like he left everything on the floor." With a bacchanal raging in the lobby and the Michigan State band playing into the wee hours of the morning, there wouldn't be much sleep for Bird and his teammates that night.

Hodges woke Bird up at 9 a.m. Sunday morning because they were supposed to attend a brunch in honor of Bird having won the Eastman Award for national player of the year. Bird was so exhausted, he asked Hodges if he could stay in bed. Some reporters at the brunch were ticked when Bird didn't show up, but even Billy Packer stepped up to his defense on this one. "Hey, how many times do you want him to get the award anyway?" he said. "He went to New York two weeks ago to receive the same award. He's going to the

NABC banquet tonight to get the award for the third time. Two out of three isn't too bad when the guy is playing for the national championship."

Later that morning, Indiana State held a closed practice at the Special Events Center. The players were in their usual great spirits. After the workout, they waited patiently while Bob Forbes, their radio play-by-play man, conducted interviews with the players for a Terre Haute TV station. Then they grabbed Forbes, lifted him up, and dumped him in a trash can as the cameras kept rolling. The Spartans, meanwhile, had gathered in a hallway to get ready to begin their own practice. As the Sycamores bounded past their Monday night opponents, they chanted and sang out buoyantly. "They weren't wrong for doing that, but we took it as a sign of disrespect," Greg Kelser says. "That was something we could use. We figured, okay, we're fired up even more now. We'll get them tomorrow."

As the Indiana State players filed past, Earvin Johnson approached Larry Bird to say hello. They hadn't spoken since they were together on the U.S. team that played at the World Invitational Tournament the previous summer. As Johnson walked toward him, Bird took one look at him and kept right on walking. Magic was stunned—and really, really pissed. "So that's how it is, huh?" he said to his teammates. "Okay, then. If that's how he wants it, that's fine with me."

"Even later, when we were driving back to the hotel, Earvin was still talking about how Bird wouldn't speak to him," says Darwin Payton, the student manager. "He kept saying, 'Okay, we'll see what happens tomorrow.' Earvin is a happy-go-lucky type of guy, but Bird was not trying to be his friend. He looked at Earvin as the enemy."

Heathcote's main objective at Michigan State's practice was naturally to teach his players how to defend Bird. He and his assistants had seen the Sycamores play for the first time the previous night, and they devised a game plan, as Heathcote puts it, "by the seat of our pants." For most of the season, Indiana State's opposing coaches had fallen into one of two camps. The first was the Dick Versace camp: do whatever it takes to stop Bird, including double and triple teams, and make the other guys beat you. The other was the Ray Meyer camp: let Bird have his points, and prevent his teammates from going off. Heathcote decided neither approach would do. He could see Bird was too good for single coverage, yet if his team overplayed Bird too much he would kill the Spartans with his passing.

Fortunately, Heathcote's innovative matchup zone was well suited to pulling off such a hybrid strategy. All season long, he had added adjustments and tweaks designed to collar an opponent's best player. Now, he and his staff came up with a four-point plan to keep a "man-and-a-half" on Bird at all times. Point one dictated that whoever was closest to Bird when he had the ball would guard him straight up. Point two was that as soon as Bird put the ball on the floor, he would be double-teamed. Point three was that the Spartans were not to go for Bird's pass fakes. And point four was to keep Bird off the offensive glass. Because the zone had been created to give players the ability to trap the ball and shift into passing lanes, Heathcote was confident that his players would be able to recover and lock down Bird's teammates if they stayed alert and communicated well.

It was a clever strategy, but besides the limited time he had to implement it, there was the larger challenge of simulating Larry Bird in practice. Bird was, after all, a player with unusual dimensions and gifts. Where in the world could Heathcote find someone who was as big as Bird, yet who also possessed the ball skills and the court sense to mimic what he did?

The answer, of course, was in his own locker room. "Earvin," Heathcote said at the start of practice, "you're going to play Bird on our scout team." Magic couldn't flip off his practice jersey fast enough. He had always worn green with the starting five, yet now he was turning himself white—literally and figuratively—and joining the second team. "Coach had never done that before, but clearly Earvin relished the opportunity," Kelser says. "It was fun to be on the scouting team. You could do what you want because you weren't yourself."

As the workout got under way, Magic went into his Larry Bird imitation. He set himself up on the block, and when the zone shifted his way he zipped the ball to open teammates. He crashed the boards and handled the ball on the perimeter. Most remarkably of all, he hit shots from outside. He made all kinds of shots from all over the floor. Heathcote kept pushing the zone farther and farther out, but it didn't matter. Everything Johnson threw up went in. Finally, Heathcote started to get angry. "Goddamit, get up on him! Check him already!" he shouted. But it didn't matter. Magic, who was supposed to be a suspect outside shooter, drilled shot after shot, all the while boasting to his teammates, "You can't guard me! I'm Larry Bird! I can't be stopped!" He was having the time of his life.

When the practice was over, Heathcote could only wonder whether his players had properly digested his four-point plan. One thing, though, was certain. Whatever Bird had in store for them Monday night, the Spartans were not going to see a better performance than the one Magic Johnson had just delivered.

Craig McKee half-expected to be stood up as he sat in his rental car outside the Hotel Utah on Sunday afternoon. The student assistant in Indiana State's sports information office had drawn the short-straw assignment to escort Larry Bird to the big pregame press conference being held for players and coaches at the Salt Lake City Hilton. To McKee's surprise, Bird was waiting for him outside the Hotel Utah just as he said he would. As the two of them rode through the city, Bird said quietly, "This sure is a pretty town." *Kid*, McKee thought, *you have no idea the sights you're going to see.*

There were some four hundred members of the media waiting for Bird at the Hilton. By this point, the vast majority of them had seen him play in person only once, and aside from the brief interaction they had with him late Saturday night they had barely heard him speak. "We all wondered if he could put a sentence together," Dick Enberg says. Bird arrived dressed casually in a white Adidas warm-up jacket and blue jeans. When he took his seat in the front of the room, someone asked, "How's your thumb?"

"Broke," Larry deadpanned.

The room busted out in laughter.

Over the next forty-five minutes, Larry proved to be everything the reporters had assumed he wasn't. He was smart. He was charming. He was funny. He was articulate, albeit not so grammatically correct. He even looked happy to be there, though when someone suggested he was enjoying himself, he replied, "That's what you think."

Bird parried the reporters' questions with humor and candor. *People who have seen you play in person think you're better than when they saw you on television,* he was told.

"Yeah, they know what they're talking about."

What do you remember about playing with Johnson last summer?

"He passed the ball to me."

You seem to have a great feeling for passing.

"My feeling about passing is that it don't matter who's doing the scoring as long as it's us. I just think when a man is open, he should get the ball whether it's thirty feet out on the wing or underneath. We had guys last year who didn't care about passing. They thought scoring was more important, but passing is more important."

Earvin Johnson looks like he's having fun on the court, but you don't.

"He's probably laughing at the opponents. But you can't have fun when the game's tied with two seconds to go and they got the ball. If you got a one-point lead, it's different, but I got to do what I do. I can't be laughing out there. Earvin's different. I just hope he's not laughing at me."

Why have you avoided interviews all season?

"We got seven guys who can play. They deserve to be talked to, too. It got so it was taking up two or three hours a day so I decided not to do interviews. If all of you was paying me, I'd enjoy it but I know that's coming. I don't mind interviews. I can handle any situation if it's all about me but I don't like it when I'm asked about my family."

So what changed your mind about doing this interview?

"Everybody wants publicity. I just thought the other guys on the team weren't getting it but now they are, so it's time to come back. We didn't expect to be here."

You didn't expect to be here?

"Did you expect us to be here?"

For the most part the reviews were positive. Billy Reed of the *Louisville Courier-Journal* suggested that if this basketball thing didn't work out for Bird, he could be on the hit TV comedy *Hee Haw*. Dave Anderson of the *New York Times* described him as "a hayseed of humor, a Herb Shriner with a jump shot." The *State Journal*'s Lynn Henning thought he came off as crude—"The hick from French Lick thing was an understatement," he says—but for the most part Bird comported himself well. "He showed his droll sense of humor that afternoon," says Andy Amey, who covered the Sycamores for the *Terre Haute Tribune*. "To me, it's still one of the best press conferences he ever had. His inner self came out."

There was nothing mixed about the reviews from Magic Johnson's Sunday press conference. When a person so obviously enjoys being somewhere, the people who are with him can't help but be seduced. "I love it. I love all this attention. As long as you got the questions, I got the answers," Johnson said. "Being in the Final Four, to get all the attention, to have your name in all the newspapers in the country, you gotta love it. All the parents from California to Germany know about it."

On the way over to the Hilton, Heathcote had sternly warned Johnson and Kelser not to say anything inflammatory, especially about Bird. Johnson was more than happy to heed that order. When someone asked him who he thought was the best player in college basketball, he didn't hesitate. "Larry Bird," he said. "I'm a fan of basketball and I'm a fan of Larry Bird, but I just have to make sure I don't get caught looking at him too much. . . . I guess I could say there's two of the best passers in the game in this matchup. It's what the whole world wants. Everyone wants to see the Magic Man against the Bird Man. It'll be something else. It will be a wild party." Some of the writers tried to criticize Bird for not being as gregarious as Magic, but Johnson came to his defense. "He comes from a different background than I do," Johnson said. "You can't knock him because he doesn't like attention."

The narrative was set. This was not a championship game between Michigan State and Indiana State. This was Magic against Bird, the best big man matchup in an NCAA final since Bill Russell led the University of San Francisco to a win over Tom Gola's LaSalle University in 1955. A flurry of headlines characterized it that way: "Bring on Bird" (*State Journal*); "Bird takes on the Magic Man" (*Dallas Morning News*); "Brace yourselves for the matchup: Bird vs. 'Magic'" (*Louisville Courier-Journal*). "These mano-a-mano things always appeal to sports fans," says Don Ohlmeyer, the former president of NBC Sports. "Magic and Bird were such attractive characters. I think it just captured people's imaginations."

Before Johnson and Bird left the Hilton, they briefly sat together for photographers. The occasion marked the first time the two of them had been photographed just by themselves. One picture was transmitted across the Associated Press wire, enabling it to be published in almost every sports section in America on Monday morning. It was a striking image: Magic's smile beamed from ear to ear, as if there were nowhere on earth he'd rather be. Larry leaned toward Magic awkwardly and proffered half a smile. They were both big men who were skilled passers and steadfast competitors. They both even wore the number 33. Yet that photograph told the broader story, quite literally in black and white: for all of their similarities, these two guys could not have been more different.

The only thing left was to find ways to fill the time until the game tipped off Monday night. Some of the Indiana State players went to see a movie on Sunday night. "When we got out of the theater, the Michigan State players were on the other side of the street," Bob

Heaton says. "We thought, Hey, those are the guys we're gonna play tomorrow night."

As game time neared, Carl Nicks understood that he would need to bring the toughness he learned while growing up on the playgrounds of Chicago. But he couldn't help but wonder if all of his teammates would exhibit that same mentality. "I think that me and Leroy and Alex, we were like, if Magic and them want to fight, we'll fight. But I didn't know what to expect from the white guys," Nicks says. "When you grow up in a city, you learn how to survive. You claw, you bite, you scratch, whatever it takes. I knew the guys from Indiana would play hard, but I just didn't know if deep down inside, they would have that type of mind-set."

On Sunday night, Johnson, Kelser, Vincent, and Payton played cards in the hotel, as always. Many of the visitors in town spent Sunday and Monday skiing, and a few attended a performance given by the Mormon Tabernacle Choir. The choir tried to pay homage to the big event by playing the Michigan State fight song, but it committed a major faux pas by playing the University of Michigan's "The Victors" instead. "Sunday and Monday really dragged," Bob Ryan says. "The anticipation for that game was electrifying. It was an atmosphere unlike any other Final Four I've been to, and I've been to more than twenty-five of them."

NBC was certainly ready. As per Don Ohlmeyer's instructions, Don McGuire had put together a pregame package on Magic and Bird, as well as a highlight reel that was going to run at halftime under the soundtrack to the song "Magic to Do" from the Broadway musical *Pippin*. To put together those segments, McGuire watched hours and hours of footage from the entire season. At that point, he had seen more of both Magic and Bird than anybody on the planet. "It was like looking at a great piece of art. Just play after play, and it wasn't just shooting. It was passing and dribbling," McGuire says. "The beauty of the way these guys played really captivated people. We just hadn't seen anything like it before."

Terry Donnelly's condition remained a concern for Michigan

State. The deep bruise he had suffered on his lower back during the win over Penn was severe enough to keep him out of practice on Sunday. Clint Thompson, the team's trainer, gave Donnelly a chemical application called DMSO that was supposed to help mask his pain. To make matters worse, Donnelly had contracted a bad virus overnight, and by Sunday afternoon he was running a 103-degree temperature. "From that afternoon on, all I had was like two pancakes," Donnelly says. "I was in bed all the way up until we got on the bus to go to the game. I wasn't sure I was going to make it because I was so dehydrated."

Jay Vincent, meanwhile, was also limited by his broken right foot, but he had decided to take a painkiller injection before the game. "We numbed it up," Vincent says. "That was the first time I had done that. It was like running out there on one foot."

Both teams conducted their standard game-day shootarounds on Monday, March 26, but as the hours passed before they headed over to the arena, Kelser developed a severe case of the butterflies. "The time was just going by so slowly. It was a snail's pace," he says. "You know where you are, what you're trying to accomplish as a group, and you're almost there. With every passing half hour, the nerves would just grow and grow. I think some nervousness is always good before a game, but this was quite unusual, so much so that I wondered if nature would take over and eventually quell itself."

Kelser didn't tell anyone how he was feeling, but Darwin Payton sensed the players were wound pretty tight. In his final pregame meeting of the season with Heathcote in the coach's hotel room, the student manager encouraged Heathcote to give his guys a chance to settle down once the game began. "The guys are more prepared and more up for this game than any game we've ever played," Payton told him. "If you could just be easier on them in the beginning of the game and allow them to play, they'll be ready."

If Magic was feeling as nervous as Kelser was, he did an excellent job of hiding it. "I just remember in warm-ups, he was incredibly confident," Mike Longaker says. Before the game, he told Johnson this game was the opportunity of a lifetime. "You bet it is," Magic said, "and when we win this game, remember that."

In the other locker room, Larry Bird was not projecting the same type of swagger. "Larry told me this was going to be our toughest game of the year," Brad Miley says. "He thought we could win, there's no doubt, but he knew we had met a team that gave us the biggest matchup problems."

Moreover, the grind of the season, the tournament, and the weekend appeared to be taking their toll on Bird. As he and Heaton were sitting on tables in the Indiana State training room getting their ankles taped by Bob Behnke and Rick Shaw, Bird turned to Heaton and asked, "You ready?"

"Yeah," Heaton said.

Bird replied, "I hope so, cuz, 'cause I ain't feeling it."

Heaton didn't think much of the comment, but Shaw was taken aback. "You better be feeling it, man," he said. "This is what we've been playing for." But Bird said nothing.

"That statement has stuck with me for all these years," Behnke says. "You don't think of Larry as sophisticated, but in a basketball sense he was. Larry had an insight about Michigan State that none of our guys did. I think he knew better than anyone else what we were getting into."

Good evening, everyone. Welcome to the Special Events Center on the campus of the University of Utah in Salt Lake City. I'm Bryant Gumbel and the fans here are going bananas. They actually think there's a doubleheader going on tonight. We do have one game. It's Indiana State against Michigan State. I say it's a doubleheader because there's a game within a game. You think Indiana State–Michigan State, you've got a Big Ten powerhouse against the unlikely dream of a school and a star that has come through thirty-three perfect outings. The game within a game? Well, you'd have had to live under a rock to have not heard about Magic Johnson or Larry Bird. How good are they? Let's put it this way.

They energize the entire floor. They not only complement all the people on their teams, they do in fact make their teams. . . .

Gumbel couldn't quite declare that the events about to unfold in Salt Lake City would be the most important thing that had happened in the world that day. After all, a few hours before tip-off, a Middle East peace agreement had been signed at the White House by President Jimmy Carter, Egyptian president Anwar Sadat, and Israeli prime minister Menachem Begin. Still, in a sporting context, at least, it was going to be a historic occasion.

As Gumbel spoke over a reel of Bird's highlights, he said, "If you haven't seen Bird, you're in for a treat." That statement spoke to the limited national exposure college basketball, and Bird in particular, had enjoyed to that point. It also underscored why the matchup would have such a lasting impact on the nation's consciousness. For many of the millions watching at home, this was their introduction to Larry Bird and Magic Johnson. And they were in for a treat.

There were, of course, going to be other players on the court, and Gumbel, Dick Enberg, Billy Packer, and Al McGuire talked about them during the pregame segment as well. When Packer mentioned Carl Nicks, NBC flashed a picture taken at that morning's shootaround of Packer standing next to Indiana State's guard. The photo was hilarious and showed what a good sport Packer could be: Nicks was wearing a T-shirt with the words "I'm with Stupid" printed on it. The finger underneath was pointed right at a smiling Packer.

Like just about everybody else in Salt Lake City, Packer and McGuire picked Michigan State to win the game. So did Ray Meyer, whose DePaul Blue Demons had defeated Penn in overtime in the just-completed third-place game. "Bird is one of the superstars of the game, but they have one on Indiana State, and Michigan State has two," Meyer told Enberg. "If they start to run with Michigan State, Michigan State will bury 'em."

Fortunately for Michigan State, Greg Kelser's nerves settled down just in time for the tip-off. As the game got under way, he relaxed further as he was able to take the measure of the Sycamores at close range. He felt the same rush of confidence he experienced in the first few minutes of the Spartans' regional final win over Notre Dame. "I knew as a team we were better than they were," Kelser says. "I even began to think to myself we had probably two or three teams in the Big Ten that were better. It's just that no one in our conference had a player of Larry's stature."

Kelser was also surprised at the outset to see that Bird had been assigned to guard him. Yes, Bird was much stronger than Kelser and was two or three inches taller, but he was also much slower. There was no way he could stay with Kelser eighteen feet from the basket. Indeed, on Michigan State's second possession, Kelser easily slipped by Bird on a backdoor cut. He took the pass from Johnson, but instead of driving for a layup he fed Ron Charles for an easy dunk. It was as if after playing with Magic Johnson for two years Kelser wanted to imitate him. Over the next few minutes, Kelser continued to exploit the matchup. He got two more easy assists, and he blew by Bird for a layup that gave the Spartans an early 11–8 lead.

Meanwhile, at the other end of the floor, Heathcote's "man-and-a-half" game plan was working beautifully. Whenever Bird cut across the lane, Charles, who was stationed in the back middle of the zone, stepped forward and bumped him. When Bird caught the ball on the wing, the guard on the top of the zone pinched over to help out his baseline teammate. Whenever Bird set up in the post, he had someone positioned directly in front and behind him. And when he did get the ball, it was difficult for him to find open cutters because the Spartans weren't running with them as they would have had they been playing man-to-man.

Even so, Bird had faced all kinds of junk defenses during his three years in college, and he had almost always found a way to dominate. That he wasn't doing so in this game was only partly attributable to Michigan State's zone. Bird was tired, he was frustrated, and he was just plain off his game. "Larry didn't say much, but I would look at him from time to time, and he didn't look the same. It concerned me big-time because he didn't get his flow going," Nicks says. "He forced shots. He missed shots he would make. He had a look on his face like, My God, I'm not playing my game. I'm letting you guys down. That was the first time I had seen that in him because all year long, couldn't nobody stop Larry. I'm telling you, nobody. I don't care who it is."

Bird picked up his second foul when he charged into Kelser with 7 minutes to play in the first half. To that point, he had made just three baskets. "Larry Bird's getting a little frustrated now because he can't find an opening in which he can get his offensive move started," Packer said. With their zone choking off Indiana State's offense, the Spartans steadily built a 9-point lead. They finally unspooled their first Magic-to-Kelser alley-oop that put them up 34–23 with 5 minutes left in the first half. Upon seeing that play, Heaton sat on the bench and thought to himself, *Man, nobody has done that to us all year.*

Michigan State was in control, but the game took a turn when Johnson picked up his third foul a minute later and had to leave the game. Indiana State had a hard time taking advantage the rest of the half, but with just 14 seconds remaining, Bird grabbed a defensive rebound and alertly shifted into Kelser's path. Kelser tried to avoid the collision, but he made just enough contact to send Bird to the floor. It was not an obvious foul, but Bird had forced the official to whistle Kelser for his third personal. "The guy had all the tricks," Kelser says. "His strength, his awareness, his feel, all the little nuances and savvy things that made up for his lack of foot speed. Even though he didn't shoot the ball as well as he would have liked to that night, he was still by far the best player we played against."

Normally automatic from the foul line, Bird sank only one of his two attempts. It was a fitting way to end a subpar first half in which he had shot just 4 for 11 from the floor and scored only 11 points. As a team, Indiana State had shot 37.9 percent (to Michigan State's 62.2 percent) and had made just 6 of 11 from the free throw line. "I think we were pretty pleased just being down by nine," Bird said years later. "We weren't playing well. I didn't hit many shots the first half. We knew we had to get back and stop the break, but we felt we had a good shot at winning it."

Bird may have been the only one on his team who felt so pleased at halftime. Indiana State had faced deficits before, most recently when it trailed Arkansas by 2 points during the Midwest Regional final. This situation, however, was different. "When we were down against Arkansas at halftime, we were thinking, it's not a big deal. We haven't put our press on. We're fine," Heaton says. "But this was something we hadn't experienced before, ever. We got into that locker room and it was like, Uh, okay, this is not Arkansas."

The Indiana State locker room was so small that Hodges had to step into the showers so he could huddle with his assistants. His primary concern was that his players were guarding Kelser too tightly on the perimeter. He much preferred Kelser to shoot jump shots than drive into the lane. Hodges also wanted to tweak the patterns Bird had been running in the half-court offense in hopes of breaking him free for better shots. Finally, Hodges told Nicks, who had shot 3 for 8 from the floor in the first half, that he needed to do a better job penetrating the Spartans' zone.

Over in the Spartans' locker room, Heathcote sensed that Indiana State would have to start shifting its defense more toward Johnson, who had 10 points in the first half despite sitting out the last 5 minutes. That meant someone else besides Kelser would have to make perimeter shots. Heathcote figured that person should be Terry Donnelly. This seemed like an unconventional choice. Not only had Donnelly averaged barely 6 points per game that season, but he was playing with a badly contused lower back and was still running a high fever. "I was really just trying to stay hydrated and conserve my energy so I could play," Donnelly says. "In a way it might have helped me because I wasn't all hyped up and off the charts like the rest of the guys. Being sick probably helped me calm down and stay more under control than I would have if I were at an emotional peak." As Heathcote addressed the team, he told Donnelly he should look to shoot the ball in the second half. It was the first time Donnelly could ever recall his coach saying that. Magic immediately jumped on the idea. "Yeah, and you can hit those shots, too. Just take 'em," he said.

Meanwhile, out on the floor Bryant Gumbel was hosting NBC's halftime show, the Pro Keds College Basketball Report. It was a primitive operation by modern standards. There was no set, no fancy props, no trappings at all. The only commercial presence was a blue and white sign with the words "Pro Keds" on it—and even that was pushed out of the frame as the camera zoomed in on Gumbel's face. After noting the point totals for Johnson, Kelser, and Bird, Gumbel said, "But perhaps the biggest story is the third team on the floor. The officials are calling 'em very close. Magic Johnson has three fouls, Gregory Kelser has three."

With Magic back on the floor, Michigan State started off the second half as impressively as it had begun the first. Kelser hit a turnaround jumper in the lane to put the Spartans up by 11. On their next possession, Johnson got by Brad Miley and started to drive to the lane. Just as Heathcote predicted, Steve Reed cheated toward the middle to block Magic's path, leaving Donnelly wide open on the right wing. Johnson passed to Donnelly, identified by Enberg as someone who "rarely shoots." The six-foot-two lefty swished a seventeen-footer to give Michigan State a 41–28 lead, its largest of the game.

Over the next minute, Bird had two of his best looks of the night but missed them both. He was now 4 for 13 from the floor. In between those attempts, Ron Charles had hit a free throw to put Michigan State up by 14. After Bird's second miss, he got his own rebound and jumped up to shoot, but instead of firing another jumper he tried to dribble and committed a turnover as he came to the floor and grabbed hold of the ball. Hodges called time-out to settle down his troops. As the Spartans ran to their huddle, Magic shouted, "We got this!"

After the teams traded baskets, Magic, again facing a double team, threw the ball up top to Kelser, who swung it left to a wide-open Donnelly. Swish. After Heaton countered with a jumper from the right corner, Donnelly nailed another one from fifteen feet. Magic ran up to Donnelly, slapped him on his rear, and said he would keep feeding him the ball. "He gave me a lot of confidence," Donnelly says. "He used to do that in practice. Earvin liked to focus on one guy who was hot and keep going to him. It usually wasn't me, but in that instance it was."

Donnelly's latest bucket gave Michigan State a 48–32 lead, and it looked like the game was about to turn into another Spartans runaway. With just over 15 minutes to play, however, Kelser committed his fourth foul when he charged into Bird. Heathcote immediately summoned him to the bench and replaced him with Jay Vincent. "I don't want to hurt the Magic fans, but I think Greg Kelser is the most important man on the Spartans," Al McGuire said.

Seizing on the opportunity, Hodges decided to put on his full-court press. Slowly but steadily, the Sycamores chipped away at the deficit. Nicks drilled a shot from seventeen feet to cut the margin to 14. Donnelly answered yet again—his fourth make in as many tries—but after Heaton sank another bucket, Magic threw an unwise lob pass to Mike Brkovich against the press, which led to a turnover. Bird was fouled, giving him a chance to trim the margin to 12, but he again went 1 for 2 from the foul line. Said Enberg, "Boy, that's not the Larry Bird who has shot Indiana State to a 33–0 year."

Heeding Hodges's halftime instructions to penetrate more, Nicks drove the lane and fed Leroy Staley for a layup to bring Indiana State to within 50–39. Now it was Heathcote's turn to call time-out. When Donnelly committed a careless turnover in the Spartans' half-court offense on the ensuing possession, McGuire said, "Greg Kelser means so much to Michigan State that it's frightening."

Indiana State clearly had the momentum now and continued its run. Bird hit a turnaround jumper to make it 50–41. A Magic Johnson basket was followed by Jay Vincent's fourth foul. After a free throw from Bird, Nicks made a steal and a basket to bring the Sycamores to within 8. Another turnover by Johnson led to a tough layup by Bird, with Charles hanging all over him. Amazingly, Indiana State was now within 6 points with 9 minutes still to play. Their fans were screaming like mad.

As Kelser sat on the bench and watched the Sycamores make their run, he had flashbacks to the previous year's regional final loss to Kentucky, when the Spartans led by 7 early in the second half but ended up losing by 3. "We let things slip away against Kentucky because of our conservativeness," he says. "When I went to the bench with the fourth foul, we became very conservative. I sat there and not only watched our run get cut off, but now we were in jeopardy of maybe even losing the game. That was not easy."

Hodges was naturally excited by the comeback, but he was also concerned. He could see his players were exhausted. For a brief moment, he considered calling a time-out to give them a chance to catch their breath. But coaches are programmed never to interrupt a game when their own team is on a run, so he decided to let them go. It was a decision he would come to regret. "That was one time I didn't go with my gut feeling," he says. "I actually started to call the time-out but decided not to."

Heathcote had seen enough. He sent Kelser back into the game. Over the next few minutes, the Spartans were unable to build another big lead, but at least they stopped throwing away possessions against the press. The teams traded baskets for the next 3 minutes. Then, with Michigan State holding a 7-point advantage with under 6 minutes to play, Heathcote sent them into their patented spread offense. They worked the ball around for almost an entire minute until Kelser found Johnson on a backdoor cut down the middle of the lane. As Heaton shifted over to try to draw the charge, Magic rose up and dunked emphatically. The guys on the Michigan State bench went nuts. "We were all freaking out," says Edgar Wilson, the graduate assistant. "He really couldn't jump, and normally he would have done his customary finger roll. But the only way he was going to score was to dunk in the guy's mug. That's what separates him from anybody I've ever been around."

The Spartans had more reason to celebrate than they immediately realized. Not only did Heaton not draw the charge, but the referee Hank Nichols called a flagrant foul on Heaton, which gave Johnson not one but two additional free throws. It was a strange call considering Heaton had ended up on his back while Johnson walked away from the play all smiles. It was even stranger considering the same call had been made by a different official against Reed in the first half when Brkovich dunked over him on a fast break. Neither Heathcote nor Hodges could remember a single flagrant foul call being made all season. Now, in the national championship game, they had seen two. "It's a very difficult call," McGuire said. "Unless you've been calling it all year, to start calling it during a championship game I don't think is right."

Of course, Indiana State didn't have much cause to complain about the officiating considering its comeback had been fueled by the Spartans' foul troubles. But when Johnson made both free throws to put Michigan State up 61–50 with 5:05 to play, the game was that much further out of reach. "I don't believe in a breaking point in a basketball game, but that play sure broke my heart," Hodges said later.

The Sycamores were not used to trailing by such a big margin that late in the game, but the Spartans were plenty accustomed to playing with a lead. Moreover, when Indiana State did have a chance to make a move, it failed to take advantage. After Nicks made two free throws to cut the score to 61–54, Bird rebounded a Reed miss and found himself with a wide-open look in the lane. In his effort to loft the ball over Kelser's outstretched hand, however, Bird overshot it badly. He slammed his hand against his thigh in frustration. Alex Gilbert got the rebound for Indiana State and was fouled by Charles—his fifth—but Gilbert missed the front end of a one-and-one. The Sycamores would end up 10 for 22 from the foul line on the night. "You still have to shoot free throws," Enberg said. "It's still fifteen feet away, and Indiana State has not been able to hit their charities. That's the difference in this game."

The Spartans were inching their way toward a title, but you couldn't tell it by looking at Heathcote. As he squirmed on the Michigan State bench in his dark green blazer, green tie, and an atrocious pair of green plaid pants, the coach looked like a man who was having his prostate examined. He turned to his assistant Dave Harshman and said, "This is hard."

Harshman couldn't help but laugh. "Did you think it was going to be easy?" he said.

The Spartans executed their spread offense with their standard efficiency, and they made enough free throws down the stretch to keep the Sycamores at bay. Over on the Indiana State sidelines, Bill Hodges knew that the season's dream ending was slipping away. "I'd never had that feeling as a head coach," he says. "You have to keep battling, but it was definitely a feeling of desperation."

As the game entered the final minute, Heathcote finally allowed himself to enjoy what was happening. He started making his way down the Spartans' bench, shaking hands and embracing everyone on the team. The first person he thanked was Darwin Payton. "More than anything else, that made me feel good about my relationship with Jud," Payton says. "It was like a father being proud of his son for an accomplishment."

With the seconds ticking away, NBC announced Johnson as the game's most valuable player. "If I could put a name on the back of his uniform, I would write 'Joy,'" Enberg said. When Johnson was fouled with 16 seconds remaining, he slapped five with Kelser and held on to Kelser's hand. Johnson then put his left hand on Kelser's head, the two exchanged a few words, and they embraced. It was a moving display of fellowship.

The only thing left to be decided was the final score. Once again, Johnson and Kelser had the last say. After Steve Reed rushed downcourt and buried a jumper with 5 seconds remaining to cut the

Spartans' margin to 9, Johnson grabbed the ball as it came through the net and shouted, "Go, Greg!" Kelser instantly took off for the other basket. With his back still turned, Johnson threw the ball blindly over his left shoulder, and it landed softly into Kelser's hands at midcourt. With nothing standing between him and the basket, Kelser ran through a variety of options in his mind for how he was going to dunk. He even momentarily considered doing a 360-degree leap. "You'd be surprised how quickly these things will flash in your head," he says. "I decided to go with something fairly safe because it just would not have seemed right to miss it." So he cradled the ball in his right hand and flushed it through as the clock reached zero.

The final score was Michigan State 75, Indiana State 64. The Sycamores' perfect season had ended imperfectly. And the Spartans were national champs.

The Michigan State players and coaches embraced and celebrated all over the court. Bird shook hands with a few of them, including Magic, and then slunk to the Indiana State bench. Somehow, Don McGuire, the NBC producer, made his way through the madness and found Magic. "Hey, what's up?!" Magic said, greeting him like old friends meeting up on a street corner. McGuire shuffled Magic through the crowd to where Gumbel was positioned along the baseline. A moment later, Jud Heathcote was standing alongside them.

Taking the throw from Enberg, Gumbel said, "Thank you, Dick. I am with two very, very happy people, Magic and Jud. Magic, not only were you a leader on offense, I thought you did a good job on Larry Bird in the zone denying him the ball."

Still gasping for air, Johnson replied, "Coach gave us a good game plan to go against Larry Bird, and all we had to do was go out and do it. And if we did it, he said we would win. That's what we done."

"Jud, I know you didn't count on Larry Bird hitting as poorly from the field as he did. Were you surprised they didn't try to force the ball into him more?"

"I think that we had a man and a half on him, Bryant, and it was tough to get it in," Heathcote said. "I thought maybe they could have gone to him a little more, but I think they worked the ball. Hey, this was a tough, tough game for us. They gave us all we wanted. We're just very, very happy to win."

Gumbel ended by asking Magic if he had just played his final college game. "I can't really say," Johnson answered. "As far as I know, right now I'll be back. Everybody's got the rumor I'm leaving, but I haven't said that."

A minute later, Gumbel was joined by Bill Hodges, who had just suffered the first loss of his head coaching career. "I'm standing with a very disappointed Bill Hodges, who concluded a super season in the worst way for him. You had trouble penetrating the Michigan State zone, didn't you?"

"First of all, Bryant, you're wrong—I'm not disappointed," Hodges said. "The Lord blessed us with a great year, and I'm extremely happy with that. I think it's not a matter of how much trouble we had with their zone. It's just, you know if we had hit our free throws, it would have been a heck of a basketball game. We had a much better free throw percentage than that [during the season]. If it had been tight, you know, and we had a chance to win, I think maybe we would have. But we can't be disappointed. Our guys played great all year. They never gave up, and I don't think they ever will."

The viewers at home had heard from all of the principals but one. Gumbel might have preferred to speak with the last before NBC went off the air, but at that moment the network had something that was worth a thousand words: a picture, beamed to the largest audience in the history of the sport, of Larry Bird sitting on the Indiana State bench, his face buried in a white towel.

The Sycamores couldn't leave the court until the completion of the awards presentation, where they received their second-place trophy and individual mementos. As Bird continued to sit with his face in a towel, Rick Shaw, the manager and assistant trainer, knelt in front of him and tried to console him. A gaggle of photographers crowded the bench, prompting assistant coach Mel Daniels to shout, "Can't you give us some damned privacy!" Finally, Brad Miley came over to Bird, looked down at him, and said, "C'mon, man, let's get that trophy. Thirty-three and one. A hell of a year. Get up."

Once the players retreated to the sanctuary of their locker room, they sat for a while in total silence. "It was the quietest locker room I've ever been in," Terry Thimlar, the assistant coach, says. Hodges mustered a few words about how they should feel proud, but they fell on deaf ears.

Bird was inconsolable. Not only had he just played—and lost—his final college game, but he had turned in by far his worst performance of the season. He finished with 19 points on 7 for 21 shooting. He went 5 for 8 from the foul line, committed 6 turnovers, and had a season-low 2 assists. "It was the biggest game of our lives, and it was so close," Bird said years later. "Coming from Terre Haute after leaving IU, I wanted so bad to bring that championship trophy home to 'em. It wasn't really the feeling I had about losing the game. It was about, all of a sudden, my career. I'm done at Indiana State. I had four good years there, and I enjoyed it. Just knowing that was coming to the end was pretty tough at the time."

Bird was by rule supposed to attend the postgame press conference, but Ed McKee, the Indiana State sports information director, knew that wasn't going to happen. Late in the second half, when it became apparent that Michigan State was going to win, McKee passed a notice along press row stating that Bird would not be available to the media. After the game, Wayne Duke of the NCAA pleaded with McKee to try to convince Bird to come to the press conference, but McKee told him, "He's not going to do it. You can do whatever you want, he's not going to do it."

McKee figured he had to at least get a statement from Larry, so he went into the locker room. He found Larry huddled by himself in the trainers' room, overcome with emotion. "He was weeping uncontrollably," McKee says. "I was sitting with him saying, 'I'm not going to ask you to go out there, but we've got to give these people something.' I asked him a few questions, and he was trying to stop crying. He managed to give me a few short answers."

McKee strung those answers to compose a statement from Bird that McKee distributed to the media: "Michigan State is an excellent team. They play very tough defense and had a real good zone. Unfortunately, the ball wouldn't drop for us and we missed too many free throws. I hate to lose, just like all the other guys on our team, but I guess we did all right. We won thirty-three games. We gave it the best we had, we just didn't hit the shots. It's been a long season, but I'd like to play Michigan State again. It certainly could be a different story."

Over in the Spartans' locker room, a different mood prevailed. The players poured water and soda on each other, and they tossed Darwin Payton into the shower, ruining the spiffy three-piece suit he had purchased the week before. Kelser and Johnson would have liked to have stayed and celebrated some more with their teammates, but they were quickly shuttled down the hall with Heathcote to meet with the media.

"We are elated," said Heathcote, who called his defensive strategy against Bird "an adjustment and a prayer." "I kept thinking every one of Bird's shots would go in. He did not have a good shooting night. Our pressure on him might have been a factor, and he just had one of those nights every player has."

"This place is glamorous. You've just got to love it," said Johnson, who had 24 points, 7 rebounds, and 5 assists in the victory. Asked yet again whether he was going to enter the NBA draft, Johnson replied, "I still don't know. I've got to enjoy this first. Then maybe in a couple of weeks I'll make up my mind."

Much of the postgame coverage touched on the surprising role that Terry Donnelly had played in the win. He made all 5 of his field goal attempts during the game, including 4 for 4 in the second half, and finished with 15 points. "Coach Heathcote told me that if Indiana State started overshifting, I might be left alone and that I should be ready to shoot," he said. "I usually don't shoot very much in a game, but the more they left me open, the more excited I got because I was hitting them." Kelser was not the least bit shocked by Donnelly's performance. "Terry was one of the better shooters on the team," he says. "He played a role, and the way Coach designed things wasn't necessarily meant for him, but we knew if he was left open he could shoot."

Just as he had done in his interview with Bryant Gumbel, Bill Hodges tried to put on his best face for the media. "Anyone disappointed with our success has to be a lesser man than I. These players are a team, a unit, a family. I love every one of them," he said. Hodges also had the unfortunate duty to inform the writers that Bird was not going to be speaking further that night. "After the game, I asked Larry if he wanted to come. He said no. I told him he had given his just due and he could just relax. Larry Bird has had a great career for us. His silence might not make everybody happy, but he does all of his talking on the floor. He's a tremendous person and he has nothing but my best wishes."

While Hodges addressed the media, Steve Reed stood barefoot in the hallway outside the Indiana State locker room and spoke of Bird's unselfishness. "He should have kept shooting the ball, but Larry Bird is that type of player," Reed said. "Coach Hodges has begged him to shoot more against a zone, but he kept trying to find the open man to dump off to tonight and he forced some passes he ordinarily wouldn't." Brad Miley added that he thought Bird was "really tired. I think that accounted for his poor shooting night." Alex Gilbert uncharitably dismissed Michigan State as "a good team, but not an exceptionally great one," while Carl Nicks griped about the officiating. "It was all very frustrating," he said, standing in the tunnel wearing a cowboy hat pulled low. "We'd get these cheap fouls called on us, then Michigan State commits murder and nothing happens."

Bird, meanwhile, had to go through the awkward routine of getting showered and dressed in a roomful of people who wanted to talk to him. When a writer approached him, Bird brushed him off by saying, "I've got to go to the training room." He later hurried through a crowded hallway to get to the bus saying, "Gettin' ready to go. Excuse me, got to go." As he rushed past, one press wag cracked, "Bird flew the coop."

"He's a sensitive guy," Daniels said. "It's going to take some time to make that transition. I'm sure when it comes, he'll accept you guys. Give him a fair shake."

As the Spartans were closing up their locker room, Heathcote overheard one writer trying to goad a few of his players into saying something highly critical of Bird. "You better cut that out or I'm going to throw you out of here," Heathcote told the reporter. "If you're looking for something to write, just write that Magic Johnson and Larry Bird are going to be two of the best players in the NBA for a long time."

In an odd way, all the hype that had fueled the runup to the game contributed to a feeling of disappointment afterward. It wasn't just that it was over. The reality was, it had not been a very good game. It wasn't particularly well played—it certainly wasn't well officiated—and though it was competitive for most of the second half, it did not end in dramatic fashion. "It was an electric moment to be there, but I think everybody was waiting for something that just never happened," says *Sports Illustrated's* Bruce Newman. "It was supposed to be this colossal showdown, and it ended up being almost a blowout."

Once the Sycamores climbed aboard the team bus, their mood started to lift. Bob Behnke, who was sitting one row behind Hodges, leaned forward and said, "You know, Coach, we're never going to get to this level again. Let's enjoy it." Hodges turned his head and replied, "There are a lot of guys who are better coaches than me who are not going to get to where we just were."

As the players rode in relative quiet, their disappointment gave way to appreciation and even relief. "I was thinking, no more practice, no more games, no more watching film," Heaton says. "Not to pat us on the back, but I remembered that a year ago I was watching Duke and Kentucky play [in the final], and now a lot of people had just watched us play. That's what went through my mind. It's over, and we did pretty well."

When they arrived back at the Hotel Utah, the team was greeted by hundreds of folks from Terre Haute who were ready to party. It didn't take much prodding to get the players to join in on the fun. "It's hard to be upset if you've won thirty-three games in a year and lost one," Steve Reed says. Even Bird lightened up and enjoyed himself. He spent much of the night holding court in a corner of the room, cheerfully downing beers, signing autographs, posing for pictures, and mingling with his fans and friends.

Not everybody was in a celebratory mood, however. At one point, Hodges stood with Richard Landini, the university's president, and John Wooden. When Wooden, who had coached for two seasons at Indiana State, complimented Hodges on a great season and said it didn't matter that they had come up short, Landini interrupted him by grumbling, "We should have won." Hodges was taken aback. "I should have quit right then," he says.

Ironically, the team that truly had reason to celebrate was not in much of a partying mood. After the game, Jud Heathcote told his players that they had just accomplished something that would become even more meaningful as time went on. He told them there would be no curfew that night. He wanted them to enjoy themselves. After he finished speaking, Kelser walked up to Heathcote and said, "Coach, we're all exhausted. We're going to bed."

When the Michigan State players got back to their hotel, Donnelly, who was still running a high fever, immediately went to his room and collapsed. Several of the other players hung out in Darwin Payton's room and drank beers that he had waiting for them in a bathtub full of ice. Eventually, there was a knock at the door. It was Walter Kelser, Greg's father. He told them there was a roomful of people across the street who had come a long way to see the Spartans play. "I know you all are tired," he said, "but if you could just go over there and put in a quick appearance, it would really give them a thrill." The players obliged and followed Mr. Kelser across the street. The show was over, but the champs had just enough energy for one last curtain call.

12

The Spartans began enjoying the public's adulation before they even got home. Their flight to Lansing on Tuesday morning connected through Chicago, and as they walked through the terminal at O'Hare hundreds of strangers applauded. Upon returning to Capital City Airport, they were greeted on the tarmac by some fifteen hundred fans. Another ten thousand waited for them in Jenison Fieldhouse for a welcome home rally while several thousand people stood outside the gym because there wasn't enough room.

"Wow!" Earvin Johnson said as he stepped to the microphone amid chants of "Two more years!" "This is really something. I'd like to thank all of you. We went to Salt Lake City with a job to do and we came back with a championship."

The next day, nearly fifteen thousand people turned out in a cold drizzle to watch the big victory parade. The Spartans' route began at the Frandor Shopping Center, trekked three miles down Michigan Avenue, and ended up at the state capitol building. Johnson and Kelser rode in an open Volkswagen convertible, trailed by a fire truck carrying the rest of the team. At one point, police momentarily lost control of the crowd, and the two of them were besieged. "My arm was nearly pulled out of my socket," Johnson said later. "I've never seen anything like this before."

Though there were limits to how often the people of Lansing would turn out—an "Appreciation Night" for local natives Johnson, Jamie Huffman, Jay Vincent, and Greg Lloyd drew just eighty-five people to a local high school gym—the team's annual Basketball Bust, held four days after the championship game, stirred unprecedented interest. All 1,760 seats were scooped up, marking the event's first-ever sellout, and a local television station aired the entire ceremony live. When Johnson was awarded the team MVP as voted upon by his players, he quipped, "I really wish that Gregory would have received this award. I wish I could give it to him but it's got my name on it."

Al McGuire was the evening's guest speaker. When he repeated his assertion that he thought Kelser was the most important player on the team, Magic and Heathcote looked at each other, and Heathcote winked. They knew better. Heathcote has since said he believes Kelser felt a tinge of jealousy for having been so consistently overshadowed by Magic (which was understandable), but the respect and affection the two teammates expressed for each other was palpable. Kelser was a senior, and most everyone believed Johnson was probably headed for the NBA as well.

"Those two were the embodiment of kids who really came from good parental stock," Lynn Henning says. "In Earvin's case, I never really saw him get churlish. There was no downside. For a kid who was that young and ballyhooed, he had a rare ability to keep things together."

There was also a lot of celebrating going on that week at NBC's headquarters in New York. The Nielsen rating for the NCAA final had come in at a cool 24.1. It was the highest rating any basketball game had ever received, but because it was within range of the numbers the tournament had been generating the previous couple of years, it was natural to assume there were bigger ratings to come. "We never really put that rating into perspective until years later," says Rex Lardner, NBC Sports' programming chief. "The game gave the public and consumers across America the idea that college basketball was becoming more of a national sport."

Indeed, people were only beginning to realize the ramifications of what had happened. In Bird's case, not all of the reaction came in the form of praise. Some members of the press took Bird to the woodshed for his decision not to face their music after the loss. New York *Daily News* columnist Dick Young called Bird a "spoiled brat" while Ray Fitzgerald of the *Boston Globe* warned Bird that his impending arrival in Boston could be unpleasant. "If he thinks he's merely moving to a bigger version of Terre Haute, where his basketball life was one big pat on the back and 'you're a wunnerful kid, Larry, and we loved you against Wichita State,' he's in for an abrupt awakening." Ten writers, in a blatant act of petulance, left Bird off their all-tournament ballots listing the top five players at the Final Four.

Even Indiana coach Bob Knight wondered if Bird would wilt under the klieg lights of the NBA without the benefit of the support system that had shielded him at Indiana State. "I think it's important what city he plays in," Knight said. "In some cities, it could all come down around him."

But the pockets of negative coverage didn't diminish the reception Bird and his teammates received when they returned to Terre Haute on Tuesday afternoon. As the players disembarked from their plane, four Air National Guard F-100 jets saluted them with a flyover. Some five thousand fans greeted them at the airport, and thousands more lined the streets to wave at their bus as it made its way down the five-mile route to the Hulman Center. "I remember saying to someone, "Man, you think there's gonna be enough people at the Hulman Center?'" Heaton says.

He needn't have worried. As the players walked down the tunnel, they emerged into an arena that was jam-packed with more than twelve thousand screaming fans. "That first glimpse of all the people in there was amazing. I'm getting shivers down my spine just thinking about it," Steve Reed says. The players bounded onto the stage like rock stars. Handing the NCAA's runner-up trophy to President Landini, Bird said, "I'd like to present this so-called second place trophy to the city of Terre Haute."

To the rest of the world, Bird may have come off as introverted and aloof, but now, in front of his home audience, he was a pure ham. He assumed the emcee duties and introduced all the coaches and players, taking every opportunity to wield his ever-sharp needle. "You know what I like about all these guys? Not a damn thing," he said. "I'd like to talk about Coach Hodges. Let me tell you, Bill Hodges ain't a third of the coach that Coach King is. When he first came here, Coach Hodges wore a size seven-and-a-half hat. Now he wears a size ten." Bringing Mel Daniels to the microphone, Bird continued, "I'm sure y'all remember Mel Daniels playing. Well keep those memories 'cause he can't play no more." When the trainer Bob Behnke said, "There will never be another Larry Bird," Bird replied, "You know, that's what I like about Doc Behnke. He knows what he's talking about."

The act was in good fun, but it degenerated into something more appropriate for a locker room than an arena full of young children, not to mention a live statewide radio audience. Terry Thimlar's allusion to the flying toilet paper in Salt Lake City led Bird to tell a scatological joke about what that paper was really used for. Rick Shaw called Bird "the meanest sonofabitch in the Valley." After tossing out another good-natured insult, Bird smiled to the crowd and said, "I guess that's why they call me the prick from French Lick."

The behavior prompted the *Spectator*, the local weekly magazine, which had written nary a critical word in three years, to publish an editorial chastising the team. "We cannot ask that the team play better basketball next year," the editorial read. "We can ask, though, that they not demean their own standards of excellence nor their standing as persons worthy of public respect by injudicious public language. Think about it."

A few days later, Bird returned to his hometown for a reception held in his honor at the French Lick Hilton. The guest speaker was none other than Billy Packer. During his speech, Packer removed his coat and tie and revealed that he was wearing a T-shirt that read, "ISU #1." As the audience roared its approval, Packer cracked, "This fat little Polock from Pennsylvania finally found a way to get McGuire off his back."

The grandest fete of all took place at Hulman Center on April 27, when the school, sensing a prime fund-raising opportunity, staged a "Larry Bird Appreciation Night." More than one thousand guests paid fifty dollars each for a dinner of beef steak and cold duck, and they were treated to a seventeen-minute multimedia presentation that used twenty slide projectors and six movie cameras to beam the show onto a screen as long as the court. Bird received a key to the city of Terre Haute from the mayor ("I thought he should have given me the jail key in case I need it tonight," Bird said), as well as a letter of congratulations from Indiana governor Otis Bowen. "The governor didn't show up tonight and I didn't show up at his dinner last night," Bird said. "So now we're even."

The dinner raised twenty-two thousand dollars to fund a scholarship that was to be awarded to a student from Bird's native Springs Valley region who demonstrated academic and athletic excellence. Bob King also announced that Indiana State was going to retire Bird's No. 33 jersey, the first time the school had ever done that. When Bird, who was the only Indiana State player not in formal attire, took his turn at the podium, he was once again relaxed and witty (and, for the most part, well behaved). When he recognized his family members who were present, Bird recalled the first time he spotted his mother sitting in an upper-level seat at an Indiana State game. "I noticed that as I scored more points and got more rebounds, she got seats closer to the court," he said. Bird also noted that his Granny Kerns was also in attendance. "I was talking to my brother before this banquet and I told him I never knew what I might say," he said. "So I told him he should be sure and steal Granny's hearing aid."

Turning serious, Bird said, "It was a great pleasure playing at Indiana State. I had some ups and downs. Next year, regardless of what happens, I hope you are behind them a hundred percent." That comment completed a wonderful send-off for a once-in-a-lifetime player. It also marked the beginning of Indiana State's plunge back to reality. "It was more sad for me than anything else," Carl Nicks says. "I knew this guy was gone, and I didn't want it to end. I was like, What are we going to do next year?"

Earvin Johnson sat in his East Lansing apartment and fielded questions from Doug Looney, a writer from *Sports Illustrated*. Looney was in town to write about Johnson's impending decision over whether to turn pro. It was hard for Looney to get answers, however, because the telephone would not stop ringing. "Hello?" Johnson said, lifting the receiver. "Donna? Donna who?"

"Excuse me," Johnson said to Looney. "I guess I decide by thinking that, well, my dream—"

Ring. "Renee? Renee who?"

"Excuse me. My dream is to play in the NBA and—"

Ring. "Lisa? Lisa who?"

Finally, he unplugged the phone. "One thing I'm always going to do is have fun," Magic said. "There is time for business, time for school and time for fun. You know, things can be happening at a party before I get there, but when I show up they just happen more."

Life had been one big party since Johnson led the Spartans to the NCAA championship, but now he was trying to get down to business. From a purely financial standpoint, his decision was a no-brainer. Johnson was guaranteed to be one of the top picks, if not the number one pick, in the upcoming NBA draft. Still, there were some people who doubted whether he could carry his college success into the pros. After all, he did not have a natural position—there was no way a six-foot-eight forward could play point guard full-time in the NBA, right?—and he had some very real limitations, from his lack of explosiveness and speed to his apparent inability to drain long-range shots. "He is not superstar material for the NBA," Joe Falls wrote in the *Detroit News*. "Maybe he can grow into it. But he isn't there yet, and some NBA scouts wonder if he will ever get there."

"I think at least half of his appeal is his enthusiasm," said Pat Williams, who at the time was the general manager of the Philadelphia 76ers. "But you have to remember that happiness and glow and joy often turn to dust in our league." Another league executive told Looney flatly, "He will not turn around a franchise."

Still, Johnson was not one to suffer from a lack of confidence. When he met with Heathcote to discuss his situation, the coach told him, "You and I might be the only two people who know how good you really are. So we're not going to even discuss the basketball part of it because you will start for whoever drafts you. Let's talk about all the other things you need to consider."

It was those other things that were giving Johnson pause. He may have looked and played like a grown man, but in reality he was a nineteen-year-old kid who had never lived away from home. The town of Lansing tugged at him, just as it had pulled him to Michigan State out of high school even though Michigan was a much better basketball school. When Johnson worked at a basketball clinic in town the week after the NCAA championship game, a youngster made him tear up by asking plaintively, "My daddy said you're going to leave us. Is that true?" A Michigan State booster raised twelve hundred dollars to place a full-page ad in the student newspaper asking Johnson to stay. His mother, Christine, also wanted Earvin to remain in school so he could get his degree. Then there was the matter of the 1980 Olympic Games in Moscow. Since professionals were not eligible to compete in those days, it appeared the only way Johnson was going to fulfill his dream of playing at the Olympics was to return for his junior season.

Dreams aside, Johnson possessed a clear-eyed understanding of the business of professional basketball. He also recognized how his value stacked up against the player with whom he was already being inextricably linked. "I don't think I'm worth as much as Bird," Johnson said. "Let's be honest. He played longer, has got the experience and the accolades and, besides, wow, he's a white superstar. Basketball sure needs him."

If this was going to be a business decision, then Johnson needed to find out just how much he was worth. So he, his father, and Charles Tucker, his longtime mentor and soon-to-be agent, flew to Los Angeles in early May to meet with Jack Kent Cooke, the owner of the Los Angeles Lakers. The Lakers were a very good team that had reached the Western Conference semifinals that season, but they had been given the top pick in the draft that had belonged to the Utah Jazz as compensation for Gail Goodrich's decision to leave L.A. and sign a free-agent contract with the Jazz. (When the Jazz finished the season tied with the Chicago Bulls for the worst record in the league, the Lakers then won a coin flip with the Bulls to secure the top pick.) Cooke had his sights set on Magic, but first they had to agree to a contract that would lure him away from Michigan State.

Johnson went to Los Angeles believing he was worth $500,000 per year. When Cooke offered him $400,000, Johnson said no thanks and told Cooke he was going back to school. Cooke asked the three of them to stay overnight in town on his dime, and they resumed negotiations in the morning. Cooke tried to convince Johnson to sign for $460,000, but he eventually relented and met Johnson's asking price. Magic knew the money was great, but the deal also offered him a chance to join a playoff team that boasted the best center in the league in Kareem Abdul-Jabbar. Magic had already taken Everett High School and Michigan State from also-rans to champions. He was ready to join a winner for once.

First, though, he had to torture himself before finalizing his decision. The NBA's deadline for underclassmen to declare their intentions was May 11. As the date got closer, Johnson started to get cold feet. The day before his press conference, he went to Jud Heathcote's office and told the coach he wanted to meet. "No, that's all right," the coach said. "I'll find out tomorrow just like everyone else." Says Heathcote, "I was hoping his heart would over-rule his mind."

That night, Johnson stood in his driveway talking to Mick Mc-Cabe, the writer from the *Detroit Free Press*. When Johnson's father got home, Earvin jumped up and moved his car out of the driveway because it was parked in his father's space. "He was just a really good kid," McCabe says. It wasn't until 4 a.m., as he sat in a se-cluded spot that only he knew about, that Earvin fully arrived at his decision.

At 10:15 in the morning on Friday, May 11, Johnson walked into a room in the basement of Michigan State's University Club wearing blue jeans and a gray T-shirt and announced to the world what had long seemed inevitable. "Next season I'll be applying for hardship to turn pro," he said. "I thought it was best for me. I haven't really had as much time as I'd like but this is the deadline and it was a tough decision. I just thought it would be a challenge going to the NBA and testing my skills." Someone asked Heathcote what he would do now that Earvin was leaving. "I thought of two things, vomit or suicide," Heathcote replied. "I still may do both."

On June 25, 1979, the Lakers made Johnson the first pick in the NBA draft. Greg Kelser was selected fourth overall by the Detroit Pistons, who were coached by the man who once tried to recruit Kelser to the University of Detroit, Dick Vitale. After Johnson signed his contract with the Lakers, one of the first things he did was buy a beautiful blue Mercedes. He bought the car in Illinois and drove it back to Lansing. Before returning to Michigan State, he stopped off at Everett High. He purposely parked the car on the front lawn so the school's security guard, John the Narc, the guy who always told John-son he wouldn't amount to anything, would have to come out and tell him to move it. As John approached the car, Magic rolled down the window and flashed a smile. "John, is that you?" he said. "I guess I didn't amount to anything, did I?"

Later that spring, Johnson finished his semester at Michigan

State, packed his belongings, and took off for Hollywood. It wasn't easy cutting the umbilical cord. The day he left for Los Angeles was the first time he saw his father cry.

Once again, Larry Bird had the opportunity to fly away from Terre Haute and join the Boston Celtics. Red Auerbach had invited Bird to join the team as soon as the basketball season was over, but Bird opted to stay in school. He was determined to graduate and, besides, he was having too much fun.

As part of Bird's requirements to complete his degree in education, he had to serve a stint as a student teacher. So on Monday, April 2, he showed up at 7:45 a.m. at West Vigo High School, where he worked for the physical education teacher and served as an assistant coach for the varsity baseball team. Bird's presence on the coaching staff made West Vigo's games quite the local happening. When one of their opponents advertised Bird's appearance, several hundred people showed up for the privilege of watching Larry stand on the field and coach third base.

Bird was so committed to his student teaching that he skipped the Wooden Award ceremony in Los Angeles, where he would have received yet another trophy as national player of the year. He also insisted to West Vigo's baseball coach, Dick Ballenger, that he personally cut the grass on the field. Nodding to where Bird was riding his mower in the distance one day, Ballenger said to a friend, "I've got the only millionaire lawn mower in the world."

The paternity suit that Jan Condra, Bird's ex-wife, had filed against him was still pending in the local courts, but he had long settled into a serious relationship with Dinah Mattingly, the girl whom he was dating when he broke up with Condra for good during his sophomore year. "I don't know how many times that poor girl stood under the basket and passed the ball back to me," Bird said of the woman who would become his wife in 1989. "Over and over, standing there, throwing it back to me so I could shoot. 'Course we've gotten in a lot of beer drinking together, too."

Bird also communicated, in his own quiet way, an appreciation for the many people who had tried to make his time in Terre Haute a little easier. When Ed McKee, the sports information director who was so often the butt of Larry's inside jokes, asked Bird to sign a photograph for him, Bird took care to use a bright red pen so his writing would stand out. In autographing the picture, Bird thanked McKee for all the work he had done on his behalf. "He put it in writing better than what he could have said," McKee says. "Larry was never dumb. He just had to get over some personal hang-ups."

When the St. Louis Cardinals asked the school if Bird would be interested in throwing out the first pitch at one of their home games, Bird borrowed a luxury motor home from a friend in town who owned a bank and brought a dozen of his buddies to the ballpark. He and Bob Heaton were invited into the press box, where they spent an inning with Jack Buck, the Cardinals' legendary play-by-play man. When Buck asked Larry during the broadcast if he could hit one of those major-league fastballs, he cracked Heaton up by answering with a simple, "Yup."

(Later that summer, Heaton went to a baseball game in Kansas City and spent a few minutes beforehand chatting with the umpires in their locker room. During batting practice a short while later, one of the umpires spotted Arkansas coach Eddie Sutton standing on the field. The umpire went up to Sutton and said, "Coach, you're not going to believe who was in our dressing room thirty minutes ago—Bob Heaton." Sutton shot him a dour look and said, "I never want to see that kid again as long as I live.")

Bird's last few weeks of student life were filled with bliss. His time as a college student was coming to an end, yet his life as a basketball player was just beginning. "About a week before he signed with the Celtics, we were in the living room, and he was saying, 'Boy, my goal in life was to play professional basketball,'" Heaton says. "He just thought it was so neat to get paid for playing basketball. He broke it down so simply. It's a game, and that's what he lived for."

That dream was within reach as long as he didn't jeopardize it by doing something stupid—like suiting up for the Indiana State baseball team. Bird loved baseball. He had been a pretty good pitcher in high school, and the previous summer he had hit 12 home runs and had 48 RBI in twenty games while playing in a local slow-pitch softball league. He used to attend Indiana State's home baseball games until he had to stop going because fans kept pestering him for autographs. One day, the team's coach, Bob Warn, had casually suggested to Bird that he get a bat and go into the game. When Bird said he would do it, Warn replied, "I'll take you up on that someday."

Someday came on April 28, when Bird played first base for the Sycamores in a doubleheader against Kentucky Wesleyan College. He struck out in his only at bat in the first game, but in the nightcap he knocked in two runs with a single to center. He also gave the fans a major scare when he collided with catcher Mark Rickard while the two of them chased a foul ball. It took Bird a few minutes to shake off the cobwebs, but Rickard was out of action for three days.

Bob Woolf, the agent whom Bird had hired to represent him in his negotiations with the Celtics, was in attendance that day, and he almost had a heart attack when he saw Bird get laid out. Then again, Woolf had already come to understand that this was no ordinary client. Bird had enlisted the help of four prominent businessmen as well as Bob King to form a committee to interview potential agents on his behalf. When the choice got narrowed down to Woolf and one other agent, Bird and the committee asked Woolf to join them for dinner. Woolf tried to impress them by saying he knew how much Tommy John (a Terre Haute native) earned as a pitcher with the New York Yankees, but Bird cut him off. "Hey, Mr. Woolf, Tommy John is a friend of mine," he said. "I don't want to know how much he makes."

After Bird selected Woolf as his agent, he and Dinah Mattingly visited Woolf in Boston. They stayed in a fancy hotel in town at Woolf's expense, but when the agent got the bill, the only items listed were three days' worth of room and tax charges. There was no room service, no special amenities—not even a phone call. It was the first and last time Woolf had that experience with any of his athlete clients.

When Bird arrived a little before halftime for a Celtics home game against the Denver Nuggets, the sparse crowd of 7,831 at Boston Garden gave him a standing ovation. He expressed optimism that his contract would get worked out soon, but the negotiations quickly became acrimonious after Woolf rejected Auerbach's first offer of $400,000 per year. When Auerbach surprised Woolf by publicly announcing that negotiations had broken off, Woolf responded through the press in kind. "[Auerbach] treats everybody like he treated the referees when he was a coach," Woolf said. "He taunts you and baits you and tries to intimidate you. He is more like a dictator than a negotiator."

Back in Terre Haute, while Bird was waiting for the contract to get worked out, Heaton asked him if he wanted to play on Heaton's softball team against a team that included Bird's older brother Mike. At first, Bird said he couldn't play because West Vigo High School had a baseball game, but when a rainstorm soaked the field and postponed that game for a few hours, Bird eagerly agreed to play center field. Early in the game, Bird dove in an unsuccessful attempt to catch a hard line drive that Mike had hit his way. As he rose to throw the ball to the infield, it sailed wildly. Bird had no idea why his throw was so off until he looked down and saw the top half of his right index finger pointed at a ninety-degree angle.

A serious break on his shooting hand was no small matter for someone hoping to make a living playing basketball. Larry managed to keep news of his injury hush-hush, even after he went to Indianapolis to have it surgically repaired. A few weeks after the surgery, he went back to Boston to go through a workout for the Celtics. He made a simple adjustment by using a different part of his hand to release the ball, and as the team brass looked on he drained shot after shot. Such was the genius of Larry Joe Bird.

The Celtics' owner, Harry Mangurian, finally stepped in to break the impasse between Woolf and Auerbach. On June 8, at a press conference attended by thirty-one radio and TV outlets, Bird signed a five-year contract with the Celtics for $3.25 million, making him the highest-paid rookie in the history of sports. "I never told Mr. Auerbach this, but I would have signed for nothing," Bird said. He added that his only regret was having to miss West Vigo's game in the regional state baseball championships that day, and he broke up the room by recounting the story of how he had gotten lost that morning while jogging through Woolf's Brookline neighborhood and had to bum a ride back from a stranger. "I guess I'm still just a hick from French Lick," Bird said with a grin.

That act, however, was not as convincing as it used to be. The people who knew Bird understood how far he had come since the day Bill Hodges and Stan Evans rolled into French Lick and found Larry carrying his grandmother's laundry. At no time was that growth more apparent than on the day Bird became the first member of his family to graduate from college. He raced back to French Lick and showed off that sheepskin. If he had come home with the NCAA championship trophy, his mama would not have been any prouder.

13

It didn't take long for Bill Hodges to realize just how different life was going to be after Larry Bird. On the first day of practice in the fall of 1979, Hodges was told his team would have to wait until the band finished its practice before taking the floor. Hodges was furious. He went to the office of Jerry Huntsman, who was serving as acting athletic director in the wake of Bob King's retirement. At first, Huntsman supported the decision to give priority to the band, but he relented when Hodges threatened to tell the local media what happened. The episode was the first of many that led Hodges to believe that he had little support from the university administration.

"They treated me like a red-headed stepchild," Hodges says. "Jerry Huntsman didn't want me to get the job in the first place, and they wanted to do everything they could to make it impossible for me to win. They did a good job, too."

Alas, Hodges had greater concerns than problems at work. His marriage had fallen apart. Hodges's wife of eleven years, Connie, never liked that her husband had to put in such long hours and traveled so much. She thought that when Hodges became a head coach things would improve, but it turned out he had to work even harder. They

separated in September 1979 and were divorced the following summer, with Connie taking custody of their two young children.

"It devastated me. I had a terrible time," Hodges says. "I couldn't
focus on anything because I really loved my wife and my kids. I went
from the highest I've ever been to the lowest I've ever been. That all
happened in one year. Can you imagine that?"

Obviously, the Sycamores were not going back to the Final Four
without Bird, but with four returning starters, there was reason to
believe they could compete for another Missouri Valley Conference
title. They lost their opener at home to Armstrong State—"I told
everyone those thumps they're hearing are people falling off the
bandwagon," says Andy Amey, the *Terre Haute Tribune* writer—but
they went on to win eleven of their next thirteen games. A midseason
injury to Bob Heaton tripped them up, however, and they dropped
eight of their last thirteen to finish the season 16–11. They ended up
tied for fifth in the conference and failed to make the NCAA tournament. "I didn't do a good job, and the kids quit on me," Hodges says.

Hodges's main problem was that he had failed to capitalize on the
success of the previous season by bringing in top-notch recruits.
Evaluating and procuring talent had always been his forte as an assistant, but, says Rick Shaw, the assistant trainer, "when he became a
head coach, he didn't have a Bill Hodges [on his staff]." Carl Nicks
was likewise disappointed. "I just thought it was a great time to get
some blue-chip guys in there, and we pretty much had the same guys
coming back," he says. "It was really frustrating to go from where we
were to being mediocre."

As Hodges tried to right the ship during the latter part of the season,
his players noticed a change in his attitude. For example, in late December, he punished Heaton and another player for violating curfew by
ten minutes. The team had operated under a curfew during Bird's senior year, too, but it was rarely enforced. "All of a sudden, he's making a
big deal out of curfew," Heaton says. "I felt like saying, Well if you got
off your ass and recruited eight months ago, we'd be in better shape."

Hodges's recruiting was also hamstrung by a new university policy forbidding him to accept any more Division I transfers. The order was issued by President Landini, who had bristled whenever Al McGuire referred to Indiana State as "Transfer U." That meant Hodges couldn't bring in players like David Magley, a guard at Kansas who wanted to transfer to Indiana State but ended up staying in Lawrence, where he was later voted All-Big Eight. Hodges tried to fill the void with junior college players, but many of them either didn't pan out or were of dubious character. In 1980–81, with Nicks, Heaton, Brad Miley, Alex Gilbert, and Leroy Staley having moved on, Steve Reed was left behind to suffer through a 9–18 season. "He forgot some of the things that had made him successful," Reed says of Hodges. "His relationship with the players and how he handled situations changed. There's no doubt his personal life affected him, and to build your whole recruiting strategy around junior college players just didn't work."

"I wasn't around the players as much. I was busy and I didn't do a good job of staying close," Hodges concedes. "I can understand why they would think I was big-headed. I don't think I was different, but I just didn't have the time to grow into the job. I was ready coaching-wise, but I wasn't ready to administrate."

As the program's fortunes went south, Hodges lost the support of a community that had grown accustomed to winning during Bird's tenure. "I think the people of Terre Haute lost sight of the fact that what had happened may never happen again," says Terry Thimlar. "There was a lot of finger-pointing going on, and it was very hard to see Bill go through that. He kind of became a changed man."

It was an increasingly volatile situation, and Hodges didn't handle it well. When the Sycamores played at Tulsa during the 1979–80 season, the game was delayed by a brief power outage. Instead of patiently waiting for the lights to come back on, Hodges went ballistic. "Bill was about ready to jump off the bridge," Tulsa coach Jim King said. "He cussed me out before the game because of the lights, and he cussed me out after the game because he said we played dirty. He called me all kinds of names. He was paranoid. The pressure was eating the guy alive."

"Last year was one of the toughest years of my life," Hodges said in November 1981. "You can start taking success for granted. You get up in the morning, and you feel like you have the world by the tail. You can become, shall we say, enamored with yourself. I think it takes a little more character to dig out of a hole in the morning."

Before the start of the 1981–82 season, Indiana State hired Beanie Cooper, a friend of Bob King's who had been the athletic director at the University of South Dakota, to be its full-time athletic director. Cooper was under pressure from the Indiana State administration to fire Hodges right away, but he decided to give the coach one more year. Hodges had reason to believe he could turn things around. He had finally landed a breakthrough recruit in Kevin Thompson, a big, strapping six-foot-eight forward whose square chin, finely combed dark hair, and glasses made him look like Clark Kent. He was also a local celebrity, having earned all-state honors at Terre Haute South Vigo High School. Thompson was no Larry Bird, but he was good enough to have an impact as a freshman, and he was the kind of recruit that can become a program's cornerstone.

During the summer before his freshman year, however, Thompson broke a rib. When the injury still had not healed by the fall, the trainer, Bob Behnke, sent him to the team's physician. The doctor performed tests that revealed the cause of Thompson's discomfort: cancer.

Hodges had grown fond of Thompson during the recruiting process, so from a personal standpoint it was disheartening to watch this healthy young man's condition deteriorate so rapidly. Meanwhile, without Thompson on the floor, the losing continued, and Hodges's situation grew increasingly dire. "I thought he was getting pretty close to a nervous breakdown," Beanie Cooper says. "I can recall one morning when we walked around the track outside my office, and Bill was coming apart. He was a very, very nice man, but he was a young coach, and he had way too much thrown at him. We had zero recruits, and the community was really down on him."

Kevin Thompson died on January 21, 1982. Hodges resigned the next day. "I just had all I could handle," he says. Cooper was so worried about Hodges's mental health that he almost forbade him to finish out the season. In the end, Cooper allowed Hodges to stay on as a lame-duck coach. He left Indiana State for good following his second consecutive 9–18 record.

Naturally, Hodges was disappointed that his time in Terre Haute had come to such a disappointing end. Still, he was just three years removed from having coached in the NCAA championship game and being named national coach of the year. Surely, he believed, he would get another opportunity soon.

He could never have imagined just how wrong he was.

Coming off a season in which their regular-season NBA ratings had dropped a whopping 29 percent from the year before, CBS made sure to milk the arrival of Magic and Bird into the pros for all it was worth. The league had put them on the cover of its media guide—the first time they had used a pair of rookies for that purpose—and CBS planned to feature them whenever possible. "I know somebody is going to say he's tired of seeing that parquet floor in Boston so often," said Joe Axelson, who had left the Kansas City Kings to become the NBA's vice president for operations. "But that's something we're willing to put up with. We think this is the best showcase we can come up with."

CBS's first national game of the week of the 1979–80 season featured the Lakers playing the Celtics at Boston Garden on Sunday, January 18. The network took the fight right to the competition by moving the tip-off of that game to 1 p.m. eastern time so it would air head-to-head with the Syracuse-Purdue game on NBC. That marked the first time that nationally televised college and pro games were beginning at the same time. "I don't know why they are doing it, and I don't want to guess," Al McGuire said. "They are coming to challenge us with the two guys that we made."

Even so, it would take a while for the NBA to take off as a television franchise. That was evident on May 16, 1980, when the Lakers faced the Philadelphia 76ers, led by their star player Julius Erving, in Game Six of the NBA Finals. The Lakers had taken a 3–2 lead in the series, but their most recent victory had come at a steep price: Kareem Abdul-Jabbar, the league's MVP, severely sprained his ankle in Game Five and was lost for the remainder of the series. Lakers coach Paul Westhead decided to make the unconventional move of inserting Magic Johnson at center for Game Six in Philadelphia. Magic responded with one of the greatest performances in NBA history, a 42-point, 15-rebound, 7-assist masterpiece that lifted the Lakers to a 123–107 series-clinching win.

CBS, however, did not even broadcast the game live. Instead, it offered a taped replay to its affiliates at 11 p.m. that night. (When George Fox, Magic's former coach at Everett High in Lansing, called Earvin Sr. after listening to the game on live radio to congratulate him, Magic's dad wasn't even aware of what had happened.) A year later, CBS struck an $88 million deal to televise the NBA playoffs for another four seasons. The contract required the network to show all the Finals games live.

McGuire's lament notwithstanding, the competition between the networks was good for the sport. But as it turned out, NBC was unable to keep pace. Shortly before NBC's deal with the NCAA was due to be renegotiated, the network got a new president in Fred Silverman, who wasn't a big sports fan and never understood why he should pay such huge rights fees to broadcast games. The network's relationship with the NCAA began to sour in 1980, when it declined the NCAA's offer for a new four-year deal. When Chet Simmons, the president of NBC Sports, informed NCAA executive director Walter Byers that the network wanted to renew only for another two years, Byers abruptly hung up on him.

The next time the deal came up, NBC, which had seen its investment in the 1980 Olympic Games go belly-up with the U.S. boycott and had just ponied up $7.5 million for a one-year deal with the Rose

Bowl, was unable to lock up the NCAA tournament during its exclusive negotiating window. "They came in and basically tried to poor-mouth what was going on," says Dave Gavitt, who was a member of the NCAA's negotiating committee. "They were saying it's hard to sell, hard to clear, blah blah blah. It wasn't where we thought we were. We thought this thing had wings for the future. The meeting was classic Byers. He stood up and closed his notebook, and he said to them, 'I want to apologize to my colleagues who I brought in from around the country to listen to that. This meeting is over.'"

The NCAA opened up the bidding to the other networks, and CBS rushed in. Not only did CBS come up with an offer for $48 million over three years (a 60 percent increase over the previous deal), it also sold the NCAA on its commitment to promote the tournament as a big-time event. Part of CBS's offer was a studio control center modeled after their successful *NFL Today* pregame show, which was designed to give the games a national feel. The NCAA also convinced the network to go one step further and produce a separate "Selection Show" to reveal the tournament bracket the Sunday before the games began. On March 4, 1981, the NCAA announced it had reached a three-year deal with CBS that would begin with the 1982 tournament. "It was obvious CBS had done a lot of homework, and they were very eager to have the tournament," says Tom Jernstedt, the NCAA's executive vice president.

The news was devastating for the folks back at 30 Rockefeller Plaza. "It was a disappointment because it wasn't over that much money," Don Ohlmeyer says. Bryant Gumbel heard about it when he called in to the office from a TWA airport lounge. "I thought, How weird. We make the tournament a big deal and basically give it away," Gumbel says.

NBC still hoped that when the new CBS deal expired, NBC could either get the tournament back or convince the NCAA to put it on both networks. So NBC continued to go full bore on its regular season college basketball programming. That, combined with the ascent of the new all-sports cable network ESPN, led to an unprecedented level of exposure for the sport. During the 1981–82 season, CBS aired six-teen regular season games and sixteen NCAA tournament games, NBC produced twenty-seven games, and ESPN did ninety-one. North Carolina coach Dean Smith marveled that his father in Kansas would be able to watch all but four of the Tar Heels' twenty-six games that season.

The added visibility also fundamentally changed the way the game was played. If that many more people were going to watch, the sport had to be more TV friendly. The biggest problem was the delay tactics coaches habitually deployed during the final minutes. As Frederick C. Klein wrote in the *Wall Street Journal* in March 1982, "Games don't end anymore—they trickle away in a stream of free throws, stalling tactics, intentional fouls and more free throws." As scoring continued to decline, the NCAA took notice. In 1985, the men's basketball rules committee added a forty-five-second shot clock (later shortened to thirty-five seconds), and the following year the committee introduced the three-point line.

CBS never let NBC enter the bidding next time around, locking up the tournament for another three years for $96 million—exactly double what it had paid previously. CBS sweetened its offer by adding prime-time slots on Thursday and Friday nights for the re-gional semifinals. The NCAA took full advantage of the bulging rev-enue stream, expanding the tournament field to sixty-four teams by 1985, rescinding the two-teams-per-conference maximum, and even registering a trademark for the term "Final Four," with a stated first use of 1978. Not for nothing did the *New York Times* in 1983 call the NCAA tournament "perhaps the fastest-growing sports event in the country."

In 1982, the Final Four was held at the Louisiana Superdome in New Orleans, where a tongue-wagging freshman named Michael Jordan sank a final jumper in the championship game to give North Carolina a win over Georgetown. That marked the first time the event had been played in a dome since 1971. "It was amazing how much bigger the thing had become in just three years," says Lynn

Henning, who was covering the Final Four for the *State Journal* that year for the first time since the Spartans had won it all. "The press conferences were bigger, the excitement was bigger. There was just a lot more mass to the thing. That's when I knew the Final Four was no longer the Final Four."

That surge debunked a widely held belief that the only reason people had been so interested in the NCAA tournament during the late 1960s and early 1970s was because they were drawn in by John Wooden's dynasty at UCLA, which produced ten championships between 1964 and 1975. One such pessimist was Eddie Einhorn, the trailblazing founder of the TVS television network who did so much to capitalize on Wooden's run. "I consider Eddie a genius, and he said to me the thing is going to crash when UCLA is no longer dominating," Billy Packer says. "This game [in 1979] showed that wasn't the case because it blew away anything UCLA did. That may be what the game did for the sport more than anything."

Just as the popularity of the NCAA tournament propelled college basketball to new heights, so, too, did the meteoric rise of ESPN. From its launch in September 1979, the network grew largely on the basis of its college basketball programming, getting particularly good notices when it showed the early round games of the 1980 NCAA tournament. ESPN later solidified its regular season imprint with a Monday night doubleheader featuring teams from the newly formed Big East Conference as well as from the Big Ten. The lead college basketball analyst, Dick Vitale, who joined the network in the fall of 1979 after being fired as the coach of the Detroit Pistons, had initially thought he would return to coaching until he attended the 1983 Final Four. "I was shocked because people were coming up to me asking for autographs and pictures," Vitale says. "I'm thinking, What the hell is this? I realized this television world is not so bad, man."

Dave Gavitt's brainchild, the Big East, rode the new wave, too. In its effort to challenge the hegemony the Atlantic Coast Conference had enjoyed for decades, the Big East held a postseason tournament that was modeled after the ACC's. In the first championship game in

March 1980, Georgetown defeated Syracuse in double overtime. Two years later, Gavitt was in Raleigh, North Carolina—the heart of ACC country—to watch Villanova defeat Memphis State in the NCAA tournament's East Regional semifinal. "When they won, all the Villanova fans started cheering, 'Big East! Big East!'" Gavitt recalls. "I thought to myself, We've made it. We burned the brand. People know who we are."

ESPN deserves much credit for fueling college basketball's popularity during the 1980s, but the growth came at a price. Never again will two wondrous college basketball players be introduced to a rapt nation at the very moment they're taking the court for the national championship. In today's world, there's no room for mystery. "ESPN has ruined everything," says Dave Kindred, the former *Washington Post* sportswriter. "If Magic and Bird came along today, we'd have twenty-nine different scouting reports on each guy. We'd have Outside the Lines, documentaries, instant classics. We'd know too much."

Ironically, the man who founded ESPN, Bill Rasmussen, echoes that lament. "When I look back at that game, the hype looks bigger than it really was, because there weren't as many ways to hype a game back then," he says. "Can you imagine today, between the way CBS covers the tournament and how ESPN covers everything, what it would be like? Everybody would know Larry Bird's shoe size, the length of Johnson's shoestrings. You might expect an old guy to say this, but it's kind of a shame."

Though Greg Kelser had been Michigan State's student-athlete poster boy as a player, the two-time academic All-American finished his senior year twenty-six credits shy of earning his degree. Jud Heathcote regularly reminded Kelser of this deficiency after he set out on his professional career with the Pistons. Two years after his senior season ended, Kelser finally completed his studies. When Kelser went to Heathcote's office to report he had turned in his final paper, Heathcote said, "I'll bet you're happy to get that anvil off your back."

"I'm happy to get *you* off my back," Kelser replied.

Unfortunately, Kelser's body did not hold up well enough to allow him to fulfill his basketball potential. A lingering knee injury helped end his NBA career after just six seasons. Heathcote was his mentor every step of the way, putting him in touch with various doctors and later helping him to make the transition to a post-playing career as a broadcaster. The relationship that had begun with so much tension and distrust evolved into a genuine friendship. "I came to understand that this man really cared about me and my well-being," Kelser says. "He stayed on me about graduating. He always called and wanted to know what was going on with my pro career. When a person shows that, you can't help but have a certain amount of admiration and affection for him."

After leading the Spartans to the 1979 NCAA championship, Heathcote coached for another sixteen years in East Lansing, but he never made it back to the Final Four. In fact, he never even got past the Sweet Sixteen. That was largely due to his innate distaste for recruiting; he rarely landed players from the well-stocked Detroit Public School League. As a result, Heathcote had to win with players like Scott Skiles, Steve Smith, Kevin Willis, and Shawn Respert, all of whom were lightly recruited out of high school but became NBA first-round draft picks under Heathcote's tutelage. (Heathcote helped Respert go from being a mediocre shooter to a great one by forcing him to take hundreds of jumpers with his left hand tied to his hip.) Heathcote coached the Spartans to the NCAA tournament seven more times, but his teams were twice victimized by bad luck. In 1986, Michigan State was playing Kansas in the Midwest Regional semifinal when the game clock was inadvertently shut off for about fifteen seconds, helping the Jayhawks come back and triumph in overtime. In 1990, the Spartans lost another overtime game in the Sweet Sixteen after Georgia Tech guard Kenny Anderson hit a shot at the end of regulation that replays showed had come after time had expired. It was as if the basketball gods were trying to make up for having bestowed Magic Johnson on Heathcote lo those many years ago.

Along the way, Heathcote became one of the most respected men in his profession. He served on the board of directors for the National Association of Basketball Coaches, where, among other things, he led the push to eliminate the consolation game at the Final Four following the 1981 tournament. ("I told people, 'You make the Final Four, you lose two games, now you come home, and everybody thinks you've had a losing season.'") He even became a bona fide media darling. Sportswriters loved his wicked sense of humor, and though Heathcote still got mad about what he read from time to time, he learned to stop holding grudges. Even Lynn Henning, his old nemesis at the *State Journal*, became one of his biggest admirers. "We were on great terms again six months later [after the championship]," says Henning, who left Lansing to become a columnist at the *Detroit Free Press*. "It ended up being one of my most gratifying relationships. There's a good guy there, a genuinely good guy, and he's the funniest guy I've ever known. He will fold up an audience better than any coach I've ever seen."

Alas, toward the end of Heathcote's career, he found himself challenged on the one thing he valued more than that NCAA championship: his integrity. In 1991, one of his players, Parish Hickman, had his scholarship revoked after he was arrested and charged with attempting to sell cocaine to an undercover police officer. (He was acquitted seven months later.) Hickman sued the school, and during a deposition he alleged that while he played for Michigan State he had received money from a booster and was paid for work he didn't do. Hickman's assertions were corroborated by a second player, but Heathcote vehemently denied them. An internal university investigation found that no serious violations had taken place, but it did uncover seven secondary infractions. In November 1994, the NCAA accepted Michigan State's five self-imposed sanctions, including a one-year period in which one coach would not be permitted to recruit off campus. Since Heathcote was nearing retirement, he designated himself to be that restricted coach. "It galls me that I've worked for years to create a reputation built on honesty and integrity, and all that hard work and effort can be shattered in an instant," he said.

Heathcote repeatedly butted heads with the Michigan State administration during his last few years. His relationship with athletic director Merrily Dean Baker was so poisoned that he had to work around her to install his top assistant, Tom Izzo, as his designated successor. Heathcote privately told his wife, Beverly, that he wanted to step aside at the end of the 1993–94 season. However, on the eve of the 1994 NCAA tournament, a confidential memo written by associate athletic director Clarence Underwood was leaked to the student newspaper. In the memo, Underwood noted that Michigan State had averaged a fifth-place finish in the Big Ten over the previous ten years and recommended to the university president that Heathcote should agree to retire at season's end or face immediate termination. Heathcote was too proud to let people think he was being forced out, so on March 30, 1994, he announced he would coach one more season and then hand the reins over to Izzo.

Everywhere the Spartans played in the Big Ten during the 1994–95 season, Heathcote was paid homage with a going-away gift. He got a putter at Purdue, a green leather recliner at Indiana, a big-screen TV at Michigan, and a football helmet with a face mask at Illinois. (The last was a nod to the time when Heathcote famously slammed a ball on the floor during a game, only to have it bounce up and bash him on the nose.) He had originally kept his retirement decision private so he could avoid just such a farewell tour, but he came to appreciate the sentiments directed his way. "I think what people are clapping for is more the situation than the person," Heathcote said. "Here's a guy who's been at one school nineteen years who's retiring. How many guys retire in our profession? Not very many. No one has retired in the nineteen years I've been in the league. I'm the first. So maybe the appreciation of the longevity is why I'm getting the standing ovation. Not because I'm Jud Heathcote."

Heathcote's final team at Michigan State was one of his best. It finished the regular season with a 22–5 record and entered the NCAA tournament ranked eleventh in the country. In their first-round game against Weber State University, the Spartans led by 9 points at halftime, but as usual Heathcote foresaw problems his players couldn't. "I told the guys the only reason we're up nine is we shot pretty well," Heathcote says. "I said they got every loose ball, they outhustled us on defense, they outhustled us on the boards. If we go out and play the same way [in the second half], we're not going to win. As I walked out I said to my assistants, 'You know, the only people in that room who believed what I said are you guys.'"

Sure enough, Weber State quickly turned Michigan State's 9-point advantage into a 10-point deficit, and Heathcote's career ended with a humiliating 79–72 loss. "I knew that the end was coming," he said. "I just didn't think it would be this soon."

Heathcote retired to his native Pacific Northwest and settled in Spokane, Washington, where he celebrated his eightieth birthday in the summer of 2007. He attends all of the home games at Gonzaga University and has lunch once a week with Zags coach Mark Few. ("He's a national treasure," Few says.) Heathcote spends much of his time sitting in a lounge chair in his den watching games on the satellite dish Izzo bought for him, but stubborn as he is he has not attended a single practice since the day he hung up his whistle. Despite having had both knees replaced, he plays golf several times a week, and he remains a highly sought-after dinner speaker, provided the audience can abide his off-color humor. "Jud was one of the great characters who came through the game of basketball," Digger Phelps says. "The game doesn't have many of those characters anymore." Mick McCabe, the *Detroit Free Press* writer, jokes, "I call him every Mother's Day, because he's the biggest mother I know."

In the fall of 2007, Heathcote sat in his den and watched a full replay of the 1979 NCAA championship game. Over the years, he had seen fragments of the game as it popped up on television, but he had watched it from beginning to end only a handful of times. He was characteristically impatient ("Is this thing ever going to end?" he moaned as the Spartans were putting the Sycamores away with repeated trips to the free throw line), and he couldn't help but train his critical ex-coach's lens on the screen. "It's harder to win each time I watch it," Heathcote said when it was over. "We get that big lead and then we fritter it away. I didn't remember the pressure bothering us as much as it did. I also didn't remember how tightly the game was called. A lot of those were phantom calls."

Having reached the twilight of his life, Heathcote is not beyond a little self-reflection. "I've always said if I had a regret, I wish I would have coached a little more positive than I did. Then again, maybe I wouldn't have been near as good a coach," he says. "I hope I'm remembered as a good coach and a good guy, a guy who cared about his players, cared about other coaches, and cared about the game. I'm not trying to say I'm a great coach or a great guy, but just steady as she goes down the middle."

Heathcote endured a serious health scare during the summer of 2008, when he developed a life-threatening infection following open-heart surgery. As a result, he had to undergo a second surgery and barely left his house for three months while he recovered. "I finally played nine holes of golf for the first time yesterday," he said that fall. "I'm doing better now, but at my age I suppose anything can happen."

He may have a few regrets, but in his core Heathcote has never changed. In the summer of 2000, Greg Kelser introduced his former coach at a large banquet in Lansing. During Heathcote's speech, he listed his four favorite players whom he had coached. The quartet included two players from Montana, Eric Hays and Micheal Ray Richardson, and two from Michigan State, Scott Skiles and Magic Johnson. Afterward, several people came up to Kelser and said they were surprised Heathcote didn't include him, considering Kelser was sitting right there. Kelser could only laugh. Heathcote's bluntness and immutability had once driven him to the brink of transferring, but as an adult Kelser came to admire Heathcote precisely because he possesses those qualities. "I always like to tell people he pushed me beyond where I would have taken myself," Kelser says. "He made you understand that you have to be willing to move beyond the point of 'good enough.' I try to apply that now to everything I do. Some days it wasn't all that much fun playing for him, and I'll grant you Jud was not for the meek of mind. But if I could turn back the clock knowing everything I know now, I would still do it."

In 1999, Larry Bird and Magic Johnson sat for an interview with Chris Myers of Fox Sports for an hourlong special to commemorate the twentieth anniversary of the 1979 NCAA championship game. When Myers asked Bird if he had ever watched a replay of the final, Bird smiled wanly and said, "Never once did."

"No desire to?" Myers asked.

"No."

Magic, of course, had watched it many times. He knew every dribble by heart. "You know what I really love? Seeing both of us young," he said. "Seeing us with the shorty shorts on, the interviews. . . . It was just a great story and that linked us together forever."

Even among people who thought Johnson and Bird would do well in the NBA, it was impossible to anticipate just how profound and immediate their impact on the league would be. During their rookie season, Bird led a Celtics team that had posted the second-worst record in the NBA the year before to a league-best 61–21 mark. He averaged 21.3 points, 10.4 rebounds, and 4.5 assists en route to being named the league's rookie of the year, but Magic again did him one better by steering the Lakers to the championship. Bird got his NBA title with Boston the following year, and before they were through, the two of them collected eight NBA titles (five for Magic, three for Bird) and six league MVP awards (three each). As their incandescent rivalry spurred the NBA to unprecedented prosperity in the late 1980s, the lore of their first meeting in the NCAA championship game grew in kind.

"Not only were they great players, but they went to two of our most storied franchises," says David Stern, who became NBA commissioner in 1984. "They played off each other so well. You had the 'Showtime' of the Lakers versus the lunch pail brigade. If the NBA had gone out of business or had stayed at the same level it was at, [the 1979 final] would not have been the iconic game it turned out to be. But as you looked back, it became a milestone, the starting point for all the things that were converging on our sport."

Their impact on the court may have been swift, but it took a while for a true friendship to develop off of it. When they first arrived in the league, Magic and Bird shared a real hostility. When Bird was negotiating his endorsement deal with Converse for his rookie season, he told the company he would sign with them as long as he was paid one more dollar than Johnson. During their first meeting as pros on December 29, 1979, Bird fouled Magic hard late in the fourth quarter, and the two of them glared at each other. When asked about their relationship after the game, Bird said, "I don't go out to eat with him. I just know him on the basketball floor, and that's it. He just came driving down the lane. If he thinks he's going to go drive the lane and I'm going to lay down, he's crazy." When the Celtics and Lakers played each other during those early years, Magic and Bird wouldn't even shake hands before tip-off.

The relationship began to thaw during the summer of 1984, when they filmed two television commercials together. They were cordial in Los Angeles while shooting a commercial for Amoco, but they really bonded when Magic came to French Lick for a Converse ad. Georgia Bird made them lunch, and afterward they sat in Bird's living room and spent time alone together for the first time. They were amazed at how much their personalities clicked (they loved dishing on who they thought were the most overrated and overpaid players in the league), and they discovered how much they had in common outside of basketball. "We found out that we were much alike. We have similar backgrounds in terms of [being] Midwest boys," Johnson said. "We just started laughing and giggling like two little boys, and it started a friendship that would last forever."

One night when Magic had to sit out a Lakers-Celtics game because of an injury, Bird came over to him before the game and promised he'd put on a show in his honor. Over the next two hours, Larry smiled at Magic as he sank jumper after jumper during a Celtics rout. When Magic learned in November 1991 that he had contracted the HIV virus, a diagnosis that at the time was considered a death sentence, Larry was one of the first people he called before revealing the news to the public. "I just remember we were both crying," Magic said. "He didn't say much because that's who Larry is, but he told me, all choked up, 'You hang in there, you're going to beat it.' There wasn't a lot to say, but it meant the world to me." They spoke at each other's retirement ceremonies, and when Magic went into the Basketball Hall of Fame in 2002, he asked Bird, not one of his former Lakers teammates, to present him for induction.

Darwin Payton, who worked for Johnson on his business ventures, says, "You know how eagles can fly higher than other birds? That's how it is with them. Eagles like to fly with eagles."

As Magic and Bird soared, for the most part, they stayed grounded in the communities that raised them. Johnson never lived in Lansing again, but his parents and much of his family still live there, and he is a frequent visitor. When Michigan State won the NCAA title in 2000, Johnson, never one to assume a low profile, stood on the court and celebrated with the players. He has been willing to help out the university from time to time by doing things like hosting donors at his house in Los Angeles, but his generosity has its limits. Says Heathcote, "It bothers me that he's never given Michigan State a dime."

Bird has kept himself even more tethered to the places where he grew up. When he won his first NBA title, he dedicated the championship to French Lick. When he won his second, he told CBS broadcaster Brent Musburger on live television, "This one was for Terre Haute." The Celtics' games had been available on live radio in Terre Haute by the time Larry arrived there. He became a partner in a hotel in town called the Boston Connection, where the place mats in the restaurant had outlines of Larry's hands, including the signature crooked finger that resulted from that softball mishap. When some local citizens started a movement to rename Indiana State's Hulman Center in his honor, Bird wrote a letter to the *Terre Haute*

Tribune asking that the name not be changed out of respect for the Hulman family.

After he signed his NBA contract, Larry built a four-bedroom ranch house in French Lick for him to live in during the off-season. (His mother lived there year-round until she died of Lou Gehrig's disease in 1996.) The house, which Larry sold in the summer of 2008, was only about three thousand square feet, but it sat on an expansive lot that included a swimming pool, a tennis court, a basketball court, and an indoor workout facility. When Larry was home, he didn't like any star treatment. One morning, he showed up at the Springs Valley High School gymnasium to work out, only to find that the cheerleading team was practicing there. The coach offered to move her girls so Larry could use half the court, but he insisted on waiting. He stretched quietly for forty-five minutes until they were through. Likewise, when Larry's former gym teacher and AAU teammate Chuck Akers was killed in a car accident in the fall of 2007, Larry drove home to pay his respects. As he stood near the back of the enormous line that filed by Akers's casket in the Springs Valley gymnasium, someone offered to bring Larry straight inside. Larry said no thanks. He'd wait just like everybody else.

While Larry has long since moved on from Terre Haute, his ex-wife and oldest daughter have stayed in the community. Jan Condra settled with Corrie Bird in Brazil, Indiana, a small town about twenty miles outside Terre Haute. Jan has been married three times since she divorced Larry—"I've kind of had a rough time finding the right guy," she says—and she works for the motor vehicles bureau in Terre Haute. Corrie, meanwhile, wore the number 33 when she played for her high school basketball team, but she still suffered discomfort from growing up without her famous father around. "The hardest part was when someone would ask me what my dad was doing, and I had to tell people I didn't see him or I don't talk to him," Corrie says. "That's when it kind of hit home."

Corrie's contact with her father has been sporadic over the years. When she was growing up, Corrie would go to Larry's house a few times during the summers when she and her mother were visiting Jan's parents in French Lick. In April 1998, after Larry became coach of the Indiana Pacers, Corrie went to a Pacers game in Indianapolis and spent several hours with her father afterward. The following month, however, Corrie was quoted at length in a *Sports Illustrated* story about professional athletes who have neglected children they fathered out of wedlock. She also appeared on an episode of *The Oprah Winfrey Show* devoted to the same topic. Corrie says Larry never told her directly that he was angry at her for going public, but she heard from other relatives that he was upset. She still invited him to her high school and college graduations (she earned her bachelor's degree in education from Indiana State in 1999) as well as her wedding in May 2008, but she wasn't surprised each time when Larry didn't show up.

"My mom thinks she's a big reason why he won't reach out to me, but that's ludicrous. I don't live with my mom. I'm not a teenager anymore," Corrie says. "I don't understand why someone won't acknowledge their own child, but that's what he chooses to do."

Bob Ryan called Bird's feat of taking Indiana State to the championship game "the greatest achievement in the history of NCAA basketball," but Larry never got over the fact that they lost the damn game. He confessed as much to Darwin Payton when he and Magic filmed that Amoco commercial in Los Angeles in 1984. "He told me during one of the breaks that that game hurt him more than any game he's ever played," Payton says. Greg Kelser also sensed that Bird brought an extra edge whenever Kelser faced him in the NBA. "I always felt like he really, really wanted to make a statement when going against me," Kelser says. "There's no question in my mind about it. To this day, I've never had a conversation with him. I never had a friendship with him nor did I seek to have one. There was no need for it."

When the Celtics beat the Lakers in the 1984 NBA Finals, Bird shook hands on the court with Magic and said, "I got you back." Johnson quickly replied, "Yeah, but I'll tell you one thing. I'm gonna win more NBA titles, but you're never gonna win a championship in college. I got it and you don't." The memory still rankles Bird. "Every time I see him, it sort of cringes me because he's got something that I can't get," Bird said. "When we was doing that little feature they had on Fox, you could tell Magic was so happy and gloating. I tell you, I wanted to throw up. Magic's a good man, and I like to be with him, but he's a jerk."

They started off as strangers, they grew into rivals, and they ultimately became close friends. But while great rivalries are by definition evenly matched, in this case only one can have the last word. When Chris Myers asked Magic Johnson during that 1999 interview what the championship game meant to him, he turned the knife one more time. "Well, I got one over on him," he said, nodding at Bird. "Just like he told you he's disappointed to this day, I know he's going to always be disappointed. We know these type of things because we're winners. We're guys who hate to lose. So I got that one, and it's special."

14

It was a typical day that could have been taking place at any high school in America first thing in the morning. Students ambled through the hallway in clusters. Teachers leaned against the walls and sipped coffee. When the bell rang, a handful of freshmen walked into their classroom, plopped down at their desks, and tried to look interested. The subject was world history. After the lights went off and the overhead projector went on, the teacher stood in the back of the room peppering his lecture with corny jokes. "Don't forget what I am—the mack daddy," he said in a low, gravelly drawl. He was wearing a short-sleeved button-down shirt and khaki pants. An ID card hung around his neck. When a young girl made a wisecrack at another student's expense, he quietly admonished her by saying, "Jasmine, no crackin' on people in here."

It was only at the end of the class that the teacher indicated that his background was not so typical after all. A boy had crumpled up a piece of paper and lofted it insouciantly toward a wastebasket. The paper hit the side of the can and landed on the floor. The miscue had nothing to do with world history, but the teacher corrected him anyway.

"That's bad form," Bill Hodges said. "I don't want to see you shoot like that. If you're gonna shoot, get some decent alignment."

The back wall of the room offered more glimpses into the teacher's unique past. Several pictures hung in rows underneath a sign that read "You Love History": Hodges's yearbook photo from Zionsville Community High School; his official air force picture (which showed traces of red hair peeking from underneath his cap); and several photos of his children and grandchildren. Pictures of the best basketball teams from each of his coaching stops were part of the tableau. Tucked into the far-upper-right corner, indistinguishable from the rest, hung the official team photo of the 1978–79 Indiana State Sycamores. The big kid with the bushy blond hair stood in the middle of the back row with his hands clasped behind his back. "Some of the guys that know sports, they really get into that," Hodges says of his students. "But a lot of them don't know anything about it. They're fourteen years old. They don't know who Larry Bird was."

There are some days when Hodges wonders if the whole thing really happened, as if it might have been some kind of weird dream. "I got a handwritten letter from John Wooden after the Final Four that I had framed. Every now and then, I walk by and read it and think, Yup, it was real," he says. Hodges hadn't the foggiest notion on that Monday night in Salt Lake City that he would end up three decades later as a history teacher at William Fleming High School in Roanoke, Virginia, but he harbors no bitterness about his fate. "I have some good memories," he says. "I have some that aren't so good, but I don't have any regrets. I had some bad breaks, but that's what life is. When you play a team game, you lose some, you win some, and you better be willing to accept both with humility."

Humility is not a problem for Bill Hodges. The basketball world has humbled him many times over. After he resigned from Indiana State in 1982, Hodges applied for jobs at dozens of colleges, but to his dismay he got just one job offer, from Palm Beach Junior College in Florida. "When you're out of coaching, people think you must have done something really bad," he says. Hodges spent a relatively content season in the Sunshine State, but in the spring of 1983 he was offered another job as an assistant at California State University–Long Beach. He jumped at the chance to return to Division I.

That turned out to be a mistake. The following spring, Long Beach's head coach, Dave Buss, was fired, and Hodges once again was out of a job. This time, he didn't get any offers. He fell into a depression and put on fifty pounds. "I had a couple of days there when I just went to the beach and watched the waves," he said. "It was a soul-searching thing. A voice inside told me not to give up. Life wouldn't have any meaning if I did."

Having been essentially banished from basketball, Hodges returned to Florida, where he took a job selling insurance and looked for ways to get back into coaching. After two years of working the phones and sending out résumés, he was hired by Georgia College, an NAIA (National Association of Intercollegiate Athletics) school in Milledgeville, Georgia. (The NAIA is separate from, and competitively inferior to, the NCAA.) It was as far from the big-time as he could get: he had only three scholarships to distribute however he liked, and the college's gymnasium was so spartan that the team had to play its home games at a high school in town. Hodges did a respectable job during his five years there, taking the Bobcats to the NAIA playoffs three times (they lost in the first round each time), but he still pined to get back into the NCAA's Division I.

Hodges no doubt suffered from the perception that the only reason he had taken Indiana State to the NCAA final was because Larry Bird was on the team. However, he also suspected that people in the Indiana State administration, in particular Richard Landini, the university president, who died in 2004, were bad-mouthing him. "I liked Landini, but after he got rid of me, boy, he stuck it in my butt for a long time without me even knowing," Hodges says. Finally, in the spring of 1991, Hodges got his Division I opportunity when he was hired by Mercer University in Macon, Georgia.

Hodges's tenure at Mercer allowed him to reconnect with some of his Indiana State roots. He hired Carl Nicks as an assistant. When he took his team to play Butler University in Indianapolis, Bob Behnke, Steve Reed, and Rick Shaw came to the game. In the spring of 1994, the Indiana State coach, Tates Locke, invited Hodges to bring his Mercer team to Terre Haute for a game. But when Hodges and his team arrived at Indiana State, the Mercer players, who naturally idolized Bird and were curious to see where he played college ball, were amazed at how little the university had done to commemorate that dream season. "You couldn't find a picture of our team anywhere," Hodges says. "There weren't any banners hanging, either. I think that was the only place in the world where they were ashamed they went to the Final Four." That aside, it was a pleasant visit. Hodges got to see a lot of old friends. He exchanged a cordial pregame handshake with Landini. And Mercer won, 81–74.

It wasn't easy winning games with a program on a limited budget, but Hodges figured if he could just get Mercer into the NCAA tournament, he could move up to a better job. Twice, the Bears reached to the final of their conference tournament, but both times they lost. After the second loss, in 1996, Hodges broke down and wept. "That was the first and only time I ever shed a tear over basketball," Hodges says. "I knew that was my last chance. I kind of knew what Larry was feeling when we lost in Salt Lake City. At the time, I thought that was just my start, but that was Larry's end."

The bottom fell out at Mercer the following season, during which five relatives of players died, and the Bears were ranked dead last in the national computer rankings. Hodges resigned in February with his team owning a 3–20 record. Figuring he was done with college coaching for good, he took a job teaching history and coaching junior varsity basketball at a middle school in Fort Myers, Florida. Then, in the spring of 1998, he got a call from a close friend, Tevester Anderson, who was the head coach at Murray State University in Kentucky. Anderson wanted to know if Hodges would join his staff as an assistant. Once again, Hodges couldn't resist the call, and that season the Racers won the Ohio Valley Conference tournament. The

OVC championship game drew national attention because of its dramatic ending, when Murray State guard Aubrey Reese dashed coast to coast and sank a game-winning layup at the buzzer.

When Hodges walked into his office the next day, the basketball secretary handed him a two-word message: "Great play."

"Who is this from?" he asked.

She replied, "He said his name was Jud."

The Racers' first-round NCAA tournament game against Ohio State was played, of all places, in the RCA Dome in Indianapolis. Hodges tried to accommodate the many local newspapers who wanted to publish profiles on him, but he sensed that Anderson was not pleased that so much attention was being lavished on an assistant. "I'd have gotten upset if I'd have been him, too," Hodges says. "The press can really wreak havoc on a basketball program."

After just one season at Murray State, Hodges left college coaching, this time for good. He figured he would retire, but after a year of fishing, playing golf, and drinking with his buddies, he decided he wanted to go back to work. "If I had done that for another year, I would have either gone crazy or become an alcoholic," he says. Hodges taught at three different high schools in Virginia and Georgia before moving to Roanoke in 2006 to live with his daughter, Zoie, and her three kids.

By his count, Hodges lived in eighteen homes in eight different states over the course of his coaching career. The specter of the 1979 NCAA final followed him wherever he went, with local newspapers revisiting his remarkable story each time he alighted in a new place. In 2005, Hodges attended a special dinner at the Final Four for all the men who had coached on college basketball's biggest stage. That night he shared a table, and more than a few laughs, with Jud Heathcote. "He claimed I ruined his life," Heathcote says. "When he told me what he was doing, I said, 'What the hell do you know about history?' He told me, 'Only what I read.'"

Actually, Hodges genuinely enjoys history, and he really likes teaching. "When they start out with me, they're still eighth graders," he says of freshman students at Fleming High. "At some point, they become used to my style of teaching and become interested in history and a light switch goes on. That's the best part."

Mostly, he enjoys living with his grandchildren, even if they seem clueless about the unique role their "Pop" played in world history. As Hodges sat on the basement couch of Zoie's house in the fall of 2007 and watched a replay of the 1979 NCAA championship game, his five-year-old granddaughter, Rylie, sat on the floor with her back to the screen and doodled. His grandson, Anderson, listened to him talk basketball and said, "You're not a coach. You're just an old man." When Hodges's face came on the screen, Anderson asked him seriously, "Did you use to be a basketball coach?"

Like Heathcote, Hodges couldn't watch the game as a casual fan. It was even more uncomfortable in his case because he knew the outcome was not going to be happy. When his daughter came downstairs to check on him, Hodges sighed and said, "Damned score hasn't changed, Zoie."

Zoie massaged his shoulders and said, "It's not gonna."

Later that evening, Hodges reflected on the game and all that has happened since. "I watched that thing and I thought, Damn, I should have gone this way [he points up], not this way [points down]," he said. "You'd think most people would be unhappy with their life, but shoot, I'm happy. I'm in good health. I wish I had a lower golf handicap. I wish I had a lady in my life who accepts me for me, who likes my grandkids. I tell you, I was proud of the way I handled my interview at the end. I had never watched that."

After Bird took over the Indiana Pacers as the team's president of basketball operations in 2003, Hodges tried to convince Bird to hire him as a scout. Bird hired Carl Nicks in 2006, but he never saw fit to throw his old college coach a bone until the spring of 2008, not long after Hodges's sixty-fifth birthday. That's when Mel Daniels, the former assistant at Indiana State, who had become the Pacers' director of player personnel, called Hodges and invited him to work for the team at the NBA's predraft camp near Orlando, Florida. It was quite the Indiana State reunion that week, with Bird, Hodges, Daniels, and Nicks all working on the same team again. The trip gave Hodges the chance to spend more time with Bird than he had at any point since Bird's senior year. "It was enjoyable," Hodges says. "Larry's still so damned quiet and reserved, and he still chews his fingernails. In some ways, he's a different person. He's back to being that real quiet guy. He'll look you in the eye now, but he doesn't have a lot to say. Like if you and I sat down, you're going to start talking and I'm going to start talking. You can sit down with Larry, and if you don't start talking, it's going to be silent."

Hodges left Orlando hoping he would find more work with the Pacers the following basketball season, maybe even as a full-time scout, but as the fall approached there was no offer. "I'm totally disappointed Larry has never given Bill a job," says a friend of both men. "Larry would still be in French Lick if it wasn't for Bob King and Bill Hodges." Even so, Hodges was looking forward to returning to teach at Fleming High for at least two more years. Despite everything, he keeps a soft spot in his heart for the place that gave him his first opportunity to be a head coach. When Indiana State fired its basketball coach, Royce Waltman, in the spring of 2007, Bob Behnke, Hodges's former trainer, called and jokingly suggested that Hodges apply for the job. "I'll go back if you will," Behnke said. Hodges couldn't help but laugh. "I don't think they'd want me at my age," he says. "But heck, I loved Terre Haute and I loved Indiana State. I'd go back tomorrow if they wanted to hire me."

It was supposed to be a friendly little game. The 1979 Spartans, led by Magic Johnson, played the Spartan All-Stars, a team of Michigan State alumni led by Scott Skiles, in the summer of 1989 to mark the tenth anniversary of the NCAA title. The game was the last one to be played in Jenison Fieldhouse before the team moved into the brand-new Breslin Center in the fall. In the spirit of the occasion, the All-Stars allowed the '79ers to reprise the opening-tip play they had used in their regional final win over Notre Dame. Without any defense, the play again worked to perfection, though this time Mike Brkovich, who was after all ten years older, scored on a layup instead of a dunk.

From then on, the game became a game. They were competitors, after all. The All-Stars wanted to shut up the guys who were always bragging about their title, and the champs were too proud to go down without a fight. Not surprisingly, Magic was the difference, going for 25 points, 17 rebounds, and 12 assists while converting the winning free throws in the final minute to give the '79ers a 95–93 win before a sellout crowd. Afterward, the champs huddled together on the court, where Greg Kelser led them in their "potential" chant. Being reunited never felt so good.

The winds of time have cast the Spartans in disparate directions, but their common experience has always brought them back together. It helped that Michigan State's hoops program has remained strong as Tom Izzo built upon, and even exceeded, the legacy bequeathed to him by Jud Heathcote. During his first thirteen years as head coach, Izzo guided the Spartans to four Big Ten championships, four Final Four appearances, and the 2000 NCAA title. Yet Izzo is the first to concede that none of his teams has captured the attention of the Spartan nation, much less the entire nation, quite the way the 1979 squad did. "It baffles me even today to say it's still the highest-rated game in history," Terry Donnelly says. "To say that I was a participant in that game and played as well as I did is really special. I love when February and March come around every year and I start getting calls from reporters who are doing articles. I get to enjoy that the rest of my life."

Ten years after that "friendly" game closed Jenison, Michigan State hosted the 1979 team again for their twenty-year reunion. This time the event was an intimate, low-key dinner at the Harley Hotel outside Lansing. A video replay of the championship game played on a television in the corner of the room, but the guys were too busy socializing with each other and their families to pay much attention. As the evening wore on, it appeared that Magic Johnson wouldn't show up, but he sauntered into the room just after the food had been cleared and held court for the next two hours. "I'll never forget that night," he told reporters. "I don't want to forget. It's so, so special to me. . . . I'm Earvin here. One of the guys. Nobody can take that away. Around here, I'm just Earvin."

At that point, Kelser sneaked up behind him and said, "Excuse me, can you come over here, Magic?" Johnson busted a gut laughing, hugged Kelser, and said, "Man, we never change, do we?"

The grandest reunion of all was the silver anniversary celebration that took place over the first weekend of November 2003. The festivities began on Saturday morning, when Michigan State unveiled a twelve-foot bronze statue of Johnson outside the Breslin Center. The sculpture, which cost $250,000, was titled *Always a Champion* and showed Johnson dribbling the ball with his right hand while directing traffic with his left. At Johnson's request, there was a serious look on his face, not a smile, which may account for why the face on the statue bears so little resemblance to the real thing. "I very rarely smiled when I was actually playing," Johnson explained. He was emotional during the ceremony inside the Breslin Center that morning. "I tell you, this is just the greatest moment," he said through tears. "Knowing that even when I die I'll still have a presence is just an unbelievable feeling." Johnson also said that weekend that he was finalizing plans to complete his communications degree in 2005, but by the fall of 2008 he was still more than fifty credits shy.

Johnson and his teammates were introduced during halftime of the Michigan–Michigan State football game later that afternoon. Then, on Sunday, Johnson suited up for the Harlem Globetrotters during an exhibition game against the current Michigan State squad. The Globetrotters won, 97–83, but Johnson, who was forty-four years old, contributed little to the victory. He had 5 points and 4 assists in sixteen minutes, and he spent most of the afternoon kibitzing on the sideline with the Globetrotters' honorary coach—one Larry Bird. Terry Donnelly had never met Bird, and when he introduced himself before the game, Larry pointed at Donnelly's championship ring and said, "If it wasn't for you, I might have one of those." Says Donnelly, "That was a pretty proud moment for me."

For the players, the best part of the weekend was Friday night, when they gathered at Izzo's house. Mike Brkovich showed up late because he wanted to defy Heathcote. ("I don't have to show up on time anymore," he boasted.) And Magic showed up late because, well, he was Magic. Izzo had arranged for a designer to produce commemorative championship posters, and the players signed each one. Once Magic finally arrived, he assembled everyone in Izzo's basement, and, still orchestrating like a point guard, he called on each guy to stand up and tell a story from the championship season. "Magic just took over," Heathcote says. "It's a good thing, too, because the Brkoviches of the world wouldn't say shit unless he made them." The session was the first time Izzo had heard the story about Heathcote's embarrassing foray behind the luggage flaps at the Capital City airport. Johnson relished in showing off his Coach Heathcote imitation, limp and all, though Heathcote got the last laugh by asking Magic why he wasn't so funny on his television talk show, which had failed so spectacularly. ("It was hard to watch that show, because it wasn't Earvin," Jud says. "It was him trying to be what he wasn't. That's why it wasn't successful.")

As Johnson's public persona grew larger than life over the years, it has been harder for his former teammates and coaches to remain in close contact with him. That, however, does not mean they have grown apart. Darwin Payton, who asked Johnson to be godfather to his sons, rarely saw Johnson after Payton stopped working for him in 1999, but every couple of months Payton rings him up just to say hello. "The best time to catch him is before he gets busy around seven in the morning. He's usually on his way to the gym," Payton says. Likewise, whenever Johnson is at the Palace of Auburn Hills, either in his capacity as part-owner of the Lakers or as a studio analyst for TNT, he makes a point to seek out Brkovich, who Johnson knows is a season ticket holder. "He'll tell a guy from the Pistons, 'Where's Mike? I want to see him.' He doesn't need to do those things, but he does," Brkovich says. Heathcote has also had minimal contact since Johnson went to the NBA—"I called him a few times early, but you could never get through," he says—but when Heathcote turned eighty, he received a fruit basket with a card that read, "Thank you for helping me become a better basketball player, a better man and a better person. Love, Earvin 'Magic' Johnson."

Johnson did get to visit with his former running mate Greg Kelser while they were both playing in the NBA. Since Kelser retired, however, those meetings have been been fewer and farther between. "Do we talk to each other every day, every week, every month? No," Kelser says. "But we were unbelievable teammates together, and out of it, we formed a great friendship and a bond that will never, ever break. We get together when we can, and whenever we do we just have the most fun."

Then again, some things never change no matter how much time passes. One morning in 2007, Kelser was walking down Rodeo Drive in Los Angeles when he heard a familiar voice call out, "Greg!" He wheeled around and there was Johnson, hurrying out of a restaurant where he was having breakfast with two business associates. Johnson invited Kelser to join them inside. When Kelser took his seat, he looked out the window toward where he had just been walking. He could only shake his head. "You couldn't see the street that well and there were a lot of people walking by," Kelser says. "The opportunity for Earvin to catch me was maybe a second, but he caught me. It reminded me how unbelievable the guy is. He just sees everything."

Thirty years later, the 1979 NCAA runner-up performance remains arguably Indiana State University's best-known achievement. That is not necessarily a good thing. While the school has often looked for ways to build upon (and profit from) the accomplishments of that team, it has also struggled at times to honor that past without trying to live up to it.

Hodges's successor as coach, Dave Schellhase, was acutely aware of how the high expectations had engulfed the previous coach. He was intent on scrubbing away any reference to the dream season that he could find. Early in his first season, Schellhase instructed Bob Behnke to throw away an original painting commemorating the team that was hanging in a hallway outside the team's locker room. Behnke took down the picture, but he didn't want to throw it in the garbage. So he carefully rolled it up and stacked it in a corner of his office.

A year later, Schellhase discovered the painting. This time, he followed Behnke outside the arena so he could watch him deposit the portrait in a dumpster. After practice a few hours later, Behnke backed his station wagon down a ramp, retrieved the portrait, and put it in his car. After getting it cleaned up and framed, he nailed it to a wall in his home, where it hangs to this day. Behnke was still on bad terms with the administration when he left the Indiana State athletics program in 1985, and in the ensuing years he refused to attend reunions and stayed away from the campus as much as possible.

A similar estrangement occurred in 1994 between the school, point guard Steve Reed, and Rick Shaw, the former manager and assistant trainer. Indiana State had decided to outsource its sports medicine program, and Reed, who had become the COO of a hospital in Terre Haute, put in a bid along with Shaw, the hospital's director of sports medicine, to run the program. When the school awarded the contract to someone else, Reed and Shaw believed the administration had not been straight with them. Shaw had helped organize the ten-year reunion—he even tried to convince Heathcote to help him set up a rematch with the '79 Spartans—but he refused to attend the twenty-year reunion even though he was invited. "When I get a piece of alumni mail from ISU, I don't even open it. It goes straight in the trash," Shaw says. "I have a real bitter feeling for ISU." Reed also declined to attend the reunion in 1999. "The whole thing seemed kind of contrived and staged. It almost felt like they just needed me to make sure everyone was there," Reed says. "The university doesn't owe me anything, but it's been a disappointment that Indiana State hasn't recognized the need to stay more connected with former athletes."

Carl Nicks was similarly put off when he returned to Terre Haute to finish up his degree in the early 1990s and asked the basketball coach, Tates Locke, if he could be a volunteer assistant. Locke turned him down flat. "He didn't directly give me a reason, but I heard they didn't want any of the guys from that team involved," Nicks says. "I even asked several times, 'Can I help you guys recruit? I've got a pipeline with the Chicago public school systems.' Did I ever get a call? No. That kind of left a bad taste in my mouth."

Hodges returned for the reunions and enjoyed himself immensely, but when he told the organizers of the twenty-year reunion he wanted to bring along his children, he was informed he would have to buy them tickets at a hundred dollars apiece. "That's pretty cheap, man," Hodges says. "I told them don't ever call me again, and they haven't."

Nor have the folks at Indiana State ever found a way to bring Stan Evans, the jilted assistant who was passed over for Hodges at the start of the 1978–79 season, back into the family. Not that Evans would be receptive if they tried. "No reunions for me. I just stay away," Evans says. "I'm not even sure what I would say to them. Forgive and forget is easier said than done."

The former players might have a greater urge to be involved with the school if the basketball team had remained successful, but unlike Michigan State, the program at Indiana State fell on hard times and stayed there. In the fifteen years after Hodges resigned, Indiana State burned through five coaches. The Sycamores did reach consecutive NCAA tournaments in 2000 and 2001 (they even got a nice dose of nostalgia in 2000 when they were sent to Salt Lake City for the first round), but over the next six years the team averaged just 9.8 wins per season, which led to Royce Waltman's firing in the spring of 2007.

In many respects, the basketball program has reflected the overall health of the university, which in 2006 saw its admissions plummet to its lowest level in forty-one years. Even the University of Southern Indiana, which used to be called ISU–Evansville, is on the verge of surpassing Indiana State's undergraduate enrollment. "[ISU's] reputation among students in town is [that it's] the school to go to if you can't get in any other one," says Andy Amey, who still works for the *Terre Haute Tribune*. "There's just a whole defeatist attitude at the university, and frankly, I'm not sure anything the athletic department does is going to overcome that."

Such was the challenge that faced Kevin McKenna, the former Creighton University assistant, when he was hired in 2007 to replace Waltman. McKenna, who is one of the lowest-paid coaches in the Missouri Valley Conference, went 15–16 in his first season. He also went out of his way to reach out to the former players (Brad Miley, for one, was a regular at practices), but unless McKenna is able to win games, he'll have a hard time getting any fans, much less the guys from the 1979 squad, excited about the program. "I'm willing to go to Peoria or Muncie or Indianapolis or Evansville—if they're going to compete and play hard and have a chance at winning," Bob Heaton says. "But I'm not going to go to Evansville if they're going to get beat by twenty-one. Why do it?"

Still, on the occasions when the school has put forth the effort to honor the 1979 NCAA runner-up, it has produced some truly memorable events. When the team assembled in Terre Haute in 1989 for the ten-year reunion, Larry Bird put up everyone in his Boston Connection hotel, and they all hung out in the restaurant together until the wee hours of the morning. At the twenty-year reunion in 1999, the university inducted the entire team into the Indiana State Hall of Fame.

That weekend was also memorable because of the presence of Bob King, who had been unable to attend the ten-year reunion. "It was absolutely glorious," Sharel King says. "We thought we had died and gone to heaven. We couldn't have been treated any better." King was in declining health, but he was lucid enough to be interviewed along with Bird in front of an audience of several thousand that had gathered in Hulman Center. Ever the raconteur, Bird delighted in telling of the time that King followed him after practice to make sure he went straight home. After King's car disappeared around the corner, Bird hopped back into his own car, picked up his buddies, and drove straight to the Ballyhoo. "So Coach King is not as slick as you think he is," Bird said with a grin.

When that interview was done, each member of the 1979 team (except Steve Reed) took the microphone and told the audience what they were currently doing. "Reporters were coming up to me and asking me what it was like. I kept telling 'em what really blows me away is that it's been twenty years since that game," Heaton says. "Now we're coming up on thirty years. That's just life, you know. It goes by so quickly." Suffice to say, Heaton, who still lives in Terre Haute, enjoys his legacy as being a man of many miracles. "I get asked all the time about hitting that last-second shot. And I always go, 'Which one?'"

Tom Crowder no longer can kick a rim and he rarely answers to "The Hulk" anymore. Yet when he was surrounded by his teammates, it was as if he had just seen them the day before. "We picked right up where we left off, like nothing had ever changed," Crowder says. "It was special because we're all getting up into that age where anything could happen to us. You read about people in the paper every day dying at all ages. I just hope I'm not the first to go."

After Bob King stepped down as athletic director, he and his wife returned to their native New Mexico. King spent the rest of his life playing golf and leveling land with his small bulldozer. When he died of heart failure in December 2004, Bird flew to Albuquerque with Mel Daniels on the Pacers' corporate jet. They both spoke at King's funeral service, which was held at the Pit at the University of New Mexico on the court that bears King's name.

By that point, people at Indiana State were long past being concerned about trying to live up to the expectations that Bird had set. If anything, they were looking for ways in which they could remind the world that he was part of the Indiana State family. Though the school had retired his jersey at Larry Bird Appreciation Night in April 1979, the university had never officially raised his No. 33 to the rafters at Hulman Center. It hoped to rectify that with a ceremony—that is, if Bird would agree to appear. "There was fear for a long, long time that Larry would not come back," says Mike McCormick, the local writer and historian. "Just because he's Larry. He was remote and supposedly pissed off for some reason. He didn't even acknowledge he was going to come back until two or three weeks beforehand."

Larry did agree to come back, partly because the school smartly coupled his jersey retirement with that of Duane Klueh, a kindly old gentleman who had been an All-American player at Indiana State under John Wooden. So on February 28, 2004, before a game between Indiana State and Northern Iowa, Larry Bird returned to Hulman Center for yet another ovation. When he was invited to the podium, he waited for the applause to end, and then, glancing at the students sitting in the bleachers behind him, he quipped, "I think that some of these folks back here stopped at the Ballyhoo on the way down here."

Bird began by congratulating Klueh. "I've always had a lot of respect for Duane Klueh," he said. "I always looked up to him when I was here. He's a great man. You can't find anybody better." He continued by paying tribute to Jim Jones, the man who coached him during his first three years at Springs Valley High and was still coaching at Terre Haute North Vigo High School. "He's a man that said, Larry, when it's all done, only the champions will be standing. Well, Coach, here I am," Bird said. Gesturing over to the current Indiana State players sitting on their bench, Bird smiled and said, "I don't know how, getting ready for a basketball game, these young men can come out here and sit like this. If it was me sitting over there, I would've already ate half the floor up."

Bird then turned to the row of chairs behind him where many of his former teammates were sitting. "I want to thank ISU for this tremendous day. It's always good to come back to Terre Haute. I'd like to thank some of my fellow teammates for being here," he said. "Nineteen seventy-nine was a very special year. It was special for one reason. We played together and we played to win. Everyone knew their roles. Everyone knew that I was going to take the majority of the shots. That's always key."

That last line elicited a round of laughter. Bird paused a moment to let it subside. "But I've always been heartbroken by the fact that I wasn't able to bring that championship trophy back to Terre Haute. I didn't play the way that I usually played. . . ."

When Bird said the word "way," his voice quavered and his eyes filled. Then he stopped talking. He took a deep breath. He raised his eyebrows and looked toward the ceiling. He absently used his right fingers to scratch the back of his left hand.

Finally, he gathered himself and delivered the epitaph for that dream season. "Hell," he said, "Magic was just too tough."

NOTES

PROLOGUE

Interviews: Dick Enberg, George Finkel, Dave Gavitt, Lynn Henning, Don McGuire, Don Ohlmeyer, Billy Packer, Bill Rasmussen, Bob Ryan, David Stern.

PAGE

1   NBC production meeting: *Los Angeles Times,* April 2, 1989; *Boston Globe,* April 2, 1998.

2   "Well, this is probably the biggest game I'll ever play in my life": *Magic vs. Bird: The 1979 NCAA Championship Game,* DVD, 2004.

4   24.1 rating, 12.1 rating, 10.7 rating: Nielsen Media Research.

5   he had friends in Denver who thought Larry was black: *Boston Globe,* April 2, 1998.

7   signed a deal a few weeks before: Bill Rasmussen, *Sports Junkies Rejoice!: The Birth of ESPN* (Hartsdale, N.Y.: QV Publishing, 1983), p. 173.

8   NCAA tournament history: http://www.ncaa.com/basketball-mens/article.aspx?id=2162.

8    $5.2 million in TV revenue; $48 million; $96 million, eleven-year, $6 billion deal: *Boston Globe,* April 2, 1998; NCAA history.

9   "Bird and Magic came along and pushed the button": *Los Angeles Times,* April 2, 1989.

CHAPTER 1

Interviews: Bob Behnke, Mike Brkovich, Bob Chapman, Terry Donnelly, Stan Evans, George Fox, Rob Gonzalez, Jud Heathcote, Bill Hodges, Jamie Huffman, Greg Kelser, Sharel King, Mike Longaker, Mick McCabe, Ed McKee, John Newton, Tom Reck, Jimmy Smith, Lane Stewart, Charles Tucker, Jay Vincent, Edgar Wilson.

PAGE

11   April 22, 1978: Earvin Johnson and Richard Levin, *Magic* (New York: Penguin Books, 1991), p. 108.

11   "If the money's right": *Detroit News*, April 22, 1978.

12   "almost 70 percent sure": *State Journal* (Lansing, Mich.), April 23, 1978.

12   "The kid's got a long way to go": Ibid.

12   "knowledgeable scouts": *Basketball Weekly*, December 13, 1978.

12   Axelson told NBA commissioner Larry O'Brien that no financial terms were discussed: Ibid.

12   five-year contract worth $225,000 per year: *State Journal*, February 22, 1979.

14   Santa Claus, Indiana: Larry Bird with Bob Ryan, *Drive* (New York: Bantam Books, 1990), p. 51.

14   He had heard of Bill Russell: Ibid., p. 52.

14   "I'm very happy that the Boston Celtics": *Terre Haute Tribune*, June 9, 1978.

14   he did not want to be required to talk to the press: *Sports Illustrated*, February 5, 1979.

16   "I definitely would have left if Bill Hodges hadn't gotten the job": Bird, *Drive*, p. 54.

17   "I had acquired sort of tunnel vision": *Terre Haute Star*, October 25, 1978.

17   "I'm still Coach King's assistant": Reporter's file for *Sports Illustrated* by Dick Denny, October 29, 1978.

17   "It's not really a problem": *Terre Haute Tribune*, November 7, 1978.

18   One of Bird's teachers humiliated him: L. Virginia Smith, *Larry Bird: From Valley Hick to Boston Celtic* (Self-published, 1982), p. 89.

19   set a city scoring record with 48 points: Fred Stabley Jr. and Tim Staudt, *Tales from the Magical Spartans: A Collection of Stories from*

the 1979 Michigan State NCAA Basketball Champions (Champaign, Ill.: Sports Publishing, 2003), p. 6.

19   five supporters were recalled: *State Journal,* October 3, 1972.

19   his two older brothers, Quincy and Larry, had had bad experiences: Johnson, *Magic,* p. 46.

19   They considered having Earvin bunk up with friends: *Detroit Free Press,* February 28, 1977.

20   "I wanted to go to Sexton": *Detroit News, Sunday News Magazine,* February 27, 1977.

20   an older white teammate appeared to be refusing to pass him the ball; cheerleader boycott threat: Earvin Johnson with William Novak, *My Life* (New York: Fawcett Books, 1992), p. 28.

20   "John the Narc": Ibid., p. 35.

22   "Everett Crushes Parkside": *State Journal,* January 25, 1975.

23   He still dominated play using mostly his left: Gregory Kelser with Steve Grinczel, *Gregory Kelser's Tales from Michigan State Basketball* (Champaign, Ill.: Sports Publishing, 2006), p. 130; Jack Ebling with John Farina, *Magic Moments* (Chelsea, Mich.: Sleeping Bear Press, 1998), p. 10.

23   "talk, talk, talk": *Detroit News, Sunday News Magazine,* February 27, 1977.

24   "People are stopping me to sign autographs": *State Journal,* November 11, 1977.

26   "Greg, don't take that shot": Kelser, *Gregory Kelser's Tales,* p. 132.

27   "I thought he was your boy": Ibid.

28   "Super Sophs: Michigan State's Classy Earvin Johnson": *Sports Illustrated,* November 27, 1978.

28   "I love to be the underdog and rise to the occasion": Ibid.

CHAPTER 2

Interviews: George Fox, Bill Frieder, Gus Ganakas, Leonard Hamilton, Jud Heathcote, Bob Heaton, Bill Hodges, Joe Kearney, Ed McKee, Carl Nicks, Billy Packer, Vern Payne, Charles Tucker, Jay Vincent, Clifton Wharton.

PAGE

29   Kentucky players dominated the starting lineup: Bird, *Drive,* p. 60; Lee Daniel Levine, *Bird: The Making of an American Sports Legend*

(New York: Berkley Books, 1989), p. 145; *Terre Haute Star*, April 14, 1978.

30   The writers picked them third, the coaches picked them second: *Terre Haute Tribune*, November 7, 1978.

30   Indiana State was nowhere to be found: Ibid., November 28, 1978.

30   "Bird will again carry the team with little help": *Playboy*, November 1978.

32   he literally could not dribble the ball past half-court: Bird, *Drive*, p. 65.

32   "best player to go this far in college without being able to shoot": *Terre Haute Tribune*, March 26, 1979.

33   "We didn't have a lot of NBA talent": Larry Bird interview with Fox Sports Net, "Magic vs. Bird: The Game That Changed the Game," March 28, 1999.

33   "If we can beat these guys, we should be able to beat anybody": *Terre Haute Tribune*, November 20, 1978.

33   each Indiana State player shook hands with Bob King: Ibid., November 26, 1978.

34   "I'm an old Purdue guy": *Terre Haute Star*, November 28, 1978.

35   There was no mention anywhere of Indiana State or Larry Bird: Ibid., December 6, 1978.

35   thirteen NBA scouts: Ibid., December 10, 1978.

36   Cincinnati, Louisville, and Memphis State had defected: *Sporting News*, February 25, 1978.

37   Then he hung up the phone and asked his assistants to find out who this Johnson fellow was: Jud Heathcote with Jack Ebling, *Jud: A Magical Journey* (Champaign, Ill.: Sagamore Publishing, 1995), p. 67; Stabley and Staudt, *Tales from the Magical Spartans*, p. 16; interview with Jud Heathcote.

39   Johnson took official visits to the University of Maryland, Notre Dame, and North Carolina State: *State Journal*, November 24, 1977.

39   slightly less than the one the station generated for that year's Super Bowl: *Sports Illustrated*, November 28, 1978.

39   "Leading the Way with Earvin and Jay": *State Journal*, November 11, 1977.

40   "I couldn't get a read on Jud and his style": Ibid., April 22, 1997.

40   "That's the only signature he'll ever get from me": Johnson, *My Life*, p. 68; Stabley and Staudt, *Tales from the Magical Spartans*, p. 18.

41   two dozen local businessmen formed a committee: *Detroit Free Press,* February 28, 1977.

42   "Every time I think I've got a moment to myself": Ibid., October 11, 1976.

42   Frieder walked along press row: Ibid., March 27, 1977.

42   "I know you want me to go to Michigan State": Author interview with Charles Tucker.

43   "I thought there might be a couple of reporters": *State Journal,* April 18, 1977.

45   "Get the papers and I'll sign": Johnson, *My Life,* p. 54; Stabley and Staudt, *Tales from the Magical Spartans,* p. 149; author interview with Vern Payne.

45   "I wish I could tell you Earvin's coming to Michigan": *State Journal,* April 21, 1977.

45   "scowling and looking exceedingly irritated": Ibid., November 24, 1977.

46   "Let's get this over with": Author interview with Charles Tucker.

46   "This is the best-kept secret of all time": *Detroit Free Press,* April 23, 1977.

46   "It's a Small World": Ibid.

46   "Am I supposed to talk in all these mikes?": Video of press conference provided by George Fox.

47   "Everybody was sort of surprised that day": *State Journal,* April 22, 1997.

47   "Vern was the key": Ibid.

48   "After I came out of shock": Ibid., April 23, 1977.

48   By 11 a.m., more than one hundred people had called Michigan State: *Detroit News,* April 23, 1977.

CHAPTER 3

Interviews: Chuck Akers, Leslie Akers, Dave Bliss, James Carnes, Kevin Carnes, Tony Clark, Jan Condra Deakins, Stan Evans, Bob Heaton, Bill Hodges, Gary Holland, Jim Jones, John Laskowski, Bob Ryan, Bob Weltlich.

PAGE

51   he didn't like crowds: *Sports Illustrated,* March 21, 1988.

51   Larry was the only one whom she couldn't tell what he was thinking: Smith, *Larry Bird,* p. 6.

51   "Larry only tells you exactly what he wants you to know": *Sports Illustrated*, January 23, 1978.

51   "It would have been difficult to find anyone": Bird, *Drive*, p. 57.

51   in and out of jobs as he battled alcoholism: Smith, *Larry Bird*, pp. 17, 52.

51   Kimball Piano Factory: *Sports Illustrated*, March 21, 1988; *Inside Sports*, October 1979; Indianapolis Star and Indianapolis News, *Larry Bird: An Indiana Legend* (Champaign, Ill.: Sports Publishing, 1999), p. iv.

51   seventeen houses in eighteen years: Levine, *Bird*, p. 48.

51   "My kids were made fun of": *Sports Illustrated*, November 9, 1981.

51   post-traumatic stress disorder, violent nightmares: Levine, *Bird,* p. 50; Smith, *Larry Bird*, p. 51.

51   "sporting a beauty of a black eye and a cut": Smith, *Larry Bird*, p. 16.

52   "Why can't we get Beezer's name in the paper": *Indianapolis Star*, March 8, 1979.

52   challenged Bird to a game of H-O-R-S-E: Bird, *Drive*, p. 35; Levine, *Bird*, p. 79; author interview with Gary Holland.

53   another player Knight was recruiting opted for the University of Cincinnati: Levine, *Bird*, p. 88.

53   Wisman's father was a mail carrier: Ibid., p. 87.

54   "I made a mistake rooming Bird with Jim Wisman": *Los Angeles Times*, May 18, 1988.

54   Wisman generously told Bird he could wear his clothes: Bird, *Drive,* p. 39.

54   especially Benson: Ibid., p. 38.

54   "A lot of times he was fairly unhappy": Levine, *Bird*, p. 89.

55   "Larry Bird is one of my great mistakes": *Playboy*, March 2001.

55   asked Wisman not to tell the coaches: Levine, *Bird*, p. 90.

55   Larry headed out to Highway 37 and stuck his thumb in the air: Bird, *Drive*, p. 41.

55   It was left to one of Bird's uncles to call Knight: *Indianapolis Star*, September 17, 1974.

55   she didn't speak to Larry for weeks: Bird, *Drive*, p. 42.

55   "I can be moody like Mom": *Sports Illustrated*, March 21, 1988.

56   "He was very unsettled": *Sports Illustrated*, February 5, 1979.

56   "I loved that job": *Sports Illustrated*, March 21, 1988.

57   Larry would spy a sharply dressed man: Bird, *Drive*, p. 44.

57   he shot himself in the head with a shotgun: Ibid., p. 16.

59   Larry told his grandmother she should go into the house without him: Smith, *Larry Bird*, p. 57.

61   "Larry was pressured into going to Indiana": *Sports Illustrated*, January 23, 1978.

62   found Larry putting up some hay: Bird, *Drive*, p. 45.

63   they'd just as soon play in their jeans: Ibid.

CHAPTER 4

Interviews: Bob Chapman, Terry Donnelly, Gus Ganakas, Jud Heathcote, Lynn Henning, Joe Kearney, Gregory Kelser, Vern Payne, Darwin Payton, Jeff Tropf, Jay Vincent, Dick Vitale, Edgar Wilson.

PAGE

65   he told his buddies he believed Michigan State was going to win the NCAA championship: Bird, *Drive*, p. 63; Larry Bird interview with Intersport, "College Basketball's Ten Greatest Shooters," April 28, 2007.

65   "for national attention, prestige and pride": *State Journal*, December 16, 1978.

66   "An eight-footer for Jay is something that he'll hit sixty percent of the time": Ibid., December 17, 1978.

66   "We got a tremendous lesson in rebounding": Ibid., December 19, 1978.

67   "There's something missing right now"; Ibid., December 21, 1978.

67   "dull and slow-paced": Ibid., December 20, 1978.

68   "The big crowd had to be disappointed": Ibid., December 21, 1978.

68   "We've played just one good half": Ibid.

69   He was followed by nine players, all of them black: Ibid., January 5, 1975; *New York Times,* January 5, 1975, and January 6, 1975; *Sporting News,* February 8, 1975.

70   "Who's in Charge Anyway?": *Sporting News*, February 8, 1975.

70   abuse of a credit card belonging to a booster: *Sporting News*, May 22, 1976.

70   the lunch ended abruptly: Heathcote, *Jud*, p. 61; author interview with Jud Heathcote.

74   He wouldn't even lend them a quarter for the soda machine: Johnson, *My Life*, p. 60.

74   "So many don't know him": *State Journal,* January 5, 1978.

75   Kelser became so furious at the public humiliation: Kelser, *Gregory Kelser's Tales*, p. 143; author interview with Greg Kelser.

75   "If anybody in this room thinks he's tougher than me": Kelser, *Gregory Kelser's Tales,* pp. 59–60; Stabley and Staudt, *Tales from the Magical Spartans*, p. 55; author interviews with Mike Brkovich, Terry Donnelly, Jud Heathcote, Greg Kelser, and Edgar Wilson.

76   Heathcote's yelling didn't bother him as much as he feared it would: Johnson, *My Life*, p. 60.

76   "I didn't come here to sit": Author interview with Darwin Payton.

78   "his arm around Jud's shoulders": Stabley and Staudt, *Tales from the Magical Spartans*, p. 162.

CHAPTER 5

Interviews: Chuck Akers, Bob Behnke, Mike Brkovich, Tony Clark, Stan Evans, Lynn Henning, Bill Hodges, Sharel King, Mike McCormick, Craig McKee, Ed McKee, Brad Miley, Carl Nicks, Darwin Payton, Steve Reed, Rick Shaw, Leroy Staley.

PAGE

81   "He's so physical": *Terre Haute Tribune*, December 13, 1978.

82   "Those magazines said all we would have would be me": Ibid., December 31, 1978.

83   He stormed into the locker room: Bird, *Drive*, p. 46; author interview with Bill Hodges.

84   "When I was younger I played for the fun of it": *Sports Illustrated*, November 9, 1981.

85   "Larry could have put that ball back up": *Terre Haute Tribune*, March 2, 1977.

86   The guy ended up on his back with a bloody nose: Levine, *Bird,* p. 132; author interviews with Bob Behnke, Steve Reed, and Rick Shaw.

87   more than one thousand spectators shy of being filled to capacity: *Terre Haute Tribune*, January 3, 1979.

87   "We knew Bird was a great one": Ibid., January 4, 1979.

87   "the fellows playing with Bird and Nicks are no slouches": Ibid., January 10, 1979.

87   "Bird's wanting to win rather than just score points is infectious": Ibid., January 15, 1979.

88   "Psychologically our opponent doesn't think we're as effective without Bird": Ibid., January 19, 1979.

89   Bird grabbed Behnke's son: Smith, *Larry Bird*, p. 167; author interview with Bob Behnke.

91   "inspired defense": *Terre Haute Tribune,* January 23, 1979.

92   "with a microphone stuck in his face there are few better": *State Journal,* January 5, 1979.

92   "I think I'd vomit": Fred Stabley Jr. and Fred Stabley Sr., *Spartan Magic* (East Lansing, Mich.: Michigan State University, 1979), p. 49.

93   Heathcote responded by scrapping his usual two-three matchup zone: *State Journal,* January 7, 1979.

94   "The publicity office was too busy taking care of football": *Sports Illustrated,* January 22, 1979.

94   "I don't think our conference publicizes basketball the way it should": *State Journal,* November 22, 1977.

94   same training table privileges as football players: *Sports Illustrated,* January 22, 1979.

94   a bomb threat had been phoned in to the arena: Ibid; *State Journal,* January 12, 1979.

95   "Everybody was playing this game up like it meant the world": Ibid.

95   Lee Rose conceded Hallman was the last person he wanted to take that shot: *State Journal,* January 14, 1979.

95   "We were tired and Purdue had the momentum": Ibid.

96   "He is a mediocre passer and ball handler": Ebling, *Magic Moments,* p. 10.

96   "I think the story is a bum rap": *State Journal,* January 16, 1979.

97   he barred reporters from the team's locker room: Ibid., January 17, 1979.

98   "I tell you, Mike can jump": Ibid., January 19, 1979.

98   "Technical fouls are the most unnecessary crime in basketball": Ibid., January 23, 1979.

98   Olson still insists was horrendous: Lute Olson and David Fisher, *Lute!: The Seasons of My Life* (New York: Thomas Dunne Books/St. Martin's Press, 2006), p. 69.

99   Heathcote chased the referees off the court: *State Journal*, January 26, 1979.

100   "I just guess we're snakebit on the road": Ibid.

CHAPTER 6

Interviews: Mike Brkovich, Gerald Busby, Terry Donnelly, Rich Falk, Rob Gonzalez, Jud Heathcote, Bob Heaton, Bill Hodges, Gregory Kelser, Sharel King, Mike Longaker, Brad Miley, Carl Nicks, Darwin Payton, Steve Reed, Clint Thompson, Charles Tucker, Jay Vincent.

PAGE

101   "It's a must win for us": *State Journal,* January 27, 1979.

102   "If I was going to try and defend our team, that's what I would do": Ibid., January 28, 1979.

102   "I might figure the season is over": Ibid.

103   "I have too much respect": Ibid.

103   Heathcote called a team meeting: Kelser, *Gregory Kelser's Tales*, pp. 80–82; Stabley and Staudt, *Tales from the Magical Spartans*, pp. 56–57; Johnson, *My Life*, p. 82.

106   "personal problems with his girl at home": *State Journal,* January 31, 1979.

106   "It's not meant to be a slap at Terry": Ibid., February 1, 1979.

106   "Now is the time our basketball players need the support and backing of our fans": Ibid., January 30, 1979.

108   his momentum carried him into the bleachers: Game and broadcast details from WTHI telecast.

111   "I think we just saw a miracle": *Terre Haute Tribune*, February 2, 1979.

111   "If we had lost that game, we probably would have lost a couple more": Indiana State Athletics Hall of Fame induction, August 1, 1999, video courtesy of Indiana State University.

112   tossed him, delighted, into a snowbank: *Washington Post*, February 9, 1979.

112   "He is relaxed and at peace with the world": *Terre Haute Tribune,* February 5, 1979.

113   he found a note from Heathcote taped to his locker: *State Journal,* February 2, 1979.

113   "That's a mile away for anybody": Game and broadcast details from WJIM-TV-6 telecast, video courtesy of Michigan State University.

114   "Earvin doesn't dominate a game as much as he controls it": *State Journal,* March 2, 1978.

115   Johnson listened to the game on the radio: Ibid., February 2, 1979.

117   "Our kids went out to prove to people that they're still a good basketball team": Ibid.

118   "It was like your eardrums had popped": Ebling, *Magic Moments,* p. 185.

CHAPTER 7

Interviews: Andy Amey, Bob Behnke, Corrie Bird, Jan Condra Deakins, Terry Donnelly, Stan Evans, Jud Heathcote, Lynn Henning, Bill Hodges, David Israel, Larry Keith, Gregory Kelser, Ed McKee, Bruce Newman, Carl Nicks, Billy Packer, Darwin Payton, Lane Stewart, Dick Versace, Edgar Wilson.

PAGE

119   National Solid Wastes Management Association: *Sports Illustrated,* February 5, 1979.

119   "Larry's not talking": Ibid.

119   "People with my talents are a dime a dozen": *Sporting News,* February 25, 1978.

120   "They shouldn't do that": *St. Louis Post-Dispatch,* February 20, 1977.

120   found a dozen or more reporters waiting by his locker: Bird, *Drive,* p. 58.

120   "Writers keep asking me about my girlfriend": *Spectator* (Terre Haute, Ind.), January 15, 1977.

120   "talks like Harpo Marx": Missouri Valley Conference program, 1977–78.

121   "College Basketball's Secret Weapon": *Sports Illustrated,* November 28, 1977.

121   "You can't tell him nothing": Ibid., January 23, 1978.

122   "their schedule was suspect": *Terre Haute Tribune*, February 7, 1979.

122   "He is uncomfortable on airplanes": *Washington Post*, February 9, 1979.

122   "a mythic, almost operatic quality": *New York Post*, January 31, 1979.

122   "Maybe it added a little to the mystique of Larry Bird": *Terre Haute Tribune*, March 21, 1979.

122   POSTGAME PROCEDURES: Reporter's file for *Sports Illustrated* by Rick Stoff, February 15, 1979.

122   "I'll tell them I asked you and you said no": Ibid.

122   He spied people he assumed were writers: Bird, *Drive*, p. 57.

123   "You gotta be careful what you say around sportswriters": *Sports Illustrated*, February 5, 1979.

123   "the most pronounced fortress mentality I've ever run up against": *Spectator*, March 3, 1979.

124   Jan filed for divorce: Bird, *Drive*, p. 47; Levine, *Bird*, p. 111.

124   a court in Terre Haute established through a blood test that Larry was the father: *Sports Illustrated*, May 4, 1998.

124   "I thought people who got divorced were the devil": Ibid., March 21, 1988.

125   Eddie cried when he read it: Smith, *Larry Bird*, p. 118.

125   "Do you think I'm afraid of anyone?": *Terre Haute Tribune*, February 6, 1979.

127   dubbed Packer "enemy number one": *Indianapolis News*, December 12, 1979.

127   "Ode to Billy Packer": *Better Times* (Terre Haute, Ind.), February 26, 1979.

128   "Indiana State is a nice team, but not a number one": *Basketball Weekly*, February 8, 1979.

128   charged into the crowd to fight some fans: *State Journal*, January 11, 1979; *Basketball Weekly*, February 1, 1979.

129   "I think I'd come up with something a little better than that": Larry Bird interview with Intersport, "College Basketball's Ten Greatest Shooters," April 28, 2007.

129   six coaches voted them fourth or lower: *Terre Haute Tribune*, February 13, 1979.

129   "There's no way a team should be number two": Ibid., February 20, 1979.

129   student body president wrote a letter to U.S. senator Birch Bayh: Reporter's file for *Sports Illustrated* by Dick Denny, March 3, 1979.

130   "Coach has given me the okay": *State Journal,* February 4, 1979.

131   "Here comes the Michigan State prestidigitator!": Game and broadcast details from NBC telecast, video courtesy of Michigan State University.

132   "Earvin can get the ball to the man for a basket": *Sporting News,* February 11, 1978.

132   the trio used those words twenty-seven times in the first half alone: *State Journal,* February 13, 1979.

134   "Our zone is the best it's been all season": Ibid., February 18, 1979.

135   he noticed that referee Charles Fouty had dropped his glasses: Ibid., February 26, 1979.

135   "one of the greatest basketball players and individuals you'll ever know": Ibid., February 25, 1979.

135   "You better get him out of here": Author interview with Mike Brkovich.

136   "I didn't figure we had to check anybody from fifty-five feet away": *State Journal,* March 3, 1979.

136   "I've seen enough for a lifetime this season": Ibid.

CHAPTER 8

Interviews: Andy Amey, Tony Clark, Tom Crowder, Wayne Duke, Bob Heaton, Bill Hodges, Jim Jones, Rex Lardner, Craig McKee, Ed McKee, Brad Miley, Carl Nicks, Billy Packer, Tom Reck, Steve Reed, Rick Shaw, Chet Simmons, Jim Simpson.

PAGE

138   Twice that first season, the collegians beat the pros in the ratings: *Sports Illustrated,* January 31, 1977.

138   "It would benefit us to run them if anybody watched": Ibid., October 16, 1978.

138   only two of the top twenty scorers were white: Ibid., February 26, 1979.

139   "How can you sell a black sport to a white public?": Ibid.

142   143,918 votes: *Terre Haute Star,* March 17, 1979.

142   accidentally knocked over a nine-year-old boy: Levine, *Bird,* p. 162; *Indianapolis Star,* February 12, 1979.

144   "You're looking in on a very frantic Wabash Valley area": Game and broadcast details from NBC telecast, video courtesy of Indiana State University.

146   "He's a big Cousy": *Basketball Weekly,* March 15, 1979.

147   "I think if we had to win the game at Wisconsin, we would have": *State Journal,* March 5, 1979.

148   Heathcote didn't like the rule: Ibid., March 11, 1979.

148   "The officiating was not equal in the second half": Reporter's file for *Sports Illustrated* by Dick Denny, March 3, 1979.

149   immediately seized his thumb in obvious pain: Game and broadcast details from WTHI telecast, video courtesy of Indiana State University.

150   Even Richard Landini and Birch Bayh were victims: Reporter's file for *Sports Illustrated* by Dick Denny, March 4, 1979.

150   "I don't like that policy": *Terre Haute Tribune,* March 4, 1979.

150   "Bird's coach": *Sporting News,* March 17, 1979.

151   "You couldn't have picked a finer guy": *Terre Haute Tribune,* March 5, 1979.

151   Auerbach instructed his lawyer to send a telegram: Reporter's file for *Sports Illustrated* by Dick Denny, March 3, 1979.

152   "It would seem everybody in the country but us has been called": *Terre Haute Star,* March 5, 1979.

152   "I can think of a number of opponents I'd rather play": *State Journal,* March 5, 1979.

153   "But not NCAA champions": *Basketball Weekly,* March 15, 1979.

153   "still sneaking up on people": *Sports Illustrated,* March 19, 1979.

CHAPTER 9

Interviews: Dave Bliss, Tom Crowder, Terry Donnelly, Eddie Einhorn, Dick Enberg, Bryant Gumbel, Bob Heaton, Lynn Henning, Bill Hodges, Jamie Huffman, John Newton, Billy Packer, Darwin Payton, Digger Phelps, Steve Reed, Terry Thimlar, Jay Vincent.

PAGE

154   "All he has to do is touch it": *Terre Haute Tribune,* March 9, 1979.

154   offered Bird a special herbal recipe: *Indianapolis Star,* March 8, 1979.

155   "We aren't going to take a chance with Larry's future": Ibid., March 12, 1979.

155   Landini agreed to close down the university on Friday: Ibid.

155   spelling Larry's last name "Byrd": *Washington Post,* March 17, 1979.

155   "should be the unanimous coach of the year": *Spectator,* March 17, 1979.

156   Packer predicted Texas, not Indiana State, would come out of the Midwest region: Ibid.

156   Bird repeated the same instruction to the point guard, Steve Reed: *Indianapolis Star,* March 12, 1979.

157   Hodges called time-out and decided to switch to a two-three zone defense: Game and broadcast details from NBC telecast, video courtesy of Indiana State University.

158   "we don't have no one-man team": *Terre Haute Tribune,* March 12, 1979.

158   "They are for real": *Indianapolis Star,* March 17, 1979.

158   "he won't be talking to the press": *Sporting News,* March 31, 1979.

158   "We get letters every day from places like New York City": *State Journal,* March 10, 1979.

159   "We spent all week preparing for Detroit": Ibid., March 11, 1979.

159   "I'd like to tell you a little about Michigan State": Ibid.

159   "Don't let anybody ever tell you that Murfreesboro is dry": Ibid.

160   "We're in for a lot of fun": Game and broadcast details from NBC telecast, video courtesy of Michigan State University.

160   he compensated by running on the outside of his foot: *State Journal,* March 12, 1979.

162   "That's what you call a good ole country butt-whipping": *New York Times,* March 12, 1979.

163   "I always wanted to see what a real live prick looked like": Associated Press, March 20, 1979; Levine, *Bird,* p. 166; Smith, *Larry Bird,* p. 114.

163   "Playing college basketball is supposed to be fun": Associated Press, March 20, 1979; *Sporting News,* March 31, 1979.

163   "I'm not a racist": *Indianapolis Star,* March 14, 1979.

163   Bird opened the game by draining a pretty rainbow jumper: Game and broadcast details from NBC Sports telecast, video courtesy of Indiana State University.

164   "We are not a catch-up team": *Terre Haute Tribune*, March 16, 1979.

165   suggested he join the Celtics immediately after Indiana State's season ended: Bird, *Drive*, p. 70.

165   "Let me tell you, Larry Bird is a hell of a basketball player": *Terre Haute Tribune*, March 16, 1979.

166   "Where the hell is Terre Haute?": Ibid., March 18, 1979.

166   "Alan Zahn just looked over this way and shrugged his shoulders": Game and broadcast details from NBC Sports telecast, video courtesy of Indiana State University.

169   "This was the greatest basketball game I've ever been associated with": *Terre Haute Tribune,* March 18, 1979.

169   "Accept us as we are": *Basketball Weekly,* March 29, 1979.

170   A second X-ray revealed that Vincent had a stress fracture: *State Journal*, March 15, 1979.

170   "We told the coaches to stay off our backs and we would play harder": *Sporting News,* March 31, 1979.

171   DeWayne Scales had been suspended: *State Journal,* March 14, 1979.

171   "It's All the Way Bobo": Ibid., March 17, 1979.

171   "It was probably my best all-around game": Ibid.

172   "Just a couple of more questions, okay?": *New York Daily News,* March 18, 1979.

173   "Earvin has got to show me that he can shoot and will shoot from the outside": *State Journal,* March 18, 1979.

174   "Not today, Irwin": Kelser, *Gregory Kelser's Tales,* p. 98.

175   "He didn't catch the ball. He just changed direction of the ball": Game and broadcast details from NBC Sports telecast, video courtesy of Indiana State University.

175   "One passes and the other one dunks": *Sports Illustrated*, March 26, 1979.

177   "This is a tribute to a great bunch": *State Journal*, March 19, 1979.

178   "If we're on top of our game, ain't nobody in the world can beat Michigan State": *Sporting News,* March 31, 1979.

178   "It would be a challenge, and I love challenges": *State Journal,* March 19, 1979.

CHAPTER 10

Interviews: Andy Amey, Mike Brkovich, Tom Crowder, Terry Donnelly, Wayne Duke, Jud Heathcote, Bob Heaton, Lynn Henning, Bill Hodges, David Israel, Larry Keith, Greg Kelser, Don McGuire, Craig McKee, Ed McKee, Joey Meyer, Malcolm Moran, Billy Packer, Darwin Payton, Steve Reed, Bob Ryan, James Salters, Terry Thimlar, Bob Weinauer (Meyer, Salters, and Weinauer interviews conducted by Steve Brauntuch).

PAGE

180   They lustily booed the UCLA band for its rudeness: *Sports Illustrated,* March 26, 1979.

180   "I don't care if we win another game": *New York Times*, March 18, 1979.

181   the arena was half empty both days: *Sports Illustrated,* March 26, 1979.

181   "Penn didn't surprise me": Ibid.

181   they were welcomed at the airport by hundreds of fans: *New York Times,* March 23, 1980.

181   "Where's Princeton now?": *State Journal*, March 23, 1979.

182   All four regional finals from the previous weekend had set new records: *Dallas Morning News,* March 21, 1979.

182   "If Indiana State with Larry Bird meets Michigan State with Earvin Johnson": *Basketball Weekly,* March 29, 1979.

183   The caption identified them simply as "Miracle Man" and "The Hulk": *Terre Haute Tribune*, March 23, 1979.

183   "Some fan grabbed it": *New York Times,* March 21, 1979.

183   "I belong in New York": Ibid.

183   "Each practice we've been attracting 200 or 300 fans": *State Journal,* March 21, 1979.

185   "We have a number of columnists in our area who think we're going to win the national title": Ibid., March 22, 1979.

185   "Heathcote has often complained": Ibid.

186   the NCAA offered a five-minute presentation on how visitors could get drinks: Ibid.

186   "We're not going to gang up on the man": Associated Press, March 24, 1979.

187   "It's nice to be an intelligent team": *State Journal*, March 24, 1979.

187   "Michigan State is nothing but a bunch of dudes playing basketball just like we are": Ibid.

188   "They won't be able to run on us like they did on Notre Dame": *Dallas Morning News,* March 23, 1979.

188   the NCAA had to turn away nearly one hundred credential requests: *Terre Haute Tribune*, March 25, 1979.

189   Center Matt White got inside of Greg Kelser for a point-blank layup: Game and broadcast details from NBC Sports telecast, video courtesy of Michigan State University.

190   "We're doing it to them, aren't we?": *Sports Illustrated,* April 2, 1979.

191   "We saw where Price said he was going to make Gregory a perimeter player": *State Journal*, March 25, 1979.

191   Because Christine Johnson was a Seventh-Day Adventist, she spent that Saturday evening in the hotel room: Ibid., March 26, 1979; Johnson, *My Life*, p. 8.

192   the "bird" is just what they flipped them: *Sports Illustrated*, April 2, 1979.

192   the reserves had scored a total of 163 points all season: Associated Press, March 24, 1979.

192   His first bucket came on a turnaround bank shot: Game and broadcast details from NBC Sports telecast, video courtesy of Indiana State University.

194   "You front him and you get a foul automatically": *New York Times,* March 25, 1979.

194   "When Aguirre got the ball in the corner": *Dallas Morning News,* March 25, 1979.

194   "The whole season has been like a dream": *Spectator,* March 31, 1979.

195   "I don't know how many times": *Dallas Morning News*, March 25, 1979.

195   "IU will not get Thomas": *Spectator*, April 7, 1979.

195   "Usually I just feel sorry for the guy who's guarding me": *New York Times*, March 25, 1979.

195   "Me and Earvin Johnson don't go matching up": *Washington Post,* March 24, 1979.

195   "I gotta go see my mother": Ibid.

196   "They are also the only one": *New York Times,* March 25, 1979.

CHAPTER 11

Interviews: Andy Amey, Bob Behnke, Mike Brkovich, Tony Clark, Terry Donnelly, Dick Enberg, Bryant Gumbel, Jud Heathcote, Bob Heaton, Lynn Henning, Bill Hodges, Greg Kelser, Mike Longaker, Don McGuire, Craig McKee, Ed McKee, Brad Miley, Bruce Newman, Carl Nicks, Don Ohlmeyer, Billy Packer, Darwin Payton, Steve Reed, Bob Ryan, Rick Shaw, Terry Thimlar, Clint Thompson, Jay Vincent, Edgar Wilson.

PAGE

197   "Hey, how many times do you want him to get the award anyway?":
        Spectator, April 14, 1979.

198   they grabbed Forbes, lifted him up, and dumped him in a trash can:
        Smith, *Larry Bird,* p. 136.

199   Four-point plan: *New York Times,* March 27, 1979.

199   "you're going to play Bird on our scout team": Kelser, *Gregory Kelser's
        Tales,* p. 104; Johnson, *My Life,* p. 89.

201   "Broke"; press conference details: *New York Times,* March 26, 1979;
        Dallas Morning News, March 26, 1979; *Terre Haute Tribune,* March
        26, 1979; *State Journal,* March 26, 1979.

202   he could be on the hit TV comedy *Hee Haw*: Smith, *Larry Bird,*
        p. 135.

202   "Herb Shriner with a jump shot": *New York Times,* March 26, 1979.

202   "I love all this attention": Ibid.

204   it committed a major faux pas by playing the University of Michigan's
        "The Victors" instead: Stabley and Staudt, *Tales from the Magical
        Spartans,* p. 90.

206   *Good evening, everyone. Welcome to the Special Events Center*: Game
        and broadcast details from NBC Sports telecast.

209   "I think we were pretty pleased just being down by nine": Larry Bird
        interview with Fox Sports, "Magic versus Bird: The Game That
        Changed the Game," March 28, 1999.

214   "that play sure broke my heart": *State Journal,* March 27, 1979.

215   "This is hard": Stabley and Staudt, *Tales from the Magical Spartans,*
        p. 96.

218   "Can't you give us some damned privacy!": *New York Daily News,*
       March 31, 1979.
218   "C'mon, man, let's get that trophy": *Washington Post,* March 27, 1979.
218   "It was the biggest game of our lives, and it was so close": Larry Bird
       interview with Fox Sports, "Magic versus Bird," March 28, 1999.
219   "Michigan State is an excellent team": *Indianapolis Star,* March 27,
       1979.
219   "an adjustment and a prayer": *State Journal,* March 27, 1979.
220   "Anyone disappointed with our success has to be a lesser man than
       I": *Spectator,* March 31, 1979.
220   "He should have kept shooting the ball": *Chicago Tribune,* March 27,
       1979.
220   Brad Miley added that he thought Bird was "really tired": Ibid.
220   "We'd get these cheap fouls called on us": *State Journal,* March 27,
       1979.
221   "Bird flew the coop": *New York Times,* March 27, 1979.
222   He spent much of the night holding court in a corner of the room:
       Spectator, April 7, 1979.

CHAPTER 12

Interviews: Bob Behnke, Jud Heathcote, Lynn Henning, Craig McKee, Carl
Nicks, Rex Lardner, Mick McCabe, John Newton.

PAGE
224   they were greeted on the tarmac by some fifteen hundred fans: *State
       Journal,* March 28, 1979.
224   The next day, nearly fifteen thousand people turned out in a cold
       drizzle: Ibid., March 29, 1979.
225   drew just eighty-five people to a local high school gym: Ibid., May 10,
       1979.
225   "I really wish that Gregory would have received this award": Ibid.,
       March 31, 1979.
226   "spoiled brat": *Daily News,* March 31, 1979.
226   "If he thinks he's merely moving to a bigger version of Terre Haute":
       Boston Globe, March 25, 1979.
226   Ten writers left Bird off their all-tournament ballots: *Basketball
       Weekly,* April 15, 1979.

226   "I think it's important what city he plays in": *New York Times,* March 28, 1979.

226   four Air National Guard F-100 jets saluted them with a flyover: Smith, *Larry Bird,* p. 144.

227   "I'd like to present this so-called second place trophy to the city of Terre Haute": Levine, *Bird,* p. 175.

227   "Not a damn thing": *Putnam County Banner Graphic,* March 28, 1979.

227   "We cannot ask that the team play better basketball next year": *Spectator,* May 12, 1979.

228   "This fat little Polock from Pennsylvania finally found a way to get McGuire off his back": Smith, *Larry Bird,* p. 154.

228   "Larry Bird Appreciation Night": *Terre Haute Tribune,* April 27, 1979, and April 28, 1979; *Indianapolis Star,* April 28, 1979.

228   "I told him he should be sure and steal Granny's hearing aid": Smith, *Larry Bird,* p. 150.

229   Earvin Johnson sat in his East Lansing apartment and fielded questions from Doug Looney: *Sports Illustrated,* March 30, 1979.

230   "He is not superstar material for the NBA": Ebling, *Magic Moments,* p. 10.

230   "I think at least half of his appeal is his enthusiasm": *Sports Illustrated,* March 30, 1979.

230   "My daddy said you're going to leave us": Johnson, *Magic,* p. 137.

230   A Michigan State booster raised twelve hundred dollars to place an ad: *Sports Illustrated,* March 30, 1979.

230   "I don't think I'm worth as much as Bird": Ibid.

231   When Cooke offered him $400,000, Johnson said no thanks and told Cooke he was going back to school: Johnson, *Magic,* p. 147.

232   "Next season I'll be applying for hardship to turn pro": *State Journal,* May 12, 1979.

232   "I guess I didn't amount to anything, did I?" Johnson, *My Life,* p. 35.

233   the first time he saw his father cry: Ibid., p. 103.

233   he showed up at 7:45 a.m. at West Vigo High School: *Terre Haute Star,* April 3, 1979.

233   he skipped the Wooden Award ceremony in Los Angeles: Levine, *Bird,* p. 181.

233   "I don't know how many times that poor girl stood under the basket":
       Sports Illustrated, March 21, 1988.

235   the previous summer he had hit 12 home runs and had 48 RBI in
       twenty games: *Indianapolis Star,* March 30, 1979.

235   Bird played first base for the Sycamores in a doubleheader against
       Kentucky Wesleyan College: Bird, *Drive,* p. 66; *Terre Haute Tribune,*
       April 27, 1979; *Indianapolis Star,* May 5, 1979.

235   he collided with catcher Mark Rickard: *Indianapolis Star,* May 5,
       1979.

235   "Hey, Mr. Woolf, Tommy John is a friend of mine": *Sports Illustrated,*
       November 9, 1981.

235   the only items listed were three days' worth of room and tax charges:
       Sports Illustrated, March 21, 1988.

236   the sparse crowd of 7,831 at Boston Garden gave him a standing ova-
       tion: Ibid.

236   "He is more like a dictator than a negotiator": *Terre Haute Tribune,*
       April 28, 1979.

236   he looked down and saw the top half of his right index finger pointed
       at a ninety-degree angle: Bird, *Drive,* p. 70.

236   a press conference attended by thirty-one radio and TV outlets: *In-
       side Sports,* October 1979.

237   He raced back to French Lick and showed off that sheepskin: Bird,
       Drive, p. 70.

CHAPTER 13

Interviews: Chuck Akers, Leslie Akers, Andy Amey, Bob Behnke, Corrie
Bird, Beanie Cooper, Jan Condra Deakins, Mark Few, George Fox, Dave
Gavitt, Bryant Gumbel, Jud Heathcote, Bob Heaton, Lynn Henning, Bill
Hodges, Tom Jernstedt, Greg Kelser, Dave Kindred, Mick McCabe, Carl
Nicks, Don Ohlmeyer, Darwin Payton, Digger Phelps, Bill Rasmussen, Steve
Reed, Bob Ryan, Rick Shaw, David Stern, Terry Thimlar, Dick Vitale.

PAGE

240   "Bill was about ready to jump off the bridge": *St. Louis Post-Dispatch,*
       December 17, 1994.

241   "Last year was one of the toughest years of my life": *New York Times,*
       November 24, 1981.

242   ratings had dropped a whopping 29 percent from the year before: Ibid., January 13, 1980.

242   "I know somebody is going to say he's tired of seeing that parquet floor in Boston so often": *Sporting News,* February 21, 1981.

242   "I don't know why they are doing it, and I don't want to guess": *New York Times,* January 13, 1980.

243   CBS struck an $88 million deal to televise the NBA playoffs for another four seasons: *Sporting News,* December 23, 1981.

243   Byers abruptly hung up on him: Eddie Einhorn with Ron Rapoport, *How March Became Madness: How the NCAA Tournament Became the Greatest Sporting Event in America* (Chicago: Triumph Books, 2006), p. 216.

243   had just ponied up $7.5 million for a one-year deal with the Rose Bowl: *New York Times,* February 15, 1981.

244    $48 million over three years: Ibid., March 5, 1981.

244   a studio control center modeled after their successful *NFL Today* pregame show: *Sports Illustrated,* March 9, 1982.

245   Dean Smith marveled that his father in Kansas would be able to watch all but four of the Tar Heels' twenty-six games: Ibid., November 30, 1981.

245   "Games don't end anymore": *Wall Street Journal,* March 2, 1982.

245   three years for $96 million: *New York Times,* November 19, 1983.

245   "perhaps the fastest-growing sports event in the country": Ibid., November 22, 1983.

248   "I'm happy to get *you* off my back": Kelser, *Gregory Kelser's Tales,* p. viii.

249   Parish Hickman had his scholarship revoked after he was arrested: *Chicago Tribune,* July 10, 1993; Associated Press, June 8, 1993.

249   seven secondary infractions: *Detroit Free Press,* November 3, 1994.

249   "It galls me": Ibid., November 22, 1994.

250   a confidential memo written by associate athletic director Clarence Underwood was leaked: *Sports Illustrated,* March 13, 1995; *Detroit Free Press,* March 31, 1994.

250   "I think what people are clapping for is more the situation than the person": *Chicago Tribune,* March 8, 1995.

251   "I knew that the end was coming": *Detroit Free Press,* March 18, 1995.

254   "I don't go out to eat with him": *New York Times,* December 30, 1979.

254   Magic and Bird wouldn't even shake hands before tip-off: Johnson, *My Life,* p. 223.

254   they sat in Bird's living room and spent time alone together for the first time: Ibid., p. 224.

254   "We found out that we were much alike": Video of Larry Bird's retirement ceremony, Boston Garden, February 4, 1993.

255   "I just remember we were both crying": *Grand Rapids Press,* September 28, 2002.

255   the place mats in the restaurant had outlines of Larry's hands: *Sports Illustrated,* March 21, 1988.

256   she died of Lou Gehrig's disease in 1996: Associated Press, October 9, 1996.

258   "Every time I see him, it sort of cringes me because he's got something that I can't get": Indiana State Hall of Fame induction ceremony, August 1, 1999, video courtesy of Indiana State University.

CHAPTER 14

Interviews: Andy Amey, Bob Behnke, Mike Brkovich, Tom Crowder, Terry Donnelly, Stan Evans, Jud Heathcote, Bob Heaton, Bill Hodges, Greg Kelser, Sharel King, Mike McCormick, Brad Miley, Carl Nicks, Darwin Payton, Steve Reed, Rick Shaw.

PAGE

261   "had a couple of days there when I just went to the beach and watched the waves": *Los Angeles Times,* November 28, 1986.

261   he had only three scholarships to distribute however he liked: Ibid.

262   five relatives of players died, and the Bears were ranked dead last in the national computer rankings: *Atlanta Journal-Constitution,* February 18, 1997.

263   "Great play": *Cleveland Plain Dealer,* March 11, 1999.

263   eighteen homes in eight different states: *Roanoke Times,* January 13, 2007.

266   a 95–93 win before a sellout crowd: *USA Today,* August 14, 1989.

266   "I'll never forget that night": *Tampa Tribune,* March 26, 1999.

267   "I very rarely smiled when I was actually playing": *State Journal,* November 2, 2003.

267   5 points and 4 assists in sixteen minutes: Associated Press, December 2, 2003.

272   "So Coach King is not as slick as you think he is": Indiana State Hall of Fame induction, August 1, 1999, video courtesy of Indiana State University.

274   "I think that some of these folks back here stopped at the Ballyhoo on the way down here": Larry Bird jersey retirement video courtesy of Jason Pensky, WTWO-TV, February 28, 2004.

ACKNOWLEDGMENTS

Whenever I told people I was writing a book about the 1979 NCAA championship game, they usually responded that it was a great idea. I agreed, but I couldn't take the credit. Rather, the idea sprung from the fertile mind of Paul Golob, the editorial director at Times Books. Paul was the editor for *Truth to Tell*, a book written by my father, Lanny, for the Free Press in 1999, and just like my dad I found Paul to be a diligent, passionate, and keenly intelligent editor who provided me with the firm guidance and friendship I needed. (Paul also came up with the title for this book. Nice work, bro.) I also benefited greatly from the enthusiastic support of the entire Henry Holt family, beginning at the top with publisher, Dan Farley, and his predecessor, John Sterling, who gave us the original green light. Thanks also to Maggie Richards and Eileen Lawrence in marketing; to Claire McKinney, Tara Kennedy, and Justin Golenbock in publicity; to Paul's able assistant, Pearl Wu; and to Nicholas Caruso, who designed the book's jacket.

I am well aware that my literary agent, David Black, has many other clients who can make him more money than I can, yet I have never felt for a moment that I was getting short shrift. David was always available to me and Paul, volunteering to read more pages than

I would have ever asked him to and making terrific suggestions on every facet of this project. Ian O'Connor was right, David: you are a mensch.

For help with my research, I am grateful to the woefully overqualified Steve Brauntuch. Steve scavenged lots of library files for me, spent hour after hour photocopying old clips, conducted several phone interviews, and meticulously fact-checked the manuscript, even though in his view I did not write enough about Penn. I also got significant help from Matt Bloom in New York, Christina Jackson in Terre Haute, Matt Benjamin in East Lansing, and the staffs at the Vigo County (Indiana) Public Library, the Capital Area District Library in Lansing, and the Library of Michigan. I am especially indebted to Joy Birdsong and Natasha Simon, who oversee the sprawling *Sports Illustrated* library in New York City.

During my time working the national college basketball beat, I have been very lucky to spend lots of time with John Lewandowski and Matt Larson from Michigan State University's sports information office. They are two of the best in the business, not to mention two of my favorite people on the planet, and their help on this project was invaluable. Writing this book also introduced me to Indiana State's terrific sports information director, John Sherman. All three guys provided me with newspaper and magazine clips, contact information for former players and coaches, DVDs of games, photographs, and answers to all kinds of nettlesome questions.

For aiding my efforts to acquire video, I give thanks to Chris Richards, the go-getting aspiring journalist from Roanoke, Virginia, who transferred Bill Hodges's game videotapes onto DVDs for me; Michigan State's Kevin Pauga, who likewise furnished me with DVDs from the Spartans' championship season; and Bernadette Cafarelli, the sports information director at Notre Dame and, for my money, the sexiest woman alive. Andy Amey, Nancy Donald, Jack Ebling, Jim Jones, Sharel King, Mike McCormick, Craig McKee, and Ed McKee also furnished me with information and assistance. I am particularly pleased that this book gave me the chance to reunite with Jason Pensky, my fellow alumnus of the Bullis School in Potomac, Maryland, who is now a revered sportscaster at Terre Haute's WTWO-TV. Besides lending me his insights on all things Indiana State, Jason provided me with the dramatic video from Larry Bird's jersey retirement ceremony that served as the final scene.

During the course of my reporting for this book, I interviewed ninety-eight people. I spoke with many of those folks several times, and more than a few of those conversations lasted upwards of three hours. I have cited them all in my endnotes so I will not list them again here, but I do want to single out two of the men who formed the heart of this narrative: Jud Heathcote and Bill Hodges. They were both gracious hosts who provided me with terrific grist for my story. As men who have devoted their adult lives to providing counsel and encouragement to young people, they have my enduring affection and respect. I would also like to thank the interview subjects who welcomed me into their homes: Bob Behnke, Mike Brkovich, George Fox, Gus Ganakas, Gary Holland (who showed me around French Lick), and Steve Reed (who got me tipsy on homemade limoncello).

During my visit to French Lick, Gary Holland and I shared some pizza with Chuck Akers, a former teacher at Larry Bird's alma mater Springs Valley High School, and Chuck's wife, Leslie. The Akerses were delightful company, and their affection for Larry was palpable. Larry owes Chuck a great deal, because if Chuck hadn't encouraged Larry to join him on an AAU basketball team during the winter of 1974–75, Larry might never have gone to college. Three weeks after my pizza lunch with the Akerses, Chuck was killed in an automobile accident. I thought of him often as I wrote this book, and I know the close-knit community of French Lick is poorer without him.

When I looked to break into broadcasting, I hoped to have an agent who could also be my friend. What I found instead was a friend who is also my agent. Thank you, Rick Diamond.

I am blessed beyond words to have a roster spot on the two finest teams in all of sports journalism: *Sports Illustrated* and CBS Sports. At CBS, Sean McManus, Tony Petitti, Harold Bryant, and Eric Mann carved out a role for me that I never would have envisioned for myself. It is an honor to work for and with them. Ditto for Tim Pernetti, who has been my anchor at CBS College Sports. I was also thrilled that this book gave me the chance to delve into college basketball history with two of my CBS colleagues: Billy Packer, who is a national treasure, and Dick Enberg, who is not only the best play-by-play man of his generation but also one of the finest gentlemen I have ever known. And, of course, I would like to offer thanks to my studio partners for the last five NCAA tournaments, Greg Gumbel and Clark Kellogg. They are the best at what they do, and they are class acts to boot.

As for SI, my gratitude begins with my two managing editors, Terry McDonell (at *Sports Illustrated*) and Paul Fichtenbaum (SI.com). David Bauer has been a valued mentor who took an interest in me from the start and always told me the straight-up truth, even when I didn't want to hear it. B. J. Schecter has remained a loyal friend and gifted editor despite his meteoric rise up the masthead. Greg Kelly read a rough draft of this manuscript and offered some terrific suggestions. My two college hoops editors, Aimee Crawford and Nina Mandell, continue to be nice to me even when I'm dodging their phone calls. Most of all, thanks to Stefanie Kaufman for hiring me during the summer of 1995. Yes, it has been that long.

Thank you, Sons of Equinunk, especially the People Helping People.

While the blame for my many shortcomings lies solely with me, all the credit for the good stuff goes to my family. So thanks to Lanny, Carolyn, Josh, and Jeremy Davis; Nevin and Elaine Gibson; David, Marlo, Jake, Sydney, and Devon Sims (and Fred); Miriam, Harvey, and Gail Cohen; and Ian, Allison, Samantha, and Benjamin Cohen.

Zachary and Noah Davis improved this book immeasurably by constantly defying their strict orders never to bother Daddy while he's working. Melissa Beth Cohen Davis remains the best person I have ever known and the best friend I have ever had. This book, like everything else I do, is for her.

INDEX

ABOUT THE AUTHOR

SETH DAVIS is an on-air studio analyst for CBS Sports coverage of NCAA basketball and is an on-air host, reporter, and analyst for the CBS College Sports Network. He is also a staff writer at *Sports Illustrated* and SI.com, where he has worked since 1995, primarily covering college basketball and golf. He is also the author of *Equinunk, Tell Your Story: My Return to Summer Camp*. A graduate of Duke University, Davis lives with his family in Ridgefield, Connecticut.